Teacher Resource Guide

Developmental Reading Assessment™

Word Analysis

by Joetta M. Beaver
In Collaboration With Reading/Classroom Teachers

D1529871

CELEBRATION PRESS
Pearson Learning Group

Author's Acknowledgments

The development of the DRA™ Word Analysis is the result of much support and encouragement from colleagues locally as well as across the United States and parts of Canada.

I am appreciative of the early work of the DRA Word Analysis drafting committee consisting of Jan Yanscik, Kathleen Taps, Wendy Roush, Patty Nichols, Jennifer Taps, and Valerie Wilson. Their suggestions were very helpful in developing and shaping the initial assessment tasks.

I am truly grateful for the ongoing support and expert advice that Jane Williams, Jan Yanscik, Michelle Bell, and Carolyn Bordelon provided over the last two years. Their suggestions and questions helped me to clarify further my own thinking and revise the assessment procedures and directions. Their encouragement helped me persevere when I thought I would never see the end.

I wish to thank all the classroom and reading teachers as well as literacy coordinators who field-tested the DRA Word Analysis materials and provided insightful suggestions for improving the assessment.

I also thank Carol Ory and Sharon Meyer, my assistants, for cheerfully doing whatever needed to be done throughout the many phases of this endeavor.

Finally, I want to express my deep appreciation to my family and friends who believe in what I am doing and patiently support my efforts.

The following people have contributed to the development of this product:

Art and Design: M. Jane Heelan, Judy Mates, Jim O'Shea
Editorial: Jessica Kear, Anne Stribling, Lynn Trepicchio
Inventory: Yvette Higgins
Marketing: Christine Fleming
Production/Manufacturing: Mark Cirillo, Helen Gocher, Cynthia Lynch
Publishing Operations: Jennifer Van Der Heide

Celebration Press
Pearson Learning Group

1-800-321-3106
www.pearsonlearning.com

Contents

Introduction

The primary goal of the *DRA*™ is to identify each student's independent *DRA* text level and to document how this changes over time. An independent text level is one in which the reader is able to decode the text with an accuracy rate of 94 percent or higher, read with at least a moderate rate of fluency, and construct meaning before, during, and after reading. Each year as teachers administer the *DRA*, they often encounter a number of students who make little or no progress in their ability to read more challenging texts due to inefficient word analysis skills and/or strategies. Some of these students are "struggling" readers who do not know how to efficiently problem-solve unknown words they meet in text. Their oral reading is often slow, choppy, and repetitious as they work to figure out words. Others are at-risk emerging readers who do not understand how oral language relates to written language or how to attend to print. To help these at-risk struggling and emerging readers, teachers need further information about their knowledge and skills in working with words in context and in isolation. The *DRA*™ *Word Analysis* was created for this very purpose.

Overview of the *DRA Word Analysis*

The *DRA Word Analysis* is a diagnostic assessment that provides classroom and reading teachers with a systematic means to observe how struggling and emerging readers attend to and work with the various components of spoken and written words. It consists of forty word analysis tasks that assess a student's level of control. The *DRA Word Analysis* is divided into five strands: (1) phonological awareness, (2) metalanguage (language used to talk about printed language concepts), (3) letter/high frequency word recognition, (4) phonics, and (5) structural analysis and syllabication. The tasks, as much as possible, reflect what developing readers need to know and do in order to successfully problem-solve unknown or less familiar words as they read meaningful texts. They are sequenced in order of difficulty based upon the performance of students at the same *DRA* text levels as well as research-based expectations for phonological awareness. The information gained from *DRA Word Analysis* will enable teachers to

1. Determine students' level of control of various word analysis tasks.

2. Document students' progress over time.

3. Group students according to their instructional needs.

4. Plan more effectively for instruction.

Development of the *DRA Word Analysis*

The *DRA Word Analysis* was developed over a period of years. Beginning in the spring of 2000, an analysis of all words included within the *DRA* leveled texts, the types of miscues children made while reading *DRA* texts, and research-based information concerning developing readers' ability to attend to and work with words was compiled. An initial draft of the *DRA Word Analysis* drew upon these three resources and was shared with a small group of highly effective classroom, reading, and speech teachers. The initial draft of the assessment was revised based on the feedback from this group.

Pilot Test

Following these initial revisions, a pilot test was conducted in one urban, one rural, and two suburban schools in central Ohio in late spring and early fall of 2002. The pilot test included a small but representative sample across racial/ethnic, gender, and grade-level groups. The major purposes of the pilot test were to

- Observe how students responded to the tasks.
- Clarify the general directions as well as the directions for each task so that they were clear and easy for teachers and students to follow.
- Clarify the assessment procedures and forms.

Discussions with teachers who administered the assessment as well as an analysis of students' behaviors and responses resulted in major revisions. Tasks were revised; some tasks were deleted while other tasks were added; teacher directions were clarified; and the assessment materials were modified.

Field Tests

Subsequently, field tests were conducted in the winter and then again in the fall of 2003 by classroom and reading teachers across the United States. Urban, suburban, rural, and small town school settings were represented. The field tests included representative samples across racial/ethnic, gender, and grade-level groups. The purposes of the field tests included verifying that

- *DRA Word Analysis* is effective in assessing students' abilities to attend to and work with components of spoken and written words.
- Information gained from the assessment provided direction for future instruction.
- Assessment tasks were organized in a logical and developmentally appropriate order.
- Designated entry-level tasks were appropriate for students reading at specific *DRA* text levels.
- Directions and forms were clear and manageable.

Teacher directions and student forms were further revised based upon teacher feedback as well as teacher and student performance. Tasks were revised and reordered based on student performance.

DRA Word Analysis Components

The *DRA Word Analysis* has three components.

1. The *Teacher Resource Guide* includes
   - Directions for the administration, recording, and scoring of each assessment task
   - Blackline masters for the
     (a) Record of Responses for each task
     (b) Spelling Check forms
     (c) Student Cumulative Record
     (d) Spelling and Oral Reading Miscues Analysis form
     (e) Group Profile forms
   - Explanation and samples of completed blackline masters
   - Sample mini-lessons and/or learning activities for word analysis tasks
   - Glossary
   - Recommended references
2. The *Student Assessment Book* includes the pictures, letters, and/or words for the assessment tasks.
3. The *DRA Word Analysis Training CD* demonstrates how different types of tasks are conducted and scored.

The *DRA™ Online Management System Release 2.7*

Built to leverage the powerful *Developmental Reading Assessment* instrument, the *DRA™ Online Management System* provides a fast, secure environment for teachers to archive and manage their students' assessment results with success.

Like previous releases of *DRA™ Online*, version 2.7 provides a secure environment for teachers to archive student assessment results. Teachers can manage *DRA™* data and provide appropriate paths for instruction and flexible grouping. And now, Release 2.7 of the *DRA Online* seamlessly supports additional components that have been created to extend the effectiveness and reach of the program including *DRA™ Word Analysis*.

Available September 2004

1. **Archive student DRA records online.**
   Assessment information is inputted into the system.

2. **Review student data that is compiled for you.**

3. **Retrieve student data for a variety of purposes.**
   Information is easily accessed and can be used to:
   • create instructional groups
   • report individual student progress
   • illustrate classroom, school, and district results

Technical Requirements: All users of the system must have a working e-mail address. District and school e-mail systems must allow delivery of bulk e-mail from Pearson Learning Group. Java-enabled browsers, like Internet Explorer 5.5 or Netscape Navigator 4.7 are required, as well as access to secure Web sites.

For more information, e-mail:
DRA.Pearson@pearsonlearning.com
To see DRA Online in action, take a tour:
www.pearsonlearning.com/dratour

Developing Proficient Readers and the *DRA Word Analysis*

Proficient readers are able to read more complex texts due to effective word analysis skills and strategies. They skillfully attend to letter information, use spelling pattern/sound relationships, and recognize familiar spelling and syllable patterns as they identify words while constructing meaning. They continue to extend and deepen their vocabularies and concepts by reading many and diverse texts. They see themselves as readers, spend time reading, and become better readers each time they read.

Struggling Readers

Most "struggling" readers, on the other hand, are unable to read more complex texts due to ineffective word analysis skills and strategies. They generally give less attention to letter information and often neglect vowel patterns within words as well as middle and ending syllables of polysyllabic words when problem-solving unknown words. They have limited reading experiences and frequently are given texts that are too difficult for them to read and comprehend independently. As a result, they do not perceive themselves as readers; they often avoid reading and are reluctant to engage with longer and/or more challenging texts.

Emerging Readers

Emerging readers are learning how speech and print are related, about letter/sound relationships, and how to attend to letters and words in text. Some emerging readers in kindergarten and beginning first grade, unlike their peers who have spent many hours listening to and "rereading" books as well as drawing and scribbling messages, come to school with very limited literacy experiences. These students like many of the struggling readers are at risk due to factors beyond their control. They need to be carefully monitored, immersed in oral and written language, introduced to rhyming and alliteration, and helped to develop basic concepts about print.

To help these at-risk emerging and/or struggling readers obtain the necessary skills and strategies to become proficient readers is a big challenge. The more teachers know about the reading process, how proficient readers attend to and analyze words while constructing meaning, and what their students currently know and can do as readers, the more successful they will be in providing developmentally appropriate instruction and learning activities for all of their students.

The *DRA Word Analysis* helps teachers determine emerging and struggling readers' levels of control in attending to and working with spoken and written words. The information gained from this assessment will enable teachers to make more effective teaching decisions to help emerging and struggling readers gain the word analysis skills and strategies needed to read and comprehend more challenging texts. The chart on pages 8–9 illustrates the alignment between the behavior of proficient readers and the *DRA Word Analysis* tasks within the five strands.

What Proficient Readers Do	Corresponding *DRA Word Analysis* Tasks
	Strand 1: Phonological Awareness
Quickly identify and generate words that rhyme with given words.	**Rhyming** **Task 1:** Students identify a picture that rhymes with the first picture in the set. **Task 13:** Students provide a word that rhymes with a word given by the teacher.
Quickly identify and generate words that begin with the same sound.	**Alliteration** **Task 2:** Students identify a picture that begins with the same sound as the first picture in the set. **Task 19:** Students provide a word that begins with the same sound as the word given by the teacher.
Quickly segment • spoken sentences into words • words into onset and rime and/or syllables.	**Segmentation** **Task 8:** Students use a number line to show the number of words in a sentence. **Task 14:** Students segment a given word by separating the onset from the rime. **Task 18:** Students clap the syllables as they say a pictured word.
Quickly identify, blend, segment, and manipulate phonemes in spoken words.	**Phonemic Awareness** **Task 3:** Students isolate the initial sound of a word given by the teacher. **Task 12:** Students repeat segmented phonemes in a word and then say the word. **Task 15:** Students repeat a word given by the teacher without the first sound(s). **Task 20:** Students repeat a word given by the teacher without the last sound(s). **Task 21:** Students segment a given word into phonemes.
	Strand 2: Metalanguage
Understand language used to talk about basic printed language concepts; continue to learn terms used to talk about printed language, i.e., *vowel, consonant, prefix, suffix, syllable,* etc.	**Task 4:** Students demonstrate that they understand language used to talk about printed language concepts using their first and last names. **Task 7:** Students demonstrate that they understand language used to talk about printed language concepts using words in sentences.
	Strand 3: Letter and Word Recognition
Automatically recognize, name, and form the uppercase and lowercase letters of the alphabet.	**Letter Recognition** **Task 5:** Students name randomly placed uppercase letters. **Task 6:** Students name randomly placed lowercase letters.
Possess a large and ever-increasing number of "sight" words automatically recognized and understood.	**High Frequency Word Recognition** **Tasks 9, 17, 22, 29:** Students read as quickly as possible lists of high frequency words that increase in difficulty.

What Proficient Readers Do	Corresponding *DRA Word Analysis* Tasks
	Strand 4: Phonics
• spell many high frequency words conventionally; • segment words into syllables, onset and rime, and phonemes as needed to sound out words; • use analogies for spelling patterns that cannot be sounded out; • reflect their current knowledge of sound/spelling patterns in their spelling approximations.	**Encoding** **Task 10:** Students spell two to three-letter high frequency words. **Task 16:** Students spell words with short vowels and common spelling patterns. **Task 27:** Students spell words with *VCe*, initial diagraphs, pre-consonant nasals, or suffixes. **Task 36:** Students spell words with *r*-controlled vowels, suffixes, initial blends, *ck*, or open first syllable. **Task 40:** Students spell words with prefixes, closed first syllables, suffixes, three-letter initial blends, diphthongs, or long vowel patterns.
Automatically • identify and associate spelling patterns with sounds; • identify letters that represent more than one sound i.e., *c* or *a*; • identify vowel patterns; • quickly blend letter sounds and generate words or names that begin with the designated sound(s).	**Decoding** **Task 11:** Students provide the phoneme for each letter and give a word or name that begins with that phoneme. **Task 25:** Students blend two to three consonant-letter sounds and say a word or name that begins with the consonant blend. **Task 26:** Students tell how the words with the same vowel are alike, say the long and short sounds of the designated vowel, and read the words in each set. **Task 32:** Students identify the vowel pattern in a set of words and read aloud the words. **Task 33:** Students blend a group of letters and give a word that makes sense and begins with those blended sounds.
Know when to • sound out words; • attend to spelling patterns and use analogies to identify unknown words.	**Substitution/Analogies** **Task 23:** Students tell how the words are alike and read aloud the rhyming words in each set. **Task 24:** Students tell how the words are alike and read aloud the words in each set. **Task 30:** Students read six sets of words with different rimes. **Task 31:** Students use parts of familiar words to problem-solve unknown words.
	Strand 5: Structural Analysis and Syllabication
Identify and isolate word parts such as affixes and base or root words; understand the meaning of commonly used prefixes and suffixes; use structural analysis to determine word meanings. Recognize and use syllable patterns to decode polysyllabic words; analyze the pattern of vowels and consonants in a word to determine where the word breaks into syllables.	**Tasks 28, 35, 38:** Students read aloud and use each word to which a suffix has been added in a sentence to demonstrate their understanding of the word. **Task 37:** Students read aloud and tell the meaning of each word to which a prefix has been added. **Tasks 34, 39:** Students read aloud a polysyllabic word, clap the syllables while saying the word, and tell where to divide the word into syllables.

General Guidelines for Administering the *DRA Word Analysis*

As with all standardized assessments, it is important that teachers are familiar with and follow the established guidelines/procedures for administering the *DRA Word Analysis* so that the results are reliable and accurate. To help teachers develop a basic understanding of how the *DRA Word Analysis* is to be administered, questions most frequently asked about the administration have been addressed below.

Who should administer the *DRA Word Analysis*?

It is highly recommended that the teacher who is responsible for teaching the student to read should administer this assessment. Even though others could give it and share the results, much is gained by administering the assessment. The teacher who gives the assessment will

- Know what is expected.
- Have the opportunity to see how the student behaves and responds to the tasks.
- Know the student better.
- Be better prepared to make developmentally appropriate instructional decisions for each student he/she assesses.

To whom should teachers administer the *DRA Word Analysis*?

The *DRA Word Analysis* is intended for

- Emerging readers in kindergarten and beginning first grade to identify their level of phonological awareness and basic knowledge of phoneme/grapheme relationships.
- Struggling readers in the latter part of first grade through third grade who are reading below grade level or designated levels of proficiency due to ineffective word-solving skills and strategies.
- Fourth- and fifth-grade students whose independent *DRA* text level is 38 or below.

The *DRA Word Analysis* is not intended for

- Students who have demonstrated adequate progress on the *DRA* and are meeting established levels of proficiency.
- Students who are able to decode a text but have difficulty demonstrating their comprehension of what they have read. These students need instruction on how to construct meaning using comprehension strategies and how to respond to and/or retell what they have read.
- Students whose silent and oral reading rates are slow but who basically make only a few miscues. These students need instruction on how to read more fluently and should participate in repeated readings of familiar texts in order to become more fluent.

When should the *DRA Word Analysis* be administered?

It is recommended that *DRA Word Analysis* be administered during the first part of the school year after the *DRA* has been administered to students in first through fifth grades. Teachers will use the information gained from the *DRA* to determine which emerging and/or struggling readers should be given this assessment. It is best to wait until midyear to give this assessment to emerging readers in kindergarten.

It is also recommended that teachers readminister the *DRA Word Analysis* midyear and at the end of the school year to

- Determine if students have gained control of those tasks that they initially demonstrated no, little, and/or some control.
- Identify a new focus of instruction for students who are still reading below a designated level of proficiency on the *DRA* due to ineffective word-solving skills and strategies.

What materials are needed to administer the *DRA Word Analysis*?

The materials needed to administer each task are listed in the beginning of the teacher directions for that task. In general, teachers will need

- A copy of the Record of Responses for each task to be administered
- A pen or pencil to record responses and observations
- A stopwatch for timed tasks
- The Student Cumulative Record for each student assessed
- A designated colored pen to record the student's total scores on his/her Student Cumulative Record

How should teachers prepare to administer the *DRA Word Analysis*?

It is important for teachers to become familiar with the directions and the guidelines for recording and scoring. In preparation, teachers should first watch the *DRA™ Word Analysis Training CD* to learn how to administer the assessment, record student responses and behaviors, score the assessment, and use the information gained from this assessment. Next, they should read and/or reread the *DRA Word Analysis* general guidelines and administration procedures for each task they plan to administer. As with all assessments, this assessment will become easier to administer, record, and score with experience, but in order to ensure inter- and intra-rater reliability, it is critical that all teachers follow the directions each time a task is administered.

Which *DRA Word Analysis* task should be administered first?

The first time the *DRA Word Analysis* is administered, the initial task is determined by the student's current independent *DRA* text level. All students will not begin with the same task. After identifying the student's independent *DRA* text level, teachers will use the chart on page 16 to determine which *DRA Word Analysis* task to administer first.
[Note: The designated entry tasks were based upon the performance of students who read the same *DRA* text levels in the 2003 field tests.]

The second and/or subsequent times the *DRA Word Analysis* is administered, teachers will assess only those tasks on which the student did not previously demonstrate control. Once the student demonstrates control of a task, it does not need to be administered again. All the other tasks previously administered will be reassessed as well as some new tasks each time the assessment is readministered. For example, if a student demonstrated control of Tasks 1 through 6 and 11 the first time the *DRA Word Analysis* was administered, the teacher would begin with Task 7 and assess 8, 9, 10, skip 11, and go on to 12, 13, etc. the second time the assessment is administered.

When should teachers stop administering *DRA Word Analysis* tasks?

Teachers are to begin with the recommended entry task and continue administering *DRA Word Analysis* tasks until the student performs any three tasks with no, little, and/or some control. Once the student has demonstrated no, little, and/or some control on any three tasks, teachers should stop assessing. The three tasks do not need to be in consecutive order. Student performance on the various *DRA Word Analysis* tasks frequently reflects previous literacy experiences and instruction or the lack of such.

How long does it take to administer the *DRA Word Analysis*?

Each assessment task takes on average two to three minutes to administer. Some of the higher-level spelling checks may take slightly longer, especially if the student is slow in responding. Generally, it is best to plan to administer as many tasks as possible within a fifteen-minute block of time. Even though the tasks vary in what students are to do, some students have a difficult time staying focused for a longer period of time.

The vast majority of emerging readers in the 2003 field tests were finished in less than twelve minutes. The early (*DRA* text levels 4–10) through extending (*DRA* text levels 28–38) readers varied in the number of tasks they completed, and some students required several sittings.

How should the information from the *DRA Word Analysis* be used?

The information gained from this assessment should be used to help make instructional decisions. Transferring the scores from the Record of Responses onto the Student Cumulative Record will enable teachers to quickly identify the strengths and instructional needs of each student assessed. Once teachers are aware of what students need to gain control, they are able to plan more effectively for instruction and monitor progress over time. Suggested mini-lessons to support student learning are listed on pages 172–232 for each strand and *DRA Word Analysis* task.

How should teachers prepare students for this assessment?

Preparation for this assessment begins with good classroom instruction. During interactive writing, shared and guided reading, mini-lessons, as well as word sorts and word wall activities, teachers should call students' attention to and teach these activities as developmentally appropriate to

- Understand language used to talk about printed language concepts.
- Identify letters and words within texts and in isolation.
- Use knowledge of sounds and spelling patterns to read and spell words.
- Identify and segment various parts of words (i.e., onsets, rimes, syllables, affixes, base words).
- Substitute onsets and rimes.
- Blend, segment, and manipulate phonemes in spoken words.
- Identify and understand common prefixes and suffixes.
- Use structural analysis to determine the meaning of words.

If teachers think their students will be unfamiliar with one or more of the *DRA Word Analysis* tasks, they may use the suggested learning activities for each task beginning on page 172 to demonstrate or explain how to do a task before administering the assessment. [Note: It is critical that you do not use the letters, words, sentences, and/or examples that are in the actual assessment tasks, for this would inflate your results.]

What are the other students doing while the teacher administers the assessment?

Students should be involved in meaningful literacy learning activities that for the most part they are able to sustain while the teacher administers the *DRA Word Analysis* to selected students. For example, students could reread familiar texts, read to a partner or volunteer, draw as a preliminary step to writing, sort words, practice forming letters, illustrate texts they have written, draw as a response to a text read, listen to stories on tape, and/or complete other assignments.

When possible, teachers could team up and work together to provide each other with time to assess the identified students. While one assesses, the other could work with the combined group of students for a period of time.

What if teachers find the terms and/or language used in the *DRA Word Analysis* unfamiliar, confusing, and/or difficult to remember?

Teachers, like the students they work with, are in the process of learning and extending their understanding of words, labels, and/or terms used to talk about language and word components. While students are learning to understand words like *first, last, consonant,* and *vowel,* teachers are learning to grasp and understand words like *phonological awareness, phoneme, alliteration, onset, rime,* etc. Several steps have been taken to help teachers grasp and develop a better understanding of the language included in the *DRA Word Analysis.*

- A general definition, when appropriate, has been included with the text the first time the word appears.
- The Student Cumulative Record is organized so teachers can see the relationship of the tasks within each strand and subset. At times, the title of the task helps to clarify the label for the strand and/or subset. For example, under "Alliteration" the titles for Tasks 2 and 19, "Distinguishes pictured words that begin with the same sound" and "Provides words that begin with the same sound," support the meaning of *alliteration.*
- A glossary including a basic definition and sometimes an example has been included on pages 233–235 as a reference.

Should the *DRA* be given before the *DRA Word Analysis* is administered a second and/or third time?

It is important that teachers administer the *DRA* first. The *DRA* will show if the students have learned how to efficiently use what they know to problem-solve unknown words while constructing meaning in a slightly more challenging *DRA* text level. That will be a true indication of progress.

If students are able to read an on-grade-level *DRA* text, then it is not necessary to readminister the *DRA Word Analysis.* For all students reading below grade level due to inefficient word analysis skills, it is recommended that teachers readminister the *DRA* and the *DRA Word Analysis* periodically (beginning of the year, midyear, and end of the year) to monitor progress and determine current instructional needs.

Administration Procedures

The administration of the *DRA Word Analysis* includes four steps. It is important that teachers are familiar with and follow the established procedures in each of the four steps for administering the *DRA Word Analysis*. This will help to ensure that the results are reliable and accurate.

Step 1: Prepare for Administering the Assessment

In preparing for the administration of the *DRA Word Analysis* teachers should:

1. Administer the *DRA* to all students to confirm each student's current independent *DRA* text level. An independent *DRA* text level is one in which the reader is able to (1) decode the text with an accuracy rate of 94 percent or higher, (2) read with at least a moderate rate of fluency, and (3) construct meaning before, during, and after reading.

2. Use the chart below to determine which students qualify for this assessment. Students whose current independent *DRA* text level falls within the designated range according to the time of year should be administered the *DRA Word Analysis*. For example, a second grader whose current *DRA* text level is 14 at the beginning of the school year would qualify for the assessment. A second grader reading *DRA* text level 18 would not qualify at the beginning of the year but would qualify midyear or at the end of the year.

Student Selection Criteria for *DRA Word Analysis*

Grade	Student's Current Independent *DRA* Text Level		
	Beginning of the Year	Midyear	End of the Year
Kindergarten	Optional	Level 1 and below	Level 2 and below
First	Level 2 and below	Level 10 and below	Level 14 and below
Second	Level 14 and below	Level 18 and below	Level 24 and below
Third	Level 24 and below	Level 30 and below	Level 34 and below
Fourth	Level 34 and below	Level 38 and below	Level 38 and below
Fifth	Level 38 and below	Level 38 and below	Level 38 and below

3. Use the chart below to determine the initial *DRA Word Analysis* task for each identified student. The column in the table delineating the range of tasks to administer is designed to help teachers plan and prepare for the tasks being administered.

Initial Task Selection Criteria for *DRA Word Analysis*

Student's Current *DRA* Text Level	Initial Task	Range of Tasks to Administer*
A–3	1	1–10
4–8	8	8–17
10–12	12	12–22
14–18	16	16–28
20–24	20	20–32
28–30	24	24–36
34 or higher	28	28–40

*Note: The number of tasks the student completes will vary based upon his/her previous experiences, strengths, and needs. For example, a student reading *DRA* text level A will more than likely complete less than ten tasks, whereas a student reading *DRA* text level 3 may complete several tasks beyond Task 10. The assessment is stopped when the student demonstrates no, little, and/or some control on any three tasks.

4. Consider how to administer the *DRA Word Analysis*. It will take approximately two minutes for most tasks. The spelling checks generally take longer. The assessment may be administered in one of two ways.

   (a) Administer the designated tasks across several sittings. For example, administer as many tasks as the student is able to complete in fifteen minutes in the morning and then after lunch continue administering tasks for another fifteen minutes or until the student demonstrates no, little, and/or some control on any three tasks.

   (b) Administer one or two of the designated tasks per day to all identified students. Stop the assessment for individual students when they demonstrate no, little, and/or some control on any three tasks.

5. Read and/or review the teacher directions for each task to be administered.

6. Make copies of the Record of Responses for the tasks to be administered. Also make a double-sided copy of the Student Cumulative Record on 11-by-17-inch paper for each identified student.

7. Fold the Student Cumulative Record in half, and write the student's name, grade, and current independent *DRA* text level on the front. Place a Record of Responses for each task to be administered within the Student Cumulative Record for easy access.

8. Select and prepare a place to administer the assessment. It is best to use a rectangular table so the teacher is able to sit near the student to point to items and/or turn pages as needed. It is also important, as much as possible, to prevent the student from observing what is being recorded during the assessment.

9. Gather all the following assessment materials:
   - Teacher directions
   - Student Assessment Book
   - Identified students' Cumulative Records
   - Record of Responses pages for the tasks to be administered
   - Stopwatch
   - Pen or pencil

Step 2: Administer the *DRA Word Analysis*

It is important for teachers to become familiar with the assessment procedures and guidelines in order to effectively and efficiently administer, record observations, and score the *DRA Word Analysis*.

Assessment Procedures

When administering the assessment, teachers are to use the following directions:

1. Follow the specific directions for each task.

   > Note: Sounds are to be given when a letter or letters appear between diagonal lines, such as /b/ or /cl/. Isolated vowel sounds are marked with phonemic symbols. For example, the short *e* sound appears /ĕ/ whereas the long *e* sound appears /ē/. Letter names are to be said when isolated uppercase letters appear, such as *L* or *TR*.

2. Use a stopwatch to document the amount of time it takes for the student to complete each designated timed task. An icon of a stopwatch 🕐 and the maximum length of time recorded in minutes and seconds have been included on timed tasks as a reminder.
   [Note: The maximum length of time was based on student performance in the 2003 field tests. On timed tasks, teachers should look for quick responses and/or automatic recognition.]

3. Before beginning the first assessment task, explain to the student that you want to learn what he/she knows and can do, so you will <u>not</u> be able to help him/her once you start a task. If he/she does not know an answer and cannot figure it out, he/she is to say, "skip" or "I don't know."

4. Write the student's name and date at the top of the Record of Responses form for each task administered.

5. Read aloud to the student all statements, words, and/or sounds that are in boldface italics.

6. Silently count "1-one-thousand, 2-one-thousand, 3-one-thousand" for a 3-second wait time. Count "1-one-thousand, 2-one-thousand, . . ." up to 8-one-thousand for an 8-second wait time. A 3-second wait time is given for letter and word recognition, whereas tasks in which students are asked to generate words or sentences permit up to an 8-second wait time.

7. Do not comment about the student's responses during the actual assessment of a task, but make positive comments and/or praise the student's efforts after each task is completed.

Recording Guidelines

1. Record your observation of the student's responses on the Record of Responses for each task in the appropriate column for the first, second, and/or third administration of the task.

2. Use the following guidelines to record the student's responses as you administer each task.

    (a) For each correct response, place a check mark.

    (b) For incorrect responses, write the incorrect response given by the student.

    (c) For self-corrected responses, place sc to the right of the incorrect response that the student self-corrected.

    (d) For each skipped or omitted item, place a dash.
    [Note: A copy of these recording guidelines has been included on the inside back cover of the book. It is recommended that you make a copy of the recording guidelines and use it as a bookmark so that you will be able to quickly refer to them, when necessary, until you become familiar with how to record the student's responses.]

3. For each timed task, record the length of time in minutes and seconds on the designated lines. Round time to the nearest second if your stopwatch shows hundredths of a second. For example, a task completed in 1:50:40 (1 minute 50 seconds 40 hundredths of a second) would be recorded as 1:51 (1 minute 51 seconds). A task completed in 2:40:23 (2 minutes 40 seconds 23 hundredths of a second) would be recorded as 2:40 (2 minutes 40 seconds).

4. Write your observations of how the student responded; his/her attitude and pace; comments made before, during, or after the task; etc. in the space provided. This information will be helpful when planning for future instruction.

Scoring Guidelines

1. Follow the specific criteria provided with each task to identify correct and self-corrected responses.

2. Add the number of correct and self-corrected responses to obtain a total score.

3. Record the total score on the designated line at the bottom of the page.

4. Use the student's total score to identify the student's level of control for the task on the chart at the top of the Record of Responses. There are four levels of control:
   • No/Little Control (0–39% correct)
   • Some Control (40–79% correct)
   • Gaining Control (80–99% correct)
   • Control (100% correct)

5. You do not need to figure the percentages; this has already been done for you.

Make a note of all other observations.

Step 3: Analyze Student Behaviors and Responses

Teachers will generally use three sources of information to prepare for and analyze students' behaviors and responses when attending to and working with words in isolation and in context. These sources are the Student Cumulative Record, the Record of Responses, and the Spelling and Oral Miscues Analysis form.

Student Cumulative Record

1. Record the date of the assessment, the student's current independent *DRA* text level, and the numbers of the first and the last task administered in the appropriate grade-level section on the front of his/her Student Cumulative Record.

2. Record the date (month/year) each task was completed in the appropriate column, depending upon his/her level of control, on the inside of the Student Cumulative Record.
   [Note: The level of control columns are further subdivided into three columns to indicate whether the assessment was the first, second, or third administration.]

3. Use the following colored pen to document progress over time:
   • Kindergarten (purple)
   • First grade (red)
   • Second grade (green)
   • Third grade (blue)
   • Fourth grade (black)
   • Fifth grade (orange)

See an example of a completed Student Cumulative Record on page 28.

Record of Responses

1. Use the Record of Responses for the three tasks performed with no, little, and/or some control to identify patterns of responding, as well as knowledge and use of various components of words.

2. Note what word components the student attended to and controlled.

3. Note what word components the student neglected to attend to and/or did not control.

4. Decide if more information is needed. If a student began the assessment with Task 8 or higher, it is strongly recommended that teachers administer the earlier tasks in the strand if that student demonstrated no, little, and/or some control on one or more of the tasks. This would enable the teacher to document the student's level of control on the more basic tasks. For instance, if a student demonstrates some control on "Using analogies to decode words," Task 31, the teacher should assess or reassess the earlier tasks (Tasks 23, 24, and 30) in the substitutions/analogies strand to see if the student demonstrates control of substituting rimes, final sounds, and/or onsets. This should be completed before selecting a focus for instruction.

Spelling and Oral Miscues Analysis

With each struggling reader, it is important for the teacher to complete a more detailed analysis of the student's spelling and oral reading miscues to see what visual information, letters, and/or spelling patterns he/she is attending to as well as neglecting when reading and writing text independently.

1. Use the two pages of the Spelling and Oral Reading Miscues Analysis form to record the student's (1) spelling within an independently written text and (2) miscues recorded in his/her current *DRA* Record of Oral Reading.

2. Note what word components the student attended to and controlled. For example, note if the student consistently controlled initial consonants, final consonants, short vowels, middle consonants, common long vowel patterns (*VCe*), etc.

3. Note what word components the student neglected to attend to and/or did not control.

4. Note if there is a pattern between what the student controlled in writing and reading. For example, note what parts of words he/she consistently controlled (onsets, endings, dominant sounds, etc.) or what is confused (letters and/or words).

See an example of a completed Spelling and Oral Miscues Analysis form on page 163.

Step 4: Identify a Focus for Instruction

The Focus for Instruction on the back of the Student Cumulative Record is designed to help teachers use the information gained from *DRA Word Analysis* and Spelling and Oral Reading Miscue Analysis to plan for instruction and implement developmentally appropriate learning activities. Use the following guidelines to help determine a focus for instruction and select related activities:

1. Identify what the student needs to learn next based on his/her responses to the three *DRA Word Analysis* tasks in which the student demonstrated no, little, and/or some control.
   [Note: Place a sticky note or in some way flag these three tasks so they are easy to access in the future.]

2. Identify what the student needs to learn next in spelling and in decoding unknown words based upon the analysis of his/her spelling approximations and oral reading miscues.

3. Determine the focus for instruction, and place the date by the strand(s) that the student is in need of instruction on the back of the Student Cumulative Record. See a completed example on page 28.

4. Review and select sample mini-lessons and/or learning activities beginning on page 172 to teach and reinforce the identified word analysis tasks.

5. Store the Record of Responses pages inside the Student Cumulative Record and the Student Cumulative Record within the *DRA* Continuum folder for each student assessed. Keeping each student's *DRA Word Analysis* forms with his/her *DRA* Continuum will enable teachers to monitor the student's progress on both assessments.

After the identification of a focus for instruction is completed, teachers may want to complete a *DRA Word Analysis* Group Profile form. The Group Profile will enable teachers to compile each student's levels of control for the tasks he/she completed in order to group the students according to instructional needs and plan more effectively for their instruction.

DRA™ *Word Analysis* Student Cumulative Record

The Student Cumulative Record provides an overview of the *DRA Word Analysis* tasks and enables teachers to

- document the student's level of performance each time a task is completed,
- show progress over time,
- identify instructional needs.

The 40 *DRA Word Analysis* tasks are grouped into the following five strands:

- Phonological Awareness
- Metalanguage
- Letter/Word Recognition
- Phonics
- Structural Analysis and Syllabication

Phonological Awareness and Phonics are further divided into subgroups. Phonological Awareness is subdivided into Rhyming, Alliteration, Phonemic Awareness, and Segmentation. Phonics is subdivided into Encoding, Decoding, Substitutions/analogies, and Syllabication.

The tasks in each strand and/or subgroup are in chronological order. For example, the subgroup *Rhyming* includes tasks 1 and 13, while Structural Analysis includes Tasks 28, 35, 37, and 38. The tasks were organized into strands so teachers can quickly identify areas of strengths and weaknesses. Also these groupings enable a teacher to identify previous tasks within a strand if the student demonstrates no, little, and/or some control on a later task. For instance, if a student demonstrates some control on "Providing words that rhyme," Task 13, the teacher should assess or reassess the earlier task within the subgroup "Distinguishing pictured rhyming words," Task 1, to see if the student demonstrates control.

[Note: The task objectives within each of the five strands are listed in the Developing Proficient Readers and the *DRA Word Analysis* chart on pages 9–10.]

After the number and the title of each task, there are four major columns denoting level of control. The first three columns are further subdivided into three sections to indicate the first, second, and/or third administration of that task. The fourth column is not subdivided because once the student demonstrates control of a task, the date is recorded and the task is not readministered. The first two columns, "No/Little Control" and "Some Control," are shaded indicating a need for further instruction. Teachers are to record the date (month/year) in the appropriate column, depending on the student's level of control, for each completed assessment task. A different color pen is used to record a student's scores for each grade level. For example, kindergarten teachers will use a purple pen, whereas third-grade teachers will use a blue pen. This way teachers, students, and parents will see progress over time.

When a teacher readministers the *DRA Word Analysis* later in the school year or the following year, the student's previous scores on the Student Cumulative Record will enable the teacher to identify the initial task, the tasks to reassess, as well as the tasks that do not need to be reassessed because the student has already demonstrated control. [<u>Note</u>: It is important that teachers administer the *DRA* again before readministering the *DRA Word Analysis*. How the student problem-solves unknown words while constructing meaning in a slightly more challenging *DRA* text level will be a true indicator of what he/she has learned.]

The Student Cumulative Record is also an organizational tool. Before administering the initial assessment, teachers may place inside the Student Cumulative Record folder a copy of the Record of Responses pages for each task they plan to administer. [<u>Note</u>: Stapling the Record of Responses pages together helps to keep them in order and from getting lost.] After the teacher has analyzed the student's performance and selected a focus for future instruction, the Record of Responses pages may be stored in the cumulative folder in preparation for the next time the assessment is given. [<u>Note</u>: It is recommended that teachers in some way designate the tasks that do <u>not</u> need to be reassessed because the student has already demonstrated control, e.g., cut off diagonally the top right-hand corner of those Record of Responses pages.]

If a student did not initially demonstrate control of a task, he/she should demonstrate greater control the next time the task is given if instruction and opportunities to practice were provided in the meantime. When progress is not made between assessments, a teacher needs to find another way to help the student learn the needed word analysis skill, strategy, and/or information.

Student Name

School

Record both the date on which the *DRA Word Analysis* is administered and the student's current *DRA* text level in the appropriate grade-level section each time the assessment is given.

Grade	Beginning of Year			Middle of Year			End of Year		
	Date	DRA Level	Tasks	Date	DRA Level	Tasks	Date	DRA Level	Tasks
Kindergarten									
First									
Second									
Third									
Fourth									
Fifth									

On the second and third pages of the Student Cumulative Record, record the date (month and year) when each task was completed in the appropriate column, depending upon his/her level of control.
[Note: The "level of control" columns are divided into three sections to indicate whether this assessment was the first, second, or third administration.]

To document progress over time, record the student's total scores using the following colors: kindergarten (purple); first grade (red); second grade (green); third grade (blue); fourth grade (black); fifth grade (orange).

DRA™ Word Analysis *Student Cumulative Record*

Task Number	Task Objective	No/Little Control			Some Control			Gaining Control			Controls
		1st	2nd	3rd	1st	2nd	3rd	1st	2nd	3rd	
Phonological Awareness											
	Rhyming										
1	Distinguishes pictured rhyming words										
13	Provides words that rhyme										
	Alliteration										
2	Distinguishes initial sounds of pictured words										
19	Provides words that begin with the same sound										
	Phonemic Awareness										
3	Isolates the initial sound of a word										
12	Blends phonemes into words										
15	Deletes onsets										
20	Deletes final sounds										
21	Segments words into phonemes										
	Segmentation										
8	Segments sentences into words										
14	Segments words into onsets and rimes										
18	Segments words into syllables I										
Metalanguage											
4	Understands words used to talk about printed language concepts I										
7	Understands words used to talk about printed language concepts II										
Letter/Word Recognition											
5	Names capital letters										
6	Names lowercase letters										
9	Recognizes high frequency words I										
17	Recognizes high frequency words II										
22	Recognizes high frequency words III										
29	Recognizes high frequency words IV										

DRA™ Word Analysis *Student Cumulative Record*

Task Number	Task Objective	No/Little Control			Some Control			Gaining Control			Controls
		1st	2nd	3rd	1st	2nd	3rd	1st	2nd	3rd	
Phonics											
	Encoding: Phoneme/grapheme relationships										
10	Spells 2–3 letter high frequency words										
16	Spells words with short vowels, high frequency words with common spelling patterns										
27	Spells words with VCe, initial digraphs, preconsonant nasals, suffixes										
36	Spells words with r-controlled vowels, suffixes, initial blends, "ck," open first syllable										
40	Spells words with prefixes, closed first syllables, suffixes, 3-letter initial blends, diphthongs, long vowel patterns										
	Decoding: Grapheme/phoneme relationships										
11	Identifies and uses initial sounds										
25	Blends and uses initial consonant sounds										
26	Identifies words with long/short vowels										
32	Identifies words with vowel patterns										
33	Blends and uses initial syllables										
	Substitutions/analogies										
23	Substitutes onsets: rhyming words										
24	Substitutes final sounds										
30	Substitutes rimes										
31	Uses analogies to decode words										
Structural Analysis and Syllabication											
28	Uses structural analysis to determine word meaning: suffixes I										
34	Segments words into syllables II										
35	Uses structural analysis to determine word meaning: suffixes II										
37	Uses structural analysis to determine word meaning: prefixes										
38	Uses structural analysis to determine word meaning: suffixes III										
39	Segments words into syllables III										

Use the tasks that the student scored "no/little" or "some" control to determine the next step and identify what he/she needs to learn next on the Focus for Instruction on the back of the folder.

What's Next? Focus for Instruction

Rhyming
___ Provide opportunities to hear and read rhymes/poetry
___ Provide opportunities to read and sing songs with rhymes
___ Provide opportunities to sort pictured rhyming words
___ Teach/support how to distinguish rhyming words
___ Teach/support how to generate words that rhyme

Alliteration
___ Read aloud books with alliteration
___ Teach/support how to distinguish words that begin with the same sound(s)
___ Provide opportunities to sort pictured-words that begin with the same sound(s)
___ Teach/support how to generate words that begin with the same sound(s)
___ Co-write alliterations using students' names

Phonemic Awareness
___ Teach/support how to isolate the initial sound of a word
___ Teach/support how to delete the initial sound of a word
___ Teach/support how to delete the final sound of a word
___ Teach/support how to blend phonemes into words
___ Teach/support how to segment words into phonemes

Segmentation
___ Teach/support segmenting sentences into words
___ Teach/support segmenting words into onsets and rimes
___ Teach/support segmenting words into syllables

Metalanguage
___ Model/support concept of a word during "shared reading" and "interactive writing" experiences
___ Model/support the meaning of "first," "last," "beginning," "end" of a word
___ Model/support the meaning of "letter," "capital letter," "lowercase letter"
___ Model/support the meaning of "letter-sound(s)"

Letter/Word Recognition
___ Teach/support the names of capital and/or lowercase letters
___ Provide opportunities to hear and read alphabet books
___ Make own alphabet book
___ Teach/support how to distinguish similar letters
___ Teach/support the formation of capital/lowercase letters
___ Teach/support high frequency words
___ Support rereading of familiar books

Encoding: Phoneme/grapheme relationships
___ Teach/support consonant sound-letter correspondences
___ Teach/support vowel sound-letter correspondences
___ Teach/support how to say a word slowly and write the sounds heard
___ Teach/support segmenting words into phonemes
___ Teach/support how to check a word to see if it looks right
___ Support use of a word wall

Decoding: Grapheme/phoneme relationships
___ Teach/support letter-sound correspondences
___ Teach/support the blending of letter/sounds grouped together
___ Teach/support how to recall words that begin with a blended group of letter(s)/sound(s)
___ Teach/support how to identify short-vowel words, i.e., CVC, CCVC, CVCC
___ Teach/support how to identify common long-vowel patterns, i.e., CV, CVV, CVCe, CVVC
___ Support word sorts
___ Use magnetic letters or cards to construct/change words

Substitutions/analogies
___ Teach/support how to substitute onsets
___ Teach/support how to substitute rimes and/or final sounds
___ Teach/support how to substitute vowels
___ Provide opportunities to do word sorts
___ Use magnetic letters to construct/change words
___ Teach/support how to use known onsets and rimes to identify unfamiliar words
___ Teach/support how to use known features of words to identify unfamiliar words (spelling patterns, suffixes, etc.)

Using structural analysis to determine word meaning
___ Teach/support how to use inflectional endings to determine word meaning (s, ed, ing, ly, er, est)
___ Teach/support how to use contractions to determine word meaning
___ Teach/support meaning of suffixes (ful, less, ness, able, etc.)
___ Teach/support meaning of prefixes (un, re, pre, etc.)

Syllabication
___ Support segmenting compound words and contractions
___ Support segmenting words with 2–3 consonants between vowels (VC/CV) into syllables
___ Support segmenting words with a consonant between two vowels (V/CV—open syllable or VC/V—closed syllable)
___ Support segmenting words with a final syllable with a consonant plus *le* (*Cle*)
___ Support segmenting words with affixes into syllables
___ Support word sorts and word hunts involving syllable patterns

Other:_____

_____

_____

_____

_____

_____

DRA™ Word Analysis *Student Cumulative Record*

Student Name Example

School

Record both the date on which the *DRA Word Analysis* is administered and the student's current *DRA* text level in the appropriate grade-level section each time assessment is given.

Grade	Beginning of Year			Middle of Year			End of Year		
	Date	DRA Level	Tasks	Date	DRA Level	Tasks	Date	DRA Level	Ta
Kindergarten									
First									
Second	9-03	4	1-19	1-04	16	5-22			
Third									
Fourth									
Fifth									

On the second and third pages of the Student Cumulative Record, record the date (month and year) when each task was completed in the appropriate column, depending upon his/her level of control.
[Note: The "level of control" columns are divided into three sections to indicate whether this assessment was the first, second, or third administration.]

To document progress over time, record the student's total scores using the following colors: kindergarten (purple); first grade (red); second grade (green); third grade (blue); fourth grade (black); fifth grade (orange).

DRA™ Word Analysis *Student Cumulative Record*

Task Number	Task Objective	No/Little Control			Some Control			Gaining Control			Controls
		1st	2nd	3rd	1st	2nd	3rd	1st	2nd	3rd	
Phonological Awareness											
	Rhyming										
1	Distinguishes pictured rhyming words										9-03
13	Provides words that rhyme										9-03
	Alliteration										
2	Distinguishes initial sounds of pictured words										9-03
19	Provides words that begin with the same sound							9/03			1-04
	Phonemic Awareness										
3	Isolates the initial sound of a word										9-03
12	Blends phonemes into words				9/03			1/04			
15	Deletes onsets										9-03
20	Deletes final sounds				1/04						
21	Segments words into phonemes				1/04						
	Segmentation										
8	Segments sentences into words				9/03			1/04			
14	Segments words into onsets and rimes							9/03			1-04
18	Segments words into syllables I							9/03			1-04
Metalanguage											
4	Understands words used to talk about printed language concepts I										9-03
7	Understands words used to talk about printed language concepts II										9-03
Letter/Word Recognition											
5	Names capital letters							9/03			1-04
6	Names lowercase letters							9/03	1/04		
	Recognizes high frequency words I							9/03			1-04
	Recognizes high frequency words II				9/03				1/04		
	Recognizes high frequency words III				1/04						

DRA™ Word Analysis *Student Cumulative Record*

Task Number	Task Objective	No/Little Control			Some Control			Gaining Control			Con
		1st	2nd	3rd	1st	2nd	3rd	1st	2nd	3rd	
Phonics											
	Encoding: Phoneme/grapheme relationships										
10	Spells 2–3 letter high frequency words										9-
16	Spells words with short vowels, high frequency words with common spelling patterns				9/03	1/04					
27	Spells words with VCe, initial digraphs, preconsonant nasals, suffixes										
36	Spells words with r-controlled vowels, suffixes, initial blends, "ck," open first syllable										
40	Spells words with prefixes, closed first syllables, suffixes, 3-letter initial blends, diphthongs, long vowel patterns										
	Decoding: Grapheme/phoneme relationships										
11	Identifies and uses initial sounds				9/03						1-
25	Blends and uses initial consonant sounds										
26	Identifies words with long/short vowels										
32	Identifies words with vowel patterns										
33	Blends and uses initial syllables										
	Substitutions/analogies										
23	Substitutes onsets: rhyming words										
24	Substitutes final sounds										
30	Substitutes rimes										
31	Uses analogies to decode words										
Structural Analysis and Syllabication											
28	Uses structural analysis to determine word meaning: suffixes I										
34	Segments words into syllables II										
35	Uses structural analysis to determine word meaning: suffixes II										
37	Uses structural analysis to determine word meaning: prefixes										
38	Uses structural analysis to determine word meaning: suffixes III										
39	Segments words into syllables III										

Use the tasks that the student scored "no/little" or "some" control to determine the next step and identify what he needs to learn next on the Focus for Instruction on the back of the folder.

DRA™ Word Analysis *Student Cumulative Record*

What's Next? Focus for Instruction

Rhyming
___ Provide opportunities to hear and read rhymes/poetry
___ Provide opportunities to read and sing songs with rhymes
___ Provide opportunities to sort pictured rhyming words
___ Teach/support how to distinguish rhyming words
___ Teach/support how to generate words that rhyme

Alliteration
___ Read aloud books with alliteration
___ Teach/support how to distinguish words that begin with the same sound(s)
___ Provide opportunities to sort pictured-words that begin with the same sound(s)
___ Teach/support how to generate words that begin with the same sound(s)
___ Co-write alliterations using students' names

Phonemic Awareness
___ Teach/support how to isolate the initial sound of a word
___ Teach/support how to delete the initial sound of a word
1/04 Teach/support how to delete the final sound of a word
9/03 Teach/support how to blend phonemes into words
1/04 Teach/support how to segment words into phonemes

Segmentation
9/03 Teach/support segmenting sentences into words
___ Teach/support segmenting words into onsets and rimes
___ Teach/support segmenting words into syllables

Metalanguage
___ Model/support concept of a word during "shared reading" and "interactive writing" experiences
___ Model/support the meaning of "first," "last," "beginning," "end" of a word
___ Model/support the meaning of "letter," "capital letter," "lowercase letter"
___ Model/support the meaning of "letter-sound(s)"

Letter/Word Recognition
___ Teach/support the names of capital and/or lowercase letters
___ Provide opportunities to hear and read alphabet books Make own alphabet book
1/04 Teach/support how to distinguish similar letters
___ Teach/support the formation of capital/lowercase letters
9/03 Teach/support high-frequency words
9/03 Support rereading of familiar books

Encoding: Phoneme/grapheme relationships
___ Teach/support consonant sound-letter correspondences
___ Teach/support vowel sound-letter correspondences
___ Teach/support how to say a word slowly and write the sounds heard
___ Teach/support segmenting words into phonemes
___ Teach/support how to check a word to see if it looks right
___ Support use of a word wall

Decoding: Grapheme/phoneme relationships
___ Teach/support letter-sound correspondences
___ Teach/support the blending of letter/sounds grouped together
___ Teach/support how to recall words that begin with a blended group of letter(s)/sound(s)
___ Teach/support how to identify short-vowel words, i.e. CVC, CCVC, CVCC
___ Teach/support how to identify common long vowel patterns, i.e. CV, CVV, CVCe, CVVC
___ Support word sorts
___ Use magnetic letters or cards to construct/change words

Substitutions/analogies
___ Teach/support how to substitute onsets
___ Teach/support how to substitute rimes and/or final sounds
___ Teach/support how to substitute vowels
___ Provide opportunities to do word sorts
___ Use magnetic letters to construct/change words
___ Teach/support how to use known onsets and rimes to identify unfamiliar words
___ Teach/support how to use known features of words to identify unfamiliar words (spelling patterns, suffixes, etc.)

Using structural analysis to determine word meaning
___ Teach/support how to use inflectional endings to determine word meaning (s, ed, ing, ly, er, est)
___ Teach/support how to use contractions to determine word meaning
___ Teach/support meaning of suffixes (ful, less, ness, able, etc.)
___ Teach/support meaning of prefixes (un, re, pre, etc.)

Syllabication
___ Support segmenting compound words and contractions
___ Support segmenting words with 2–3 consonants between vowels (VC/CV) into syllables
___ Support segmenting words with a consonant between two vowels (V/CV—open syllable or VC/V—closed syllable)
___ Support segmenting words with a final syllable with a consonant plus le (Cle)
___ Support segmenting words with affixes into syllables
___ Support word sorts and word hunts involving syllable patterns

Other:_____
_____
_____
_____
_____

Teacher Directions for *DRA*™ *Word Analysis* Tasks

Specific teacher directions for each of the 40 *DRA Word Analysis* tasks are included in this section. The task number and objective(s) are identified at the top of the page. The directions for each task are divided into three sections. The first section, "Prior to the Assessment," lists the materials needed for the administration of the task. The second section, "Administering the Assessment," provides the directions for a demonstration and shared demonstration of the task, and the actual task assessment. The last section, "After the Assessment," includes guidelines for scoring the student's responses and determining the next step.

It is important for teachers to follow the specific directions for administering, (i.e., say, point, don't point, etc.). All statements, words, sounds that are in bold are to be read aloud to the student. Sounds are to be given when a letter or letters appear between diagonal lines, such as /b/ or /cl/. Isolated vowel sounds are marked, such as the short *e* sound appears /ĕ/ while the long *e* sound appears /ē/.

A stopwatch is used in some tasks to document the amount of time it takes for the student to complete designated "timed" tasks. In timed tasks teachers are looking for quick and/or automatic responses. An icon of a stopwatch has been included on timed tasks. Each timed task has a maximum length of time recorded in minutes and seconds after the objective.

A 3-second wait time is given for letter and word identification, while for tasks in which students are asked to generate words or sentences, up to 8 seconds is allowed. Teachers are to count "1-one-thousand, 2-one-thousand, 3-one-thousand" for a 3-second wait time and up to "8-one-thousand" for an 8-second wait time.

It is highly recommended that teachers do not comment on the student's responses during the actual assessment of a task, but they are encouraged to make positive comments and/or praise the student's efforts after the task is completed.

Distinguishing pictured rhyming words

Objective: To identify a picture in a set that rhymes with the first picture

Prior to the Assessment

Assemble the following materials:
- *Student Assessment Book:* Task 1
- *Record of Responses:* Task 1
- Folded sheet of plain paper (optional)

Administering the Assessment

Use the *Recording Guidelines* provided in General Directions, page 18, to record your observation after <u>each</u> response in the *Record of Responses*.

Demonstration
1. Say: ***In each row there are two pictured words that rhyme. I will ask you to point to a picture that rhymes with the first picture in each row. I will show you what to do.***
   [<u>Note</u>: You may use a folded sheet of plain paper to cover the pictures below the row on which you are focusing if it is helpful for the student.]
2. Point to each picture as you say: ***Glue, tree, cat, two.*** Pause between the words, but do <u>not</u> say, "and."
3. Point to the glue, and say: **Glue *ends with* /oo/**
4. Point to the tree, and say: **Tree *ends with* /ee/. Glue, tree *do not rhyme.***
5. Point to the cat, and say: **Cat *ends with* /at/. Glue, cat *do not rhyme.***
6. Point to the two and say: **Two *ends with* /oo/. Glue, two *rhyme.***

Shared Demonstration
1. Say: ***Let's do one together now.***
2. Point to each picture in the second row as you say: ***Nose, top, rose, shoe. Now, you say each one.*** Wait while student says each one. Give the name of the picture if the student has difficulty recalling the name.
3. Then, say: ***Point to a picture that rhymes with* nose.**
   - If CORRECT, say: ***That's right.* Nose, rose *rhyme.***
   - If INCORRECT, say: ***Let's say together, nose, top, rose, shoe.*** Point to each picture as you both say: ***Nose, top, shoe, rose.*** Point to the nose, and say: **Nose *ends with* /ōz/.** Point to top, and say: **Top *ends with* /op/. Nose, top *do not rhyme.*** Point to rose, and say: **Rose *ends with* /ōz/. Nose, rose *rhyme.*** Point to shoe and say: **Shoe *ends with* /oo/. Nose, shoe *do not rhyme.***
4. Say: ***Do you understand what to do?*** Repeat directions and/or demonstrations if necessary. ***If you cannot find a word that rhymes, say "I don't know."***

Assessment

1. Start with the first set of pictures and say: ***train, duck, wing, rain.***
   [<u>Note</u>: STOP THIS TASK if the student responds incorrectly to the first three sets of pictures.]
2. Say: ***Now you say each one.*** Wait while the student responds. Say the name of the picture if the student has difficulty recalling the name.
3. Then, say: ***Point to a picture that rhymes with train.***
4. Continue the task. Follow the same procedures as above using the remaining sets of pictures.

After the Assessment

Scoring Guidelines
- Count each identified picture that rhymes with the first picture in the set as 1 point. See an example of a completed *Record of Responses* for this task below.

| Total score: 8 |

Determining Next Step
- Continue on to Task 2, "Distinguishing initial sounds of pictured words."

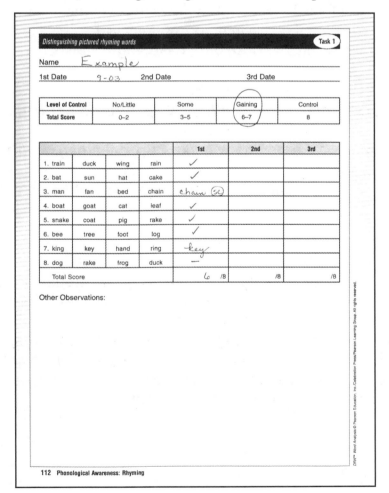

Task 2

Distinguishing initial sounds of pictured words

Objective: To identify a picture in a set that begins with the same sound as the first picture

Prior to the Assessment

Assemble the following materials:
- *Student Assessment Book:* Task 2
- *Record of Responses:* Task 2
- Folded sheet of plain paper (optional)

Administering the Assessment

Use the *Recording Guidelines* provided in General Directions, page 18, to record your observation after <u>each</u> response in the *Record of Responses*.

Demonstration
1. Say: ***In each row there are two pictured words that begin with the same sound. I will ask you to point to a picture that begins with the same sound as the first picture in each row. I will show you what to do.***
   [<u>Note</u>: You may use a folded sheet of plain paper to cover the pictures below the row on which you are focusing if it is helpful for the student.]
2. Point to each picture as you say: **Cup, bird, cake, log.** Pause between the words, but do <u>not</u> say "and."
3. Point to cup, and say: **Cup** *begins with /k/.*
4. Point to bird, and say: **Bird** *begins with /b/.* **Cup, bird** *do not begin with the same sound.*
5. Point to cake, and say: **Cake** *begins with /k/.* **Cup, cake** *begin with the same sound.*
6. Point to log and say: **Log** *begins with /l/.* **Cup, log** *do not begin with the same sound.*

Shared Demonstration
1. Say: ***Let's do one together.***
2. Point to each picture in the second row as you say: **Duck, mouse, leaf, door.** ***Now, you say each one.*** Wait while the student says each one. Give the name of the picture if the student has difficulty recalling the name.
3. Then, say: ***Point to a picture that begins with the same sound as*** duck.
   - If CORRECT , say: ***You are right.*** **Duck, door** *begin with the same sound.*
   - If INCORRECT , say: ***Let's say together*** duck, mouse, leaf, door. Point to each picture as you both say: **Duck, mouse, leaf, door.**

Point to the duck, and say: **Duck** *begins with /d/.*
Point to the mouse, and say: **Mouse** *begins with /m/.* **Duck, mouse** *do not begin with the same sound.*
Point to the leaf and say: **Leaf** *begins with /l/.* **Duck, leaf** *do not begin with the same sound.*
Now, point to the door, and say: **Door** *begins with /d/.* **Duck, door** *begin with the same sound.*

4. Say: ***Do you understand what to do?*** Repeat directions and/or demonstrations if necessary. ***If you cannot find a word that begins with the same sound, say, "I don't know."***

Assessment

1. Start with the first set of pictures and say: ***bike, bat, hand, scissors.***
   [Note: STOP THIS TASK if the student responds incorrectly to the first three rows of pictures.]
2. Say: ***Now you say each one.*** Wait while the student responds. Say the name of the picture if the student has difficulty recalling the name.
3. Then, say: ***Point to a picture that begins with the same sound as bike.***
4. Continue the task. Follow the same procedures as above using the remaining sets of pictures.

After the Assessment

Scoring Guidelines
- Count each identified picture that begins with the same sound as the first picture in the set as 1 point.

Total score: 8

Determining Next Step
- Continue on to Task 3, "Isolating the initial sound of a word (Auditory/Oral)."

Isolating the initial sound of a word (Auditory/Oral)

Objective: To repeat a word given and provide the onset of the word

Prior to the Assessment

Assemble the following materials:
- *Student Assessment Book:* No accompanying page for this task
- *Record of Responses:* Task 3

Administering the Assessment

Use the *Recording Guidelines* provided in General Directions, page 18, to record your observation after <u>each</u> response in the *Record of Responses.*

Demonstration
1. Say: ***I will say a word. Then you will say the same word. Next, you will tell me the first sound in the word. I'll show you what to do.***
2. Say: ***Lock.*** (Pause) ***/l/.*** (Pause) ***/l/ is the first sound in lock.***

Shared Demonstration
1. ***Let's do one together.*** Say: **Kite. *Now you say* kite.** Wait while the student responds.
2. Then say: ***Tell me the first sound in* kite.** (/k/)
   - If CORRECT , say: ***That's right. /k/ is the first sound in* kite.**
   - If INCORRECT , say: ***Kite. /k/ /ite/.*** (Pause) ***/k/.*** (Pause) ***/k/ is the first sound in* kite. *Now, you say* kite, /k/.**
3. Say: ***Do you understand what to do?*** Repeat directions and/or demonstrations if necessary. ***If you do not know the first sound and cannot figure it out, say "I don't know."***

Assessment
1. Use the words listed in the *Record of Responses* for this task.
   [<u>Note</u>: STOP THIS TASK if the student responds incorrectly to the first three words.]
   Say: ***Pig. Now you say* pig.** Wait while the student responds.
2. Then say: ***Tell me the first sound in* pig.**
3. Continue the task; follow the same procedures as above using the remaining words listed in the *Record of Responses.*
   - If the student gives the CORRECT name of the letter instead of the sound, say: ***What sound does the letter make?***
   - If the student gives the INCORRECT letter name instead of the sound, go on to the next word.

After the Assessment

Scoring Guidelines

- Count each initial sound that the student correctly isolated as 1 point.
  [Note: The student must say the first sound by itself and not with other additional sounds. For example, if the student adds a vowel sound such as /mī/ (mice) or /ně/ (net), his/her response is not counted as correct.]

See an example of a completed *Record of Responses* for this task below.

Total score: 10

Determining Next Step

- Continue on to Task 4, "Understanding words used to talk about printed language concepts I."

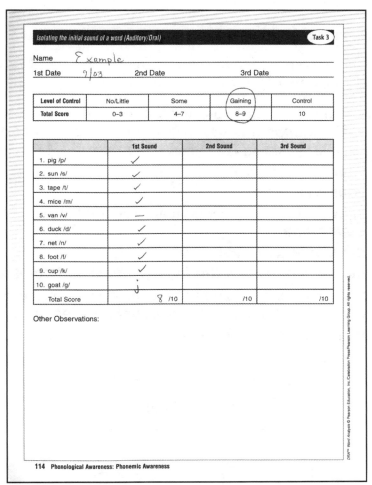

Isolating the initial sound of a word (Auditory/Oral)   Task 3

Name   Example
1st Date   9/03   2nd Date   3rd Date

Level of Control	No/Little	Some	Gaining	Control
Total Score	0–3	4–7	8–9	10

	1st Sound	2nd Sound	3rd Sound
1. pig /p/	✓		
2. sun /s/	✓		
3. tape /t/	✓		
4. mice /m/	✓		
5. van /v/	—		
6. duck /d/	✓		
7. net /n/	✓		
8. foot /f/	✓		
9. cup /k/	✓		
10. goat /g/	ɟ		
Total Score	8 /10	/10	/10

Other Observations:

114 Phonological Awareness: Phonemic Awareness

Understanding words used to talk about printed language concepts I

Objective: To demonstrate an understanding of words used to talk about printed language concepts, such as *name, first, last, letter,* and *capital* or *uppercase letter*

Prior to the Assessment

Assemble the following materials:

- *Student Assessment Book:* No accompanying page for this task
- *Record of Responses:* Task 4
- Two small sheets of paper (one blank and one with the student's first and last name printed neatly in fairly large manuscript letters); see Sample Sketch A below.

Administering the Assessment

Use the *Recording Guidelines* provided in General Directions, page 18, to record your observation after <u>each</u> response in the *Record of Responses*.

1. Place the paper with the student's first and last names on the table in front of the student and say: **What does this say?** (Pause) **If you do not know, say "I don't know."** (Say the child's first and last names if he/she does not recognize them.)
2. Say: **Point to your first name.**
3. Say: **Point to your last name.**
4. Cover up the student's last name. See Sample Sketch B below. Say: **Point to the first letter in your name.**
5. Say: **Point to the last letter in your name.**
6. Say: **Tell me the name of each letter in your name as I point to it.**
7. Cover up the student's first name and uncover his/her last name. See Sample Sketch C below. Say: **Point to a capital or uppercase letter.**
8. Say: **Tell me the name of each letter in your last name as I point to it.**

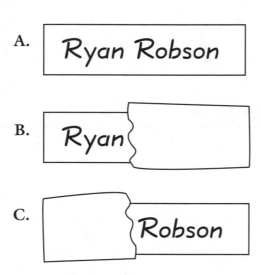

A. Ryan Robson

B. Ryan

C. Robson

After the Assessment

Scoring Guidelines
- Count each correct or self-corrected response as 1 point.
  [Note: The student must correctly name each letter in his/her first and last names to receive credit. Partial responses may be noted as an observation.]

See an example of a completed *Record of Responses* for this task below.

Total score: 8

Determining Next Step
Continue on to Task 5, "Recognizing capital letters" (Timed).

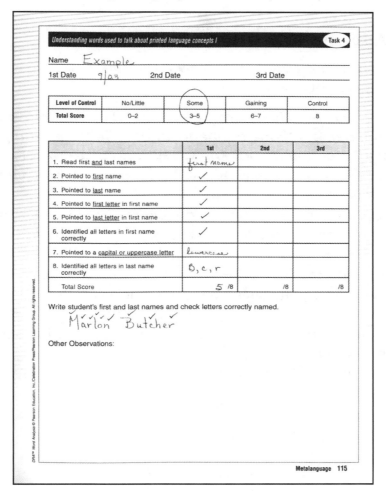

Understanding words used to talk about printed language concepts I | Task 4

Name Example

1st Date 9/03   2nd Date   3rd Date

Level of Control	No/Little	Some	Gaining	Control
Total Score	0–2	3–5	6–7	8

	1st	2nd	3rd
1. Read first _and_ last names	first name		
2. Pointed to _first_ name	✓		
3. Pointed to _last_ name	✓		
4. Pointed to _first letter_ in first name	✓		
5. Pointed to _last letter_ in first name	✓		
6. Identified all letters in first name correctly	✓		
7. Pointed to a _capital or uppercase letter_	lowercase		
8. Identified all letters in last name correctly	B, c, r		
Total Score	5 /8	/8	/8

Write student's first and last names and check letters correctly named.

Marlon Butcher

Other Observations:

Metalanguage 115

Task 5

Recognizing capital letters

Objective: To recognize and name capital letters within the specified time
(1 minute 30 seconds)

Prior to the Assessment

Assemble the following materials:
- *Student Assessment Book:* Task 5
- *Record of Responses:* Task 5
- Stopwatch

Administering the Assessment

Use the *Recording Guidelines* provided in General Directions, page 18, to record your observation after <u>each</u> response in the *Record of Responses.*

1. Point to the letters and say: ***These are called capital or uppercase letters. Each letter has a name. Tell me the name of each letter as you point to it. If you come to a letter you do not know, say "I don't know" or "skip."***
2. Show the student how to point to each letter while moving left to right, top to bottom starting with the first letter.
3. Then say: ***Do you understand what to do?*** Repeat directions if necessary.
   [<u>Note</u>: If student is unable to point to the letters, you may point to each letter for him/her.]
4. Say ***Begin now,*** as you start the stopwatch.
5. If the student does not respond after a 3-second wait time, tell him/her to go on to the next letter.
6. Stop the stopwatch after the last letter is named, or stop this task when the maximum length of time has been reached.
   [<u>Note</u>: Maximum length of time is 1 minute 30 seconds.]

After the Assessment

Scoring Guidelines

Letter confusions are <u>not</u> to be included in the total score.

- Place an X on top of the check mark that indicated a correct response for all letters that were confused with other letters.
  (<u>For example</u>, if the student correctly identified *C* and then identified the letter *G* as *C*, an X will indicate that the letter *C* was confused with another letter and will not be included in the total score.)
- Count each letter correctly named or self-corrected and <u>not</u> confused with other letters as 1 point.

See an example of a completed *Record of Responses* for this task below.

Total score: 26

Determining Next Step

Continue on to Task 6, "Recognizing lowercase letters" (Timed).

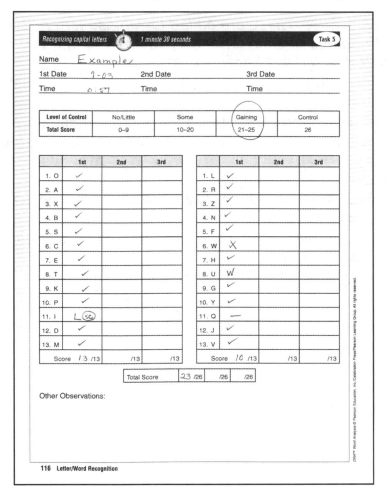

Recognizing lowercase letters

Objective: To recognize and name lowercase letters within the specified time
(1 minute 30 seconds)

Prior to the Assessment

Assemble the following materials:
- *Student Assessment Book:* Task 6
- *Record of Responses:* Task 6
- Stopwatch

Administering the Assessment

Use the Recording Guidelines provided in General Directions, page 18, to record your observation after <u>each</u> response in the *Record of Responses.*

1. Point to the letters and say: ***These are called lowercase letters. Each letter has a name. Tell me the name of each letter as you point to it. If you come to a letter you do not know, say "I don't know" or "skip."***
2. Show the student how to point to each letter while moving left to right, top to bottom starting with the first letter.
3. Then say: ***Do you understand what to do?*** Repeat directions, if necessary.
   [<u>Note</u>: If the student is unable to point to the letters, you may point to each letter for him/her.]
4. Say ***Begin now,*** as you start the stopwatch.
   [<u>Note</u>: If the student does not respond after a 3-second wait time, tell him/her to go on to the next letter.]
5. Stop the stopwatch after the last letter is named, or stop this task when the maximum length of time has been reached.
   [<u>Note</u>: Maximum length of time is 1 minute 30 seconds.]

After the Assessment

Scoring Guidelines

Letter confusions are <u>not</u> to be included in the total score.

- Place an X on top of the check mark that indicated a correct response for all letters that were confused with other letters.
  (<u>For example</u>, if the student correctly identified *n* and then identified the letter *h* as *n*, an X will indicate that the letter *n* was confused with another letter and will not be included in the total score.)
- Count each letter named correctly or self-corrected and <u>not</u> confused with other letters as 1 point.

See an example of a completed *Record of Responses* for this task below.

Total score: 26

Determining Next Step

Continue on to Task 7, "Using words used to talk about printed language concepts II." STOP ASSESSING if the student (1) has demonstrated "no/little" or "some" control on any three tasks or (2) is becoming distracted.

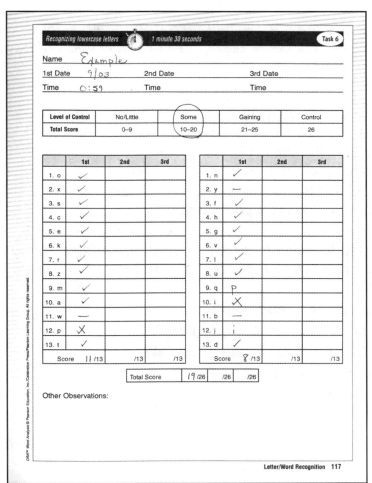

Recognizing lowercase letters	1 minute 30 seconds			Task 6

Name Example

1st Date	9/03	2nd Date		3rd Date
Time	0:59	Time		Time

Level of Control	No/Little	Some	Gaining	Control
Total Score	0–9	10–20	21–25	26

	1st	2nd	3rd		1st	2nd	3rd
1. o	✓			1. n	✓		
2. x	✓			2. y	—		
3. s	✓			3. f	✓		
4. c	✓			4. h	✓		
5. e	✓			5. g	✓		
6. k	✓			6. v	✓		
7. r	✓			7. l	✓		
8. z	✓			8. u	✓		
9. m	✓			9. q	P		
10. a	✓			10. i	✗		
11. w	—			11. b	—		
12. p	✗			12. j	i		
13. t	✓			13. d	✓		
Score	11 /13	/13	/13	Score	8 /13	/13	/13

Total Score	19 /26	/26	/26

Other Observations:

Letter/Word Recognition 117

Understanding words used to talk about printed language concepts II

Objective: To demonstrate an understanding of words used to talk about printed language concepts, such as *word, letter, first, last, begin, end,* and *sound*

Prior to the Assessment

Assemble the following materials:
- *Student Assessment Book:* Task 7
- *Record of Responses:* Task 7
- A blank sheet of paper

Administering the Assessment

Use the *Recording Guidelines* provided in General Directions, page 18, to record your observation after <u>each</u> response in the *Record of Responses*.

Shared Demonstration
Say: **This is a story about a cat. We will read it together.** Point to each word in the first line as you read, **"My cat is black."** (Pause) **Now you point to each word as you read it.**

Assessment
1. Point to the second line but <u>not to each word</u> and say: **This says "My cat is on the mat." Point to each word as you read it.**
   [<u>Note.</u> If a student is matching one-to-one and stops because of an unknown word, say the word so he/she can go on.]
2. Point to the third line <u>but not to each word</u> and say: **This says "My cat is playing now." Point to each word as you read it.**
3. Cover the first two lines with a sheet of paper. See Sample Sketch A. Say: **Now I am going to ask you to point to certain words and letters. If you do not know an answer and cannot figure it out, say "I don't know" or "skip."** Then say: **Point to the word is.**
4. Ask: **What letter does is end with?**
5. Ask: **What letter does playing begin with?**
6. Ask: **What is the first letter in the word cat?**
7. Ask: **What sound does cat begin with?**
8. Ask: **What sound does cat end with?**

After the Assessment

Scoring Guidelines

- Count each correct or self-corrected response as 1 point.
  [Note: When the student is asked to point to and read each word, he/she must say each word as he/she points to it to be counted as correct.]

Total score: 8

Determining Next Step

- Continue on to Task 8, "Segmenting sentences into words."
- STOP ASSESSING if the student (1) has demonstrated "no/little" or "some" control on any three tasks or (2) is becoming distracted.

My cat is playing now.

Understanding words used to talk about printed language concepts II   9

Sample Sketch A

Segmenting sentences into words

Objective: To use a number line to show the number of words in a given sentence

Prior to the Assessment

Assemble the following materials:
- *Student Assessment Book:* Task 8
- *Record of Responses:* Task 8

Administering the Assessment

Use the *Recording Guidelines* provided in General Directions, page 18, to record your observation after <u>each</u> response in the *Record of Responses*.

Demonstration
1. Say: **This is a number line. You are to use the number line to show each word you hear in a sentence. I'll show you what to do.**
2. Say: **My car is yellow.**
   [<u>Note</u>: Be sure to enunciate the words in each sentence clearly, but do not pause between words.]
3. Use the number line to show each word as you repeat **My car is yellow.**

Shared Demonstration
1. Say: **Let's do one together. Rabbits can hop.** Then, say: **Now use the number line to show each word as you say, "Rabbits can hop."**
   - If CORRECT , say: **That's right.**
   - If INCORRECT , say: **Watch me as I do it.** Use the number line to show each word as you say: **Rabbits can hop.** (Pause) **Now you do it.**
2. Say: **Do you understand what to do?** Repeat directions and/or demonstrations if necessary.

Assessment
Use the sentences included in the *Record of Responses* for this task.
[<u>Note</u>: STOP THIS TASK if the student responds incorrectly to the first three sentences.]
1. Say: **Use the number line to show each word as you say, "Dogs can run fast."**
   [<u>Note</u>: Be sure to enunciate the words in each sentence clearly, but <u>do not</u> pause between words.]
2. Continue with the remaining sentences listed in the *Record of Responses*. If the student cannot remember what to do, say: **Use the number line to show each word as you say,** _____ (insert sentence).
   [<u>Note</u>: The student is asked to show the number of words, <u>not</u> tell how many words.]

After the Assessment

Scoring Guidelines

The student receives credit for word boundaries. For instance, if the student points to the numbers 1 and 2 for *bears,* number 3 for *sleep,* and number 4 for *in caves,* he/she <u>does not</u> receive credit for that sentence, even though he/she ended on the correct number.

- Count each sentence in which the student pointed to the correct number for each word as 1 point.

See an example of a completed *Record of Responses* for this task below.

Total score: 7

Determining Next Step

- Continue on to Task 9, "Recognizing high frequency words I" (Timed).
- STOP ASSESSING if the student (1) has demonstrated "no/little" or "some" control on any three tasks or (2) is becoming distracted.

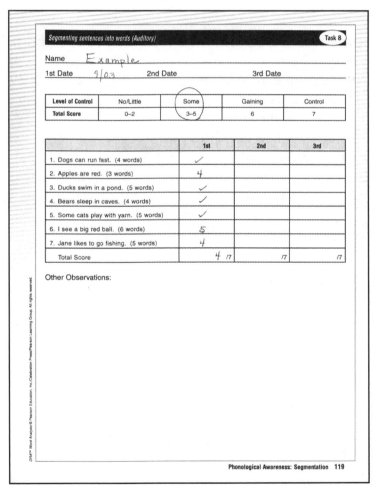

Task 9

Recognizing high frequency words I

Objective: To quickly read aloud the words in each column within the specified time (1 minute 30 seconds)

Prior to the Assessment

Assemble the following materials:
- *Student Assessment Book:* Task 9
- *Record of Responses:* Task 9
- Stopwatch

Administering the Assessment

Use the *Recording Guidelines* provided in General Directions, page 18, to record your observation after <u>each</u> response in the *Record of Responses*.

Assessment
1. Say: ***These are some words you will find in books. Please point to and read each word. Begin by reading the words in the first column, then in the second. If you don't know a word, say "skip" and go on. Do you understand what to do?*** Repeat directions, if necessary.
2. Say: ***Begin now,*** as you start the stopwatch.
   [<u>Note</u>: If the student does not respond after a 3-second wait time, tell him/her to go on to the next word.]
3. Stop the stopwatch when the student reads the last word or is unable to locate other known words; STOP this task when the maximum length of time has been reached.
   [<u>Note</u>: Maximum length of time is 1 minute 30 seconds.]

After the Assessment

Scoring Guidelines

Words confused with other words or words that are sounded out are <u>not</u> to be included in the total score.

- Place an X on top of the check mark if the word was sounded out and not quickly recognized.
- Place an X also on top of the check mark of words that were confused with another word. For example, if the student identified *is* correctly and then later said *is* for *it*, the word *is* would not be included in the total score.
- Count each word read correctly or self-corrected and <u>not</u> sounded out or confused with other words as 1 point.

See an example of a completed *Record of Responses* for this task below.

Total score: 20

Determining Next Step

- Continue on to Task 10, "Spelling Check I."
- STOP ASSESSING if the student (1) has demonstrated "no/little" or "some" control on any three tasks or (2) is becoming distracted.

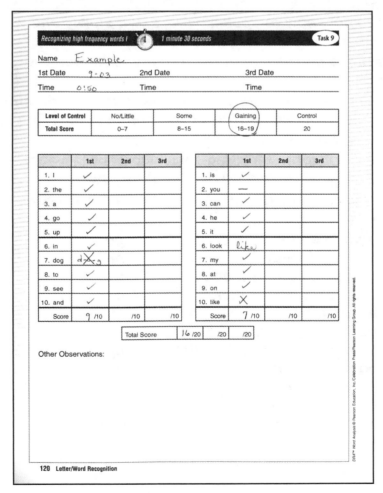

Spelling Check I

Objective: To accurately spell each component of (1) two-letter words and (2) high frequency words with common spelling patterns

Prior to the Assessment

Assemble the following materials:
- *Student Assessment Book:* No accompanying page for this task
- *Record of Responses:* Task 10
- *Spelling Check I* form

Administering the Assessment

Use the *Recording Guidelines* provided in General Directions, page 18, to record your observation after <u>each</u> response in the *Record of Responses*.

Assessment
1. Say: ***I am going to ask you to spell some words. Try to spell each word the best you can. Some words will be easy to spell; some words will be harder. When you don't know how to spell a word, say it slowly and write down all the sounds you hear.*** Repeat the directions if necessary.
2. Say: ***Write your name on the line at the top of your paper.*** Give students adequate time to respond.
3. Then say: ***I will say each spelling word by itself and in a sentence. I will then say the word again. Write each word by the number I say. Do you understand what to do?*** Repeat directions if necessary.
4. Enunciate each spelling word clearly, and give student adequate time to respond. Say: ***Number 1. no*** (Pause) ***I have <u>no</u> pencil.*** (Pause) ***no***
5. Continue the assessment using the remaining words and sentences; follow the same procedures as above.

2.	go	I <u>go</u> home after school.	go
3.	he	<u>He</u> is my friend.	he
4.	we	<u>We</u> are going to the park.	we
5.	on	The cat sat <u>on</u> the mat.	on
6.	at	I am <u>at</u> school.	at
7.	is	The flower <u>is</u> pretty.	is
8.	up	The monkey climbed <u>up</u> the tree.	up
9.	my	You are <u>my</u> friend.	my
10.	to	We like <u>to</u> read.	to
11.	the	<u>The</u> cat is playing.	the
12.	see	I <u>see</u> a red ball.	see

6. Collect the student's paper when he/she has completed this task.

After the Assessment

Scoring Guidelines

The words in Spelling Check I are grouped into sets with common features.

- Set 1: Count each initial consonant and long vowel spelled correctly as 1 point.
- Set 2: Count each short vowel and final consonant spelled correctly as 1 point.
- Set 3: Count each initial consonant(s) and spelling pattern spelled correctly as 1 point. [Note: Correct responses must have the letters written in the correct sequential order. Reversed or inverted letters, such as *b* for *d*, *t* for *f*, are not counted as correct. Make note of the improper use of capital letters.]

See an example of a completed *Record of Responses* for this task below.

Total score: 24

Determining Next Step

- Continue on to Task 11, "Identifying and using initial sounds" (Timed).
- STOP ASSESSING if the student (1) has demonstrated "no/little" or "some" control on any three tasks or (2) is becoming distracted.

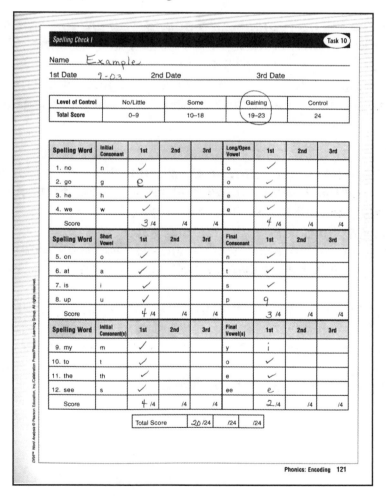

Spelling Check I — Task 10

Name _Example_

1st Date _9-03_   2nd Date _____   3rd Date _____

Level of Control	No/Little	Some	Gaining	Control
Total Score	0–9	10–18	19–23	24

Spelling Word	Initial Consonant	1st	2nd	3rd	Long/Open Vowel	1st	2nd	3rd
1. no	n	✓			o	✓		
2. go	g	e			o	✓		
3. he	h	✓			e	✓		
4. we	w	✓			e	✓		
Score		3 /4	/4	/4		4 /4	/4	/4

Spelling Word	Short Vowel	1st	2nd	3rd	Final Consonant	1st	2nd	3rd
5. on	o	✓			n	✓		
6. at	a	✓			t	✓		
7. is	i	✓			s	✓		
8. up	u	✓			p	q		
Score		4 /4	/4	/4		3 /4	/4	/4

Spelling Word	Initial Consonant(s)	1st	2nd	3rd	Final Vowel(s)	1st	2nd	3rd
9. my	m	✓			y	i		
10. to	t	✓			o	✓		
11. the	th	✓			e	✓		
12. see	s	✓			ee	e		
Score		4 /4	/4	/4		2 /4	/4	/4

Total Score	20 /24	/24	/24

Phonics: Encoding 121

Task 11

Identifying and using initial sounds

Objective: To (1) provide the phoneme for each letter and (2) give a word or name which begins with that phoneme within the specified time (4 minutes)

Prior to the Assessment

Assemble the following materials:
- *Student Assessment Book:* Task 11
- *Record of Responses:* Task 11
- Stopwatch

Administering the Assessment

Use the *Recording Guidelines* provided in General Directions, page 18, to record your observation after <u>each</u> response in the *Record of Responses.*

Demonstration
1. Say: ***Each of these letters represents a sound. You are to point to each letter, tell me the sound it makes, and then tell me a word or name which begins with that sound. I'll show you what to do.***
2. Point to the starred example and say: ***/t/. Ted. Ted begins with /t/.***
3. Say: ***Do you understand what to do?*** Repeat directions and/or demonstration if necessary.

Assessment
1. Say: ***Start with the first letter in the first column, then the second column. If you do not know the sound a letter makes or a word that begins with that sound, say "skip" and go on to the next letter.***
2. Say: ***You may begin now,*** as you start the stopwatch.
   a. If the student has difficulty remembering the task, ask: ***What sound does that letter make?*** and ***What word begins with that sound?*** as the student points to each letter.
   b. If the student does not respond after an 8-second wait time, tell him/her to go on to the next letter.
3. Stop the stopwatch when student completes the task or the maximum length of time has been reached.
   [<u>Note</u>: Maximum length of time is 4 minutes.]

After the Assessment

Scoring Guidelines

Sounds confused with other sounds are not included in the total score.

- Place an X on top of the check mark that indicated a correct response for all sounds that were confused with other sounds. (For example, if the student correctly said /m/ for the letter *m* and then said /m/ for the letter *n*, an X will indicate that the /m/ was confused with another sound and will not be included in the total score.)
- Count each correct or self-corrected sound not confused with other sounds as 1 point.
- Count each correct or self-corrected word or name beginning with the designated sound as 1 point.
  [Note: Do *not* count a word if it begins with a different sound than what the student said. For example, if the student said /ŏ/ for the letter *o* and then provided the word *ocean*, he/she would receive 1 point for the short *o* sound and zero points for the word because *ocean* begins with a long *o* sound.]

See an example of a completed *Record of Responses* for this task below.

| Total score: 48 |

Determining Next Step

- Continue on to Task 12, "Blending phonemes into words (Auditory/Oral)."
- STOP ASSESSING if the student (1) has demonstrated "no/little" or "some" control on any three tasks or (2) is becoming distracted.

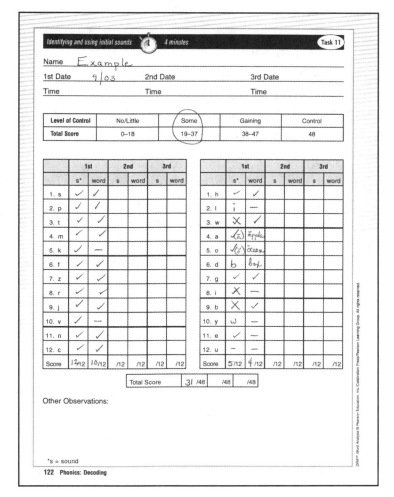

Blending phonemes into words (Auditory/Oral)

Objective: To listen to the individual phonemes in a word and then say the word

Prior to the Assessment

Assemble the following materials:
- *Student Assessment Book:* No accompanying page for this task
- *Record of Responses:* Task 12

Administering the Assessment

Use the *Recording Guidelines* provided in General Directions, page 18, to record your observation after <u>each</u> response in the *Record of Responses*.

Demonstration
1. Say: *I am going to say each sound in a word. You are to listen to the sounds and then tell me the word. I'll show you what to do.*
   [<u>Note</u>: Make sure that you say each sound individually with less than a second interval between sounds. Do <u>not</u> blend the sounds together.]
2. Then say: */p/ /ĭ/ /g/* (pig). (Pause) **Pig.** (Pause) */p/ /ĭ/ /g/ is* **pig.**
3. Say: *Let's do one together. /k/ /ī/ /t/.* Repeat once or twice if needed.
4. Then ask: *What word do these sounds make?* (kite) Wait while the student responds.
   - If CORRECT, say: *That's right.*
   - If INCORRECT, say: */k/ /ī/ /t/ is* **kite.**
5. Say: *Do you understand what to do?* Repeat the directions and/or demonstration, if necessary. Say: *If you cannot figure out the word the sounds make, say "skip."*

Assessment
Use the words listed in the *Record of Responses* for this task.
[<u>Note</u>: STOP THIS TASK if the student responds incorrectly to the first three words.]
1. Say: */sh/ /ōō/* (shoe). Wait while the student responds.
   - If the student has difficulty remembering the task, ask: *What word do the sounds /sh/ /ōō/ make?*
   - If he/she does not respond after a 4-second wait time, say: *Let's try another one.* Go on to the next word.
2. Continue the task; follow the same procedures as above using the remaining words.

After the Assessment

Scoring Guidelines

- Count each word blended accurately or self-corrected as 1 point.

See an example of a completed *Record of Responses* for this task below.

Total score: 8

Determining Next Step

- Continue on to Task 13, "Providing words that rhyme (Auditory/Oral)."
- STOP ASSESSING if the student (1) has demonstrated "no/little" or "some" control on any three tasks or (2) is becoming distracted.

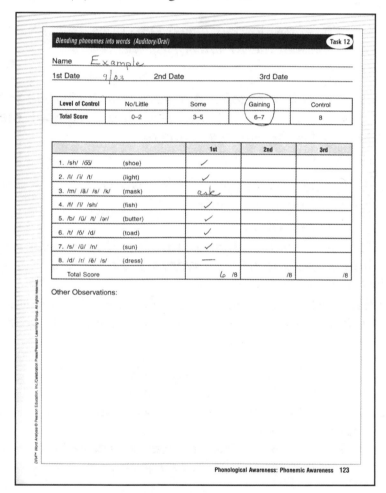

Blending phonemes into words (Auditory/Oral) — Task 12

Name: Example

1st Date: 9/03   2nd Date: _____   3rd Date: _____

Level of Control	No/Little	Some	Gaining	Control
Total Score	0–2	3–5	6–7	8

		1st	2nd	3rd
1. /sh/ /oo/	(shoe)	✓		
2. /l/ /ī/ /t/	(light)	✓		
3. /m/ /ă/ /s/ /k/	(mask)	ask		
4. /f/ /ĭ/ /sh/	(fish)	✓		
5. /b/ /ŭ/ /t/ /ar/	(butter)	✓		
6. /t/ /ō/ /d/	(toad)	✓		
7. /s/ /ŭ/ /n/	(sun)	✓		
8. /d/ /r/ /ĕ/ /s/	(dress)	—		
Total Score		6 /8	/8	/8

Other Observations:

Phonological Awareness: Phonemic Awareness   123

Task 13

Providing words that rhyme (Auditory/Oral)

Objective: To provide a word that rhymes with each word given by the teacher

Prior to the Assessment

Assemble the following materials:
- *Student Assessment Book:* No accompanying page for this task
- *Record of Responses:* Task 13

Administering the Assessment

Use the *Recording Guidelines* provided in General Directions, page 18, to record your observation after <u>each</u> response in the *Record of Responses*.

Demonstration
Say: ***I will say a word. You will then tell me a word which rhymes with that word. I'll show you what to do.*** (Pause) ***Cat.*** (Pause) ***Mat. The words*** cat, mat ***rhyme because they each end with the same sounds /at/.***

Shared Demonstration
1. Say: ***Let's do one together.*** (Pause) ***Run.*** (Pause) ***Now tell me a word that rhymes with*** run. Wait while the student responds.
   - If CORRECT , say: ***That's right.***
   - If INCORRECT , say: **Run, fun *rhyme.* Run, fun *rhyme because we hear the same sounds at the end of both words. We hear* /un/ *at the end of* run. We hear /un/ *at the end of* fun.**
2. Say: ***Do you understand what to do?*** Repeat directions and/or demonstrations if necessary. ***If you do not know and cannot think of a word that rhymes, say "skip."***

Assessment
Use the words listed in the *Record of Responses* for this task.
[<u>Note:</u> STOP THIS TASK if the student responds incorrectly to the first three words or if the student takes longer than 2 minutes.]
1. Say: ***Chair.*** (Pause) ***Tell me a word that rhymes with*** chair. If he/she does not respond after an 8-second wait time, say: ***Let's try another one.*** Go on to the next word.
2. Continue the task; follow the same procedures as above using the remaining words.

After the Assessment

Scoring Guidelines

- Count each correct or self-corrected rhyming word as 1 point.

See an example of a completed *Record of Responses* for this task below.

Total score: 8

Determining Next Step

- Continue on to Task 14, "Segmenting words into onsets and rimes (Auditory/Oral)."
- STOP ASSESSING if the student (1) has demonstrated "no/little" or "some" control on any three tasks or (2) is becoming distracted.

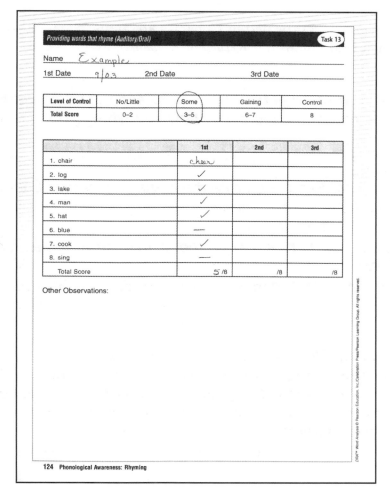

Providing words that rhyme (Auditory/Oral)   Task 13

Name   Example

1st Date   9/03   2nd Date   3rd Date

Level of Control	No/Little	Some	Gaining	Control
Total Score	0–2	3–5	6–7	8

	1st	2nd	3rd
1. chair	cheer		
2. log	✓		
3. lake	✓		
4. man	✓		
5. hat	✓		
6. blue	—		
7. cook	✓		
8. sing	—		
Total Score	5 /8	/8	/8

Other Observations:

124   Phonological Awareness: Rhyming

Task 14

Segmenting words into onsets and rimes (Auditory/Oral)

Objective: To segment a given word by separating the onset from the rime

Prior to the Assessment

Assemble the following materials:
- *Student Assessment Book:* No accompanying page for this task
- *Record of Responses:* Task 14

Administering the Assessment

Use the *Recording Guidelines* provided in General Directions, page 18, to record your observation after <u>each</u> response in the *Record of Responses.*

Demonstration
Say: ***First I will say a word. I will then ask you to separate the beginning sound or sounds from the rest of the word. I'll show you what to do.*** (Pause) ***Mat.*** (Pause) ***/m/*** (Pause) ***/at/***

Shared Demonstration
1. Say: ***Now you do one. Sand. Separate the beginning sound from the rest of the word.*** Wait while the student responds.
   - If CORRECT , say: ***That's right.***
   - If INCORRECT , say: ***Let's separate the word*** sand ***together. /s/*** (Pause) ***/and/. Now you do it.***
2. Say: ***Do you understand what to do?*** Repeat the directions and/or demonstration if necessary.

Assessment
Use the words listed in the *Record of Responses* for this task.
[<u>Note</u>: STOP THIS TASK if the student responds incorrectly to the first three words.]
1. Say: ***Chair.*** (Pause) ***Separate the beginning sounds from the rest of the word.*** Wait while the student responds. If the student does not respond after a 4-second wait time, say: ***Let's try another one.*** Go on to the next word.
2. Continue the task; follow the same procedures as above using the remaining words.

After the Assessment

Scoring Guidelines
- Count each word clearly segmented into onset and rime as 1 point.

See an example of a completed *Record of Responses* for this task below.

Total score: 8

Determining Next Step
- Continue on to Task 15, "Deleting onsets (Auditory/Oral)."
- STOP ASSESSING if the student (1) has demonstrated "no/little" or "some" control on any three tasks or (2) is becoming distracted.

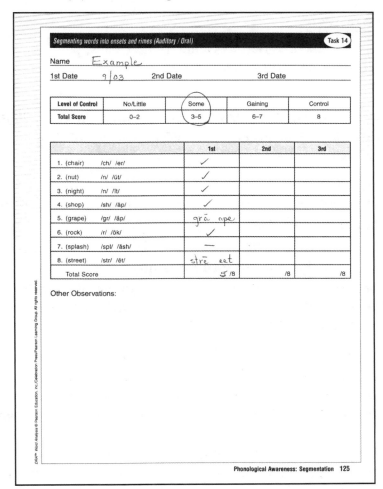

Segmenting words into onsets and rimes (Auditory / Oral) — Task 14

Name: Example

1st Date: 9/03 2nd Date: 3rd Date:

Level of Control	No/Little	Some	Gaining	Control
Total Score	0–2	3–5	6–7	8

		1st	2nd	3rd
1. (chair)	/ch/ /er/	✓		
2. (nut)	/n/ /ŭt/	✓		
3. (night)	/n/ /īt/	✓		
4. (shop)	/sh/ /ŏp/	✓		
5. (grape)	/gr/ /āp/	grā ape		
6. (rock)	/r/ /ŏk/	✓		
7. (splash)	/spl/ /ăsh/	—		
8. (street)	/str/ /ēt/	strē eet		
Total Score		5 /8	/8	/8

Other Observations:

Phonological Awareness: Segmentation 125

Task 15

Deleting onsets (Auditory/Oral)

Objective: To (1) repeat a word given by the teacher and then (2) say the same word without the first sound or sounds

Prior to the Assessment

Assemble the following materials:
- *Student Assessment Book:* No accompanying page for this task
- *Record of Responses:* Task 15

Administering the Assessment

Use the *Recording Guidelines* provided in General Directions, page 18, to record your observation after <u>each</u> response in the *Record of Responses*.

Demonstration
Say: ***I will say a word. You will then say the same word. Next, I will ask you to say that word without the first sound. I'll show you what to do.*** (Pause) ***Cat.*** (Pause) ***Now I'll say cat without /k/.*** (Pause) ***/at/.***

Shared Demonstration
1. Say: ***Let's do one together. Sit. You say sit.*** Wait while the student responds.
2. Then say: ***Now say sit without /s/.*** (/it/)
   - If CORRECT , say: ***That's right.***
   - If INCORRECT , say: ***Sit. Sit without /s/ is /it/.***
3. Say: ***Do you understand what to do?*** Repeat the directions and/or demonstration if necessary. ***If you do not know and cannot figure out how to say the word without the first sound, say "skip."***

Assessment
Use the words listed in the *Record of Responses* for this task.
[<u>Note:</u> STOP THIS TASK if the student responds incorrectly to the first three words.]
1. Say: ***Call. Now you say call.*** Wait while the student responds. ***Now say call without /k/.***
   - If the student has difficulty remembering the task, repeat the direction.
   - If he/she does not respond after a 4-second wait time, say: ***Let's try another one.*** Go on to the next word.
2. Continue the task. Follow the same procedures as above using the remaining words.

After the Assessment

Scoring Guidelines

- Count each word correctly said without the onset or self-corrected as 1 point.

See an example of a completed *Record of Responses* for this task below.

Total score: 9

Determining Next Step

- Continue on to Task 16, "Spelling Check II."
- STOP ASSESSING if the student (1) has demonstrated "no/little" or "some" control on any three tasks or (2) is becoming distracted.

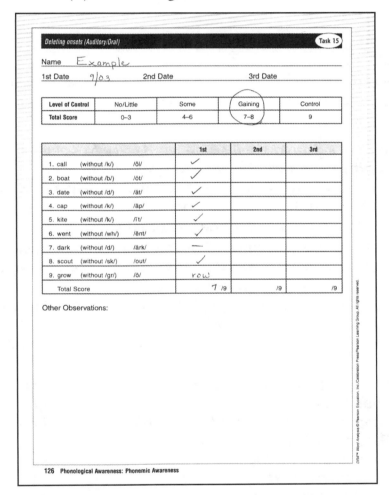

Deleting onsets (Auditory/Oral)   Task 15

Name   Example

1st Date   9/03   2nd Date   3rd Date

Level of Control	No/Little	Some	Gaining	Control
Total Score	0–3	4–6	7–8	9

		1st	2nd	3rd
1. call	(without /k/) /ôl/	✓		
2. boat	(without /b/) /ōt/	✓		
3. date	(without /d/) /āt/	✓		
4. cap	(without /k/) /ăp/	✓		
5. kite	(without /k/) /īt/	✓		
6. went	(without /wh/) /ĕnt/	✓		
7. dark	(without /d/) /ärk/	—		
8. scout	(without /sk/) /out/	✓		
9. grow	(without /gr/) /ō/	row		
Total Score		7 /9	/9	/9

Other Observations:

126   **Phonological Awareness: Phonemic Awareness**

Spelling Check II

Objective: To accurately spell each component of (1) three-letter words with short vowels and (2) high frequency words with common spelling patterns

Prior to the Assessment

Assemble the following materials:
- *Student Assessment Book:* No accompanying page for this task
- *Record of Responses:* Task 16
- *Spelling Check II* form

Administering the Assessment

Use the *Recording Guidelines* provided in General Directions, page 18, to record your observation after <u>each</u> response in the *Record of Responses*.

Assessment

1. Say: ***I am going to ask you to spell some words. Try to spell each word the best you can. Some words will be easy to spell; some words will be harder. When you don't know how to spell a word, say it slowly and write down all the sounds you hear.*** Repeat the directions if necessary.
2. Say: ***Write your name on the line at the top of your paper.***
3. Then say: ***I will say each spelling word by itself and in a sentence. I will then say the word again. Write each word by the number I say. Do you understand what to do?*** Repeat directions if necessary.
4. Enunciate each spelling word clearly, and give student adequate time to respond.
   Say: ***Number 1. not*** (Pause) ***The dog will <u>not</u> stop barking.*** (Pause) ***not***
5. Continue the assessment using the remaining words and sentences; follow the same procedures as above.

2.	can	We <u>can</u> read lots of books.	can
3.	got	I <u>got</u> a new bike.	got
4.	had	I <u>had</u> a good breakfast this morning.	had
5.	bus	Sam rides the <u>bus</u> to school.	bus
6.	sit	I like to <u>sit</u> with my friends.	sit
7.	pet	The teacher had a <u>pet</u> rabbit.	pet
8.	bug	The <u>bug</u> had red spots.	bug
9.	day	One <u>day</u> I hope to go to the zoo.	day
10.	look	"<u>Look</u> at me," said the boy.	look
11.	will	Sara <u>will</u> take the book to the library.	will
12.	call	I will <u>call</u> you tonight.	call

6. Collect the student's paper when he/she has completed the task.

After the Assessment

Scoring Guidelines

The words in Spelling Check II are grouped into two sets with common features.

- Set 1: Count each initial consonant, short vowel, and final consonant spelled correctly as 1 point.
- Set 2: Count each initial consonant and each rime/spelling pattern spelled correctly as 1 point.
  [Note: Correct responses must have the letters written in the correct sequential order to be counted as correct. Reversed letters, such as *b* for *d*, *t* for *f*, are <u>not</u> counted as correct. Make note of the improper use of capital letters.]

See an example of a completed *Record of Responses* for this task below.

Total score: 32

Determining Next Step

- Continue on to Task 17, "Recognizing high frequency words II" (Timed).
- STOP ASSESSING if the student (1) has demonstrated "no/little" or "some" control on any three tasks or (2) is becoming distracted.

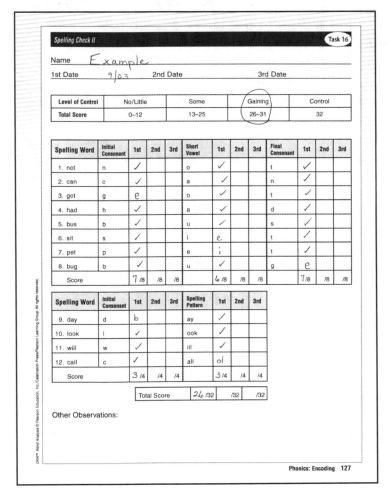

Task 17

Recognizing high frequency words II

Objective: To quickly read aloud the words in each column within the specified time (1 minute 30 seconds)

Prior to the Assessment

Assemble the following materials:
- *Student Assessment Book:* Task 17
- *Record of Responses:* Task 17
- Stopwatch

Administering the Assessment

Use the *Recording Guidelines* provided in General Directions, page 18, to record your observation after <u>each</u> response in the *Record of Responses*.

Assessment
1. Say: **These are some words you will find in books. Please read each word. Begin by reading the words in the first column, then in the second, and so on. If you don't know a word, say "skip" and go on to the next word. Do you understand what to do?** Repeat directions if necessary.
2. Say: **You may begin now,** as you start the stopwatch.
   [<u>Note</u>: If the student hesitates after a 3-second wait time, tell her/him to read the next word or look for other known words in the column.]
3. Stop the stopwatch when the student reads the last word or is unable to locate other known words; STOP this task when the maximum length of time has been reached.
   [<u>Note</u>: Maximum length of time is 1 minute 30 seconds.]

After the Assessment

Scoring Guidelines

Words confused with other words or words that are sounded out are <u>not</u> to be included in the total score.

- Place an X on top of the check mark if the word was sounded out and not quickly recognized.
- Place an X also on top of the check mark of words that were confused with another word. For example, if the student identified *had* correctly and also said *had* for *have*, the word *had* would <u>not</u> be included in the total score.
- Count each word read correctly or self-corrected and <u>not</u> sounded out or confused with other words as 1 point.

See an example of a completed *Record of Responses* for this task below.

Total score: 30

Determining Next Step

- Continue on to Task 18, "Segmenting words into syllables I."
- STOP ASSESSING if the student (1) has demonstrated "no/little" or "some" control on any three tasks or (2) is becoming distracted.

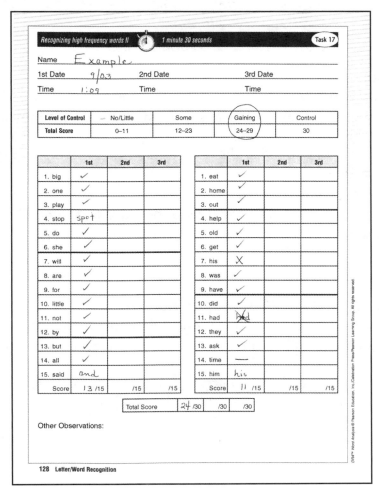

| Recognizing high frequency words II | | 1 minute 30 seconds | | | Task 17 |

Name: Example

| 1st Date | 9/03 | 2nd Date | | 3rd Date | |
| Time | 1:09 | Time | | Time | |

Level of Control	— No/Little	Some	Gaining	Control
Total Score	0–11	12–23	(24–29)	30

	1st	2nd	3rd			1st	2nd	3rd
1. big	✓				1. eat	✓		
2. one	✓				2. home	✓		
3. play	✓				3. out	✓		
4. stop	spot				4. help	✓		
5. do	✓				5. old	✓		
6. she	✓				6. get	✓		
7. will	✓				7. his	X		
8. are	✓				8. was	✓		
9. for	✓				9. have	✓		
10. little	✓				10. did	✓		
11. not	✓				11. had	X̶h̶a̶d̶		
12. by	✓				12. they	✓		
13. but	✓				13. ask	✓		
14. all	✓				14. time	—		
15. said	and				15. him	his		
Score	13 /15	/15	/15		Score	11 /15	/15	/15

| Total Score | 24 /30 | /30 | /30 |

Other Observations:

128 Letter/Word Recognition

Task 18

Segmenting words into syllables I

Objective: To (1) say the name of a pictured object, and (2) clap the syllables while saying the word again

Prior to the Assessment

Assemble the following materials:
- *Student Assessment Book:* Task 18
- *Record of Responses:* Task 18

Administering the Assessment

Use the *Recording Guidelines* provided in General Directions, page 18, to record your observation after <u>each</u> response in the *Record of Responses*.

Demonstration
1. Say: **When I say a word slowly, I can hear and clap the parts of that word. These parts are called syllables. You will say the name of the picture, and then clap the syllables as you say its name again. I'll show you what to do.**
2. Point to the starred example and say: **Elephant.**
3. Clap each syllable as you say *elephant.* **El·e·phant.** (3 claps)

Shared Demonstration
1. Say: **Let's do one together.**
2. Point to the second starred example and say: **Now you say** monkey *as you clap the* **syllables.** Wait while the student responds.
   [<u>Note</u>: The student is asked to clap the number of syllables. He/she is <u>not</u> asked to tell the number of syllables.]
   - If CORRECT , say: **That's right.**
   - If INCORRECT , say: **Let's say and clap** monkey *together. Mon·key.* (2 claps)
3. Say: **Do you understand what to do?** Repeat the directions and/or demonstration if necessary.

Assessment
1. Say: **You may begin with the first picture now.**
   [<u>Note</u>: If the student is uncertain, say: **volcano.** Do <u>not</u> emphasize the syllable breaks.]
2. Continue the assessment; follow the same procedures as above with the remaining pictures.
   [<u>Note</u>: If the student says *bike* for *motorcycle, TV* for *television, hippo* for *hippopotamus,* and/or *bug* for *caterpillar,* ask him or her to clap the parts in the word *motorcycle, television, hippopotamus,* and/or *caterpillar.*]

After the Assessment

Scoring Guidelines

- Count each word correctly segmented into syllables (initially or self-corrected) as 1 point.

    [Note: The student receives credit for clapping to indicate syllable boundaries. For instance, for the picture *grasshopper* if the student claps twice for *grass*, once for *hopper*, he/she <u>does not</u> receive credit for that item.]

  See an example of a completed *Record of Responses* for this task below.

  Total score: 8

Determining Next Step

- Continue on to Task 19, "Providing words that begin with the same sound (Auditory/Oral)."
- STOP ASSESSING if the student (1) has demonstrated "no/little" or "some" control on any three tasks or (2) is becoming distracted.

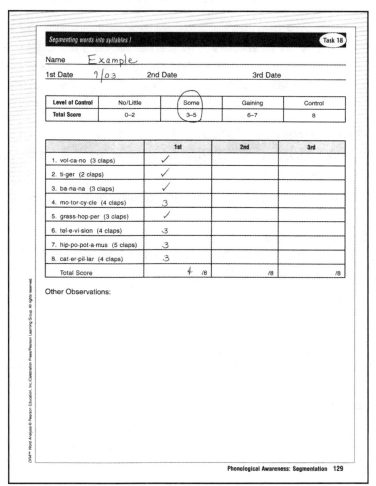

| Segmenting words into syllables I | | | Task 18 |

Name: Example
1st Date: 9/03   2nd Date: 3rd Date:

Level of Control	No/Little	Some	Gaining	Control
Total Score	0–2	3–5	6–7	8

	1st	2nd	3rd
1. vol·ca·no (3 claps)	✓		
2. ti·ger (2 claps)	✓		
3. ba·na·na (3 claps)	✓		
4. mo·tor·cy·cle (4 claps)	3		
5. grass·hop·per (3 claps)	✓		
6. tel·e·vi·sion (4 claps)	3		
7. hip·po·pot·a·mus (5 claps)	3		
8. cat·er·pil·lar (4 claps)	3		
Total Score	4 /8	/8	/8

Other Observations:

Phonological Awareness: Segmentation 129

Providing words that begin with the same sound (Auditory/Oral)

Objective: To provide a word that begins with the same sound as the word given by the teacher

Prior to the Assessment

Assemble the following materials:
- *Student Assessment Book:* No accompanying page for this task
- *Record of Responses:* Task 19

Administering the Assessment

Use the *Recording Guidelines* provided in General Directions, page 18, to record your observation after <u>each</u> response in the *Record of Responses*.

Demonstration
Say: ***I will say a word. You will then say the same word. Next, you will tell me another word that begins with the same sound. I'll show you what to do.*** (Pause) ***Hat.*** (Pause) ***House.*** (Pause) ***Hat, house*** *begin with the same sound* **/h/.**

Shared Demonstration
1. Say: ***Now let's do one together. Can. You say can.*** Wait while the student responds.
2. Then say: ***Now tell me another word that begins with the same sound as*** **can.**
   - If CORRECT , say: ***That's right.***
   - If INCORRECT , say: **Can, cat** *begin with the same sound.* **Can, cat** *begin with /k/.*
3. Say: ***Do you understand what to do?*** Repeat directions and/or demonstrations if necessary. ***If you do not know another word that begins with the same sound and cannot think of one, say "skip."***

Assessment

Use the words listed in the *Record of Responses* for this task.
[<u>Note</u>: STOP THIS TASK if the student responds incorrectly to the first three words or if the student takes longer than 2 minutes.]
1. Say: ***Man. Now you say man.***
2. Then say: ***Tell me another word that begins with the same sound as*** **man.**
   [<u>Note</u>: If he/she does not respond after an 8-second wait time, say: ***Let's try another one.*** Go on to the next word.]
3. Continue the task; follow the same procedures as above using the remaining words.

After the Assessment

Scoring Guidelines

- Count each word that begins with the same sound as the given word as 1 point.

See an example of a completed *Record of Responses* for this task below.

Total score: 8

Determining Next Step

- Continue on to Task 20, "Deleting final sounds (Auditory/Oral)."
- STOP ASSESSING if the student (1) has demonstrated "no/little" or "some" control on any three tasks or (2) is becoming distracted.

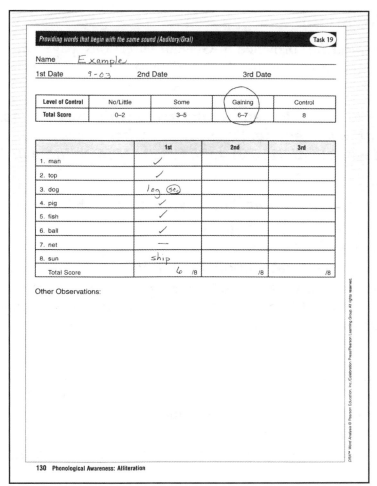

Providing words that begin with the same sound (Auditory/Oral)   Task 19

Name   Example

1st Date   9-03   2nd Date   3rd Date

Level of Control	No/Little	Some	Gaining	Control
Total Score	0–2	3–5	6–7	8

	1st	2nd	3rd
1. man	✓		
2. top	✓		
3. dog	log (se)		
4. pig	✓		
5. fish	✓		
6. ball	✓		
7. net	—		
8. sun	ship		
Total Score	6 /8	/8	/8

Other Observations:

DRA™ Word Analysis © Pearson Education, Inc./Celebration Press/Pearson Learning Group. All rights reserved.

130   Phonological Awareness: Alliteration

Task 20

Deleting final sounds (Auditory/Oral)

Objective: To (1) repeat a word given by the teacher and (2) then say the same word without the last sound(s)

Prior to the Assessment

Assemble the following materials:
- *Student Assessment Book:* No accompanying page for this task
- *Record of Responses:* Task 20

Administering the Assessment

Use the *Recording Guidelines* provided in General Directions, page 18, to record your observation after <u>each</u> response in the *Record of Responses*.

Demonstration
Say: **I will say a word. You will then say the same word. Next, I'll ask you to say that word without the last sound. I'll show you what to do.** (Pause) **Meat.** (Pause) **Now I'll say meat without /t/.** (Pause) **/mē/.** (Pause) **Meat** *without /t/ is /mē/.*

Shared Demonstration
1. Say: **Let's do one together. Goat. You say goat.** Wait while the student responds.
2. Then say: **Now say goat without /t/.** /gō/
   - If CORRECT , say: **That's right.**
   - If INCORRECT , say: **Goat** *without /t/ is /gō/.*
3. Say: **Do you understand what to do?** Repeat the directions and/or demonstration if necessary. **If you do not know and cannot figure out how to say the word without the last sound, say "skip."**

Assessment
Use the words listed in the *Record of Responses* for this task.
[<u>Note</u>: STOP THIS TASK if the student responds incorrectly to the first three words.]
1. Say: **Note. You say note.** Wait while the student responds.
2. Then say: **Now say note without /t/.**
   [<u>Note</u>: If he/she does not respond after a 4-second wait time, say: **Let's try another one.** Go on to the next word.]
3. Continue the task. Follow the same procedures as above using the remaining words.

After the Assessment

Scoring Guidelines
- Count each correct or self-corrected response as 1 point.

See an example of a completed *Record of Responses* for this task below.

Total score: 9

Determining Next Step
- Continue on to Task 21, "Segmenting words into phonemes (Auditory/Oral)."
- STOP ASSESSING if the student (1) has demonstrated "no/little" or "some" control on any three tasks or (2) is becoming distracted.

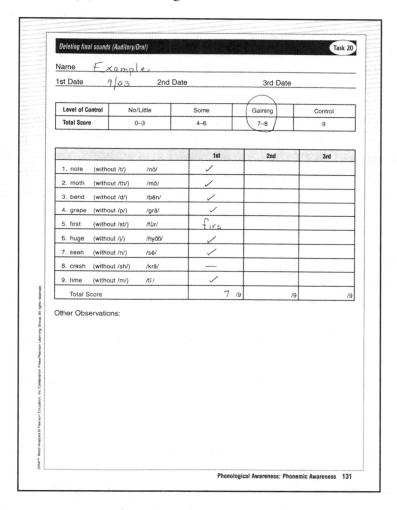

Deleting final sounds (Auditory/Oral) — Task 20

Name: *Example*

1st Date: 9/03   2nd Date: 3rd Date:

Level of Control	No/Little	Some	Gaining	Control
Total Score	0–3	4–6	7–8	9

		1st	2nd	3rd
1. note (without /t/) /nō/		✓		
2. moth (without /th/) /mô/		✓		
3. bend (without /d/) /bĕn/		✓		
4. grape (without /p/) /grā/		✓		
5. first (without /st/) /fûr/		firs		
6. huge (without /j/) /hyōō/		✓		
7. seen (without /n/) /sē/		✓		
8. crash (without /sh/) /krā/		—		
9. time (without /m/) /tī/		✓		
Total Score		7 /9	/9	/9

Other Observations:

Phonological Awareness: Phonemic Awareness   131

Task 21

Segmenting words into phonemes (Auditory/Oral)

Objective: To segment a given word into phonemes

Prior to the Assessment

Assemble the following materials:
- *Student Assessment Book:* Task 21
- *Record of Responses:* Task 21
- 4 coins or counters placed on the line below the four boxes

Administering the Assessment

Use the *Recording Guidelines* provided in General Directions, page 18, to record your observation after <u>each</u> response in the *Record of Responses*.

Demonstration

Say: ***Sometimes when we are writing a word that we don't know, we say the word slowly so we can hear <u>each</u> sound. In this task you are to think just about the sounds in the words and not the letters. I will say a word. You are then to say each sound in the word as you push up a coin/counter. I'll show you what to do.*** (Pause) ***Block.*** Push up a coin/counter with your index finger for each sound as you segment *block: /b/ /l/ /o/ /k/* (4 coins).

Shared Demonstration

1. Say: ***Fish. Now you say each sound in*** fish ***as you push up a coin/counter to show the number of sounds you hear.*** Wait while the student responds.
   - If CORRECT , say: ***That's right.***
   - If INCORRECT , say: ***Let me show you.*** Push up a coin/counter for each sound as you segment *fish: /f/ /i/ /sh/.* ***Now you say each sound in*** fish ***as you push up the coins/counters.***
2. Say: ***Do you understand what to do?*** Repeat the directions and/or demonstration, if necessary.

Assessment

Use the words listed in the *Record of Responses* for this task.
[<u>Note</u>: STOP THIS TASK if the student responds incorrectly to the first three words.]

1. Say: ***Say lad. Now say each sound in*** lad ***as you push up the coins/counters to show the number of sounds you hear.*** Wait while the student responds.
2. Continue the task; follow the same procedures as above.

After the Assessment

Scoring Guidelines
- Count each word successfully segmented into phonemes as 1 point.

See an example of a completed *Record of Responses* for this task below.

Total score: 8

Determining Next Step
- Continue on to Task 22, "Recognizing high frequency words III" (Timed).
- STOP ASSESSING if the student (1) has demonstrated "no/little" or "some" control on any three tasks or (2) is becoming distracted.

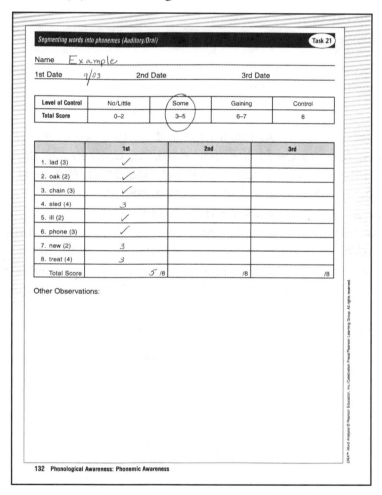

Segmenting words into phonemes (Auditory/Oral)   Task 21

Name Example

1st Date 9/03   2nd Date   3rd Date

Level of Control	No/Little	Some	Gaining	Control
Total Score	0–2	3–5	6–7	8

	1st	2nd	3rd
1. lad (3)	✓		
2. oak (2)	✓		
3. chain (3)	✓		
4. sled (4)	3		
5. ill (2)	✓		
6. phone (3)	✓		
7. new (2)	3		
8. treat (4)	3		
Total Score	5 /8	/8	/8

Other Observations:

132 Phonological Awareness: Phonemic Awareness

Recognizing high frequency words III

Objective: To quickly read aloud the words in each column within the specified time (1 minute 30 seconds)

Prior to the Assessment

Assemble the following materials:
- *Student Assessment Book:* Task 22
- *Record of Responses:* Task 22
- Stopwatch

Administering the Assessment

Use the *Recording Guidelines* provided in General Directions, page 18, to record your observation after <u>each</u> response in the *Record of Responses*.

Assessment
1. Say: **These are some words you will find in books. Please read each word. Begin by reading the words in the first column, then in the second, and so on. If you don't know a word, say "skip" and go on to the next word. Do you understand what to do?** Repeat directions if necessary.
2. Say: **You may begin now,** as you start the stopwatch.
   [<u>Note</u>: If the student hesitates after a 3-second wait time, tell her/him to read the next word or look for other known words in the column.]
3. Stop the stopwatch when the student reads the last word or is unable to locate other known words; STOP this task when the maximum length of time has been reached.
   [<u>Note</u>: Maximum length of time is 1 minute 30 seconds.]

After the Assessment

Scoring Guidelines

Words confused with other words or words that are sounded out are not to be included in the total score.

- Place an X on top of the check mark if the word was sounded out and not quickly recognized.
- Place an X also on top of the check mark that indicates a correct response of all words that were confused with another word. For example, if the student identified *then* correctly and also said *then* for *them,* the word *then* would not be included in the total score.
- Count each word read correctly or self-corrected and <u>not</u> sounded out or confused with other words as 1 point.

See an example of a completed *Record of Responses* for this task below.

Total score: 50

Determining Next Step

- Continue on to Task 23, "Substituting onsets: rhyming words."
- STOP ASSESSING if the student (1) has demonstrated "no/little" or "some" control on any three tasks or (2) is becoming distracted.

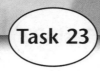

Task 23

Substituting onsets: rhyming words

Objective: To (1) tell how each set of words is alike, and (2) read aloud the rhyming words in each set

Prior to the Assessment

Assemble the following materials:
- *Student Assessment Book:* Task 23
- *Record of Responses:* Task 23

Administering the Assessment

Use the *Recording Guidelines* provided in General Directions, page 18, to record your observation after <u>each</u> response in the *Record of Responses*.

Shared Demonstration
1. Say: **The words in each set are alike in some way. First, I will ask you to tell me how the words in the set are alike. You will then read aloud the three words. Let's do the starred example together.**
2. Point to the starred box and ask: **How are these words alike?** (they all rhyme; end with *ike*)
   - If CORRECT, say: **That's right.**
   - If INCORRECT , say: **Each word ends with the letters ike.**
3. Then ask: **How will those letters sound together?** (/īk/)
   - If CORRECT, say: **That's right.**
   - If INCORRECT , say: **/īk/** (Pause) **The letters ike says /īk/.**
4. Then, say: **Now read aloud each word**.
   [<u>Note</u>: If the student does not know a word within this set, tell him/her the word in the shared demonstration only.]
5. Say: **Do you understand what to do?** Repeat the directions and/or demonstration, if necessary. Say: **If you do not know a word and cannot figure it out, say "skip" and go on to the next word.**

Assessment
1. Say: **Begin with box number 1. How are these words alike?** Wait while the student responds.
2. Then ask: **How will those letters sound together?**
3. Say: **Now read aloud each word.**
4. Continue the task. Follow the same procedures as above using the remaining eight sets of words.

After the Assessment

Scoring Guidelines

- Count each statement that accurately tells how the words within a set are alike as 1 point. [Note: If letter names are given, they must be in sequential order from left to right to be considered correct.]
- Count each group of common letters accurately blended together as 1 point. (/an/, /il/, /at/, /en/, /ōld/, etc.)
- Count each word read accurately or self-corrected as 1 point.

See an example of a completed *Record of Responses* for this task below.

Total score: 45

Determining Next Step

- Continue on to Task 24, "Substituting final sounds."
- STOP ASSESSING if the student (1) has demonstrated "no/little" or "some" control on any three tasks or (2) is becoming distracted.

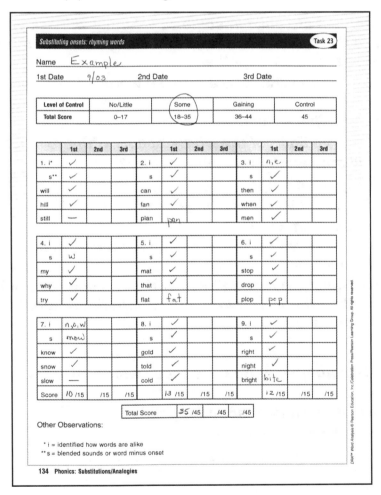

Task 24

Substituting final sounds

Objective: To (1) tell how each set of words is alike, and (2) read aloud the words in each set

Prior to the Assessment

Assemble the following materials:
- *Student Assessment Book:* Task 24
- *Record of Responses:* Task 24

Administering the Assessment

Use the *Recording Guidelines* provided in General Directions, page 18, to record your observation after <u>each</u> response in the *Record of Responses.*

Shared Demonstration
1. ***The words in each set are alike in some way. First, I will ask you to tell me how the words in the set are alike. You will then read aloud the three words. Let's do the starred example together.***
2. Point to the starred box and ask: ***How are these words alike?*** (they each begin with the letters *bi*)
   - If CORRECT, say: ***That's right.***
   - If INCORRECT, say: ***Each of the words begins with the letters*** bi.
3. Then ask: ***How will those letters sound together?*** (/bi/)
   - If CORRECT, say: ***That's right.***
   - If INCORRECT, say: ***/bĭ/*** (Pause) ***The letters*** bi ***says /bĭ/.***
4. Say: ***Now read aloud each word.***
   [Note: If the student does not know a word within this set, tell him/her the word in the shared demonstration only.]
5. Say: ***Do you understand what to do?*** Repeat the directions and/or demonstration, if necessary. ***If you do not know a word and cannot figure it out, say "skip" and go on to the next word.***

Assessment
1. Say: ***Begin with box number 1. How are these words alike?*** Wait while the student responds.
2. Then ask: ***How will those letters sound together?***
3. Say: ***Now read aloud each word.***
4. Continue the task. Follow the same procedures as above using the remaining eight sets of words.

After the Assessment

Scoring Guidelines

- Count each statement that accurately tells how the words within a set are alike as 1 point.
  [Note: If letter names are given, they <u>must</u> be in sequential order from left to right to be considered correct.]
- Count each group of common letters accurately blended together as 1 point. (/wĭ/, /hĭ/, /hō/, /dŏ/, etc.)
- Count each word read accurately or self-corrected as 1 point.

See an example of a completed *Record of Responses* for this task below.

Total score: 45

Determining Next Step

- Continue on to Task 25, "Blending and using initial consonant sounds" (Timed).
- STOP ASSESSING if the student (1) has demonstrated "no/little" or "some" control on any three tasks or (2) is becoming distracted.

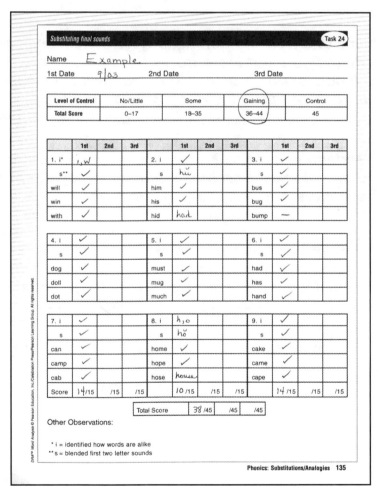

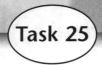

Task 25

Blending and using initial consonant sounds

Objective: To (1) blend two to three consonant letter sounds, and
(2) say a word or name that begins with consonant blend within the
specified time (2 minutes 30 seconds)

Prior to the Assessment

Assemble the following materials:
- *Student Assessment Book:* Task 25
- *Record of Responses:* Task 25
- Stopwatch

Administering the Assessment

Use the *Recording Guidelines* provided in General Directions, page 18, to record your
observation after <u>each</u> response in the *Record of Responses*.

Demonstration
1. Say: **When we come to a word we don't know, we sometimes have to blend the
   beginning sounds to figure out the word. In this task you are to tell me how
   the two or three letters sound together. Then you will tell me a word or name
   that begins with those sounds. I'll show you what to do.**
2. Point to the letters in the starred example and say: **/gr/.** (Pause) **Grapes. Grapes
   begin with /gr/.**
3. Say: **Do you understand what to do?** Repeat the directions and/or demonstration,
   if necessary. **If you do not know how the letters sound together or a word that
   begins with those letters, say "skip" and go on to the next one.**

Assessment
1. Say: **You may begin the first one now,** as you start the stopwatch
   - If the student has difficulty remembering the task, ask: **How do these letters
     sound?** and/or **What word or name begins with those sounds?**
   - If the student hesitates after a 8-second wait time, tell her/him to go on to the next
     one.
2. Stop the stopwatch when the student completes the task or STOP this task when the
   maximum length of time has been reached.
   [<u>Note</u>: Maximum length of time is 2 minutes 30 seconds.]

After the Assessment

Scoring Guidelines
- Count each group of sounds correctly blended together as 1 point.
- Count each word beginning with the designated consonant blend as 1 point.
  [Note: Nonsense words are not included in the total score.]

See an example of a completed *Record of Responses* for this task below.

Total score: 24

Determining Next Step
- Continue on to Task 26, "Identifying words with long and short vowels."
- STOP ASSESSING if the student (1) has demonstrated "no/little" or "some" control on any three tasks or (2) is becoming distracted.

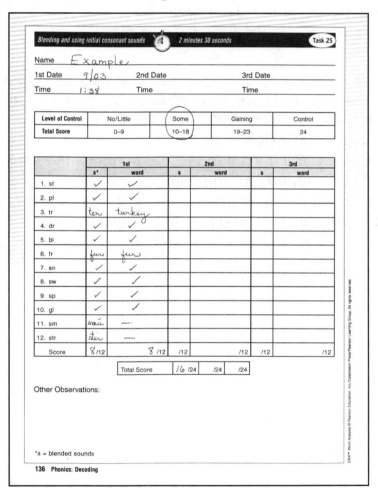

Blending and using initial consonant sounds   2 minutes 30 seconds   Task 25

Name: Example
1st Date: 9/03   2nd Date: 3rd Date:
Time: 1:38   Time: Time:

Level of Control	No/Little	Some	Gaining	Control
Total Score	0–9	10–18	19–23	24

| | 1st | | 2nd | | 3rd | |
	s*	word	s	word	s	word
1. st	✓	✓				
2. pl	✓	✓				
3. tr	ter	turkey				
4. dr	✓	✓				
5. bl	✓	✓				
6. fr	fur	fur				
7. sn	✓	✓				
8. sw	✓	✓				
9. sp	✓	✓				
10. gl	✓	✓				
11. sm	smü	—				
12. str	stir	—				
Score	8/12	8 /12	/12	/12	/12	/12

Total Score	16 /24	/24	/24

Other Observations:

*s = blended sounds

136   Phonics: Decoding

Task 26

Identifying words with long and short vowels

Objective: To (1) tell how the words are alike in each set, (2) say the long and short sounds of the designated vowel, and (3) read the words in the set

Prior to the Assessment

Assemble the following materials:
- *Student Assessment Book:* Task 26
- *Record of Responses:* Task 26

Administering the Assessment

Use the *Recording Guidelines* provided in General Directions, page 18, to record your observation after <u>each</u> response in the *Record of Responses*.

Assessment

1. Say: **The words in each set contain long and short vowel sounds. I will give you the directions as you do the first set. Look at the words in the first set and tell me how the words are alike.** Wait while the student responds.
   - If CORRECT , say: **That's right.**
   - If INCORRECT , say: **Each word in this set contains the letter o.**
2. Ask: **What are the two sounds for the letter o?** (/ŏ/; /ō/)
3. Then say: **Now read aloud the words. If you don't know a word, do your best to figure it out or say, "skip," and go on to the next word.**
4. Continue the assessment for the remaining 4 sets; follow the same procedures as above.

After the Assessment

Scoring Guidelines

- Count each correct sound as 1 point.
- Count each word read correctly or self-corrected as 1 point.

See an example of a completed *Record of Responses* for this task below.

Total score: 30

Determining Next Step

- Continue on to Task 27, "Spelling Check III."
- STOP ASSESSING if the student (1) has demonstrated "no/little" or "some" control on any three tasks or (2) is becoming distracted.

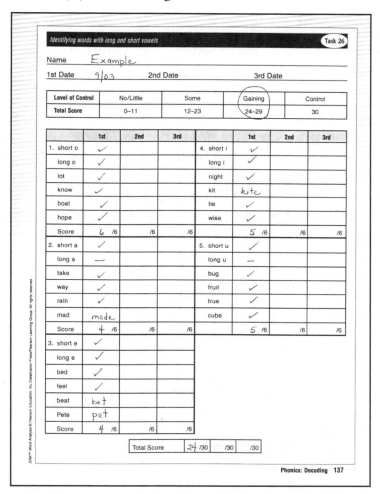

Identifying words with long and short vowels — Task 26

Name: Example

1st Date: 9/03   2nd Date: 3rd Date:

Level of Control	No/Little	Some	Gaining	Control
Total Score	0–11	12–23	(24–29)	30

	1st	2nd	3rd		1st	2nd	3rd
1. short o	✓			4. short i	✓		
long o	✓			long i	✓		
lot	✓			night	✓		
know	✓			kit	kite		
boat	✓			tie	✓		
hope	✓			wise	✓		
Score	6 /6	/6	/6		5 /6	/6	/6
2. short a	✓			5. short u	✓		
long a	—			long u	—		
take	✓			bug	✓		
way	✓			fruit	✓		
rain	✓			true	✓		
mad	made			cube	✓		
Score	4 /6	/6	/6		5 /6	/6	/6
3. short e	✓						
long e	✓						
bed	✓						
feel	✓						
beat	bet						
Pete	pet						
Score	4 /6	/6	/6				

Total Score	24 /30	/30	/30

Phonics: Decoding   137

Spelling Check III

Objective: To accurately spell each component of words with (1) VCe vowel patterns, (2) preconsonant nasals, (3) initial digraphs, and (4) suffixes

Prior to the Assessment

Assemble the following materials:
- *Student Assessment Book:* No accompanying page for this task
- *Record of Responses:* Task 27
- *Spelling Check III* form

Administering the Assessment

Use the *Recording Guidelines* provided in General Directions, page 18, to record your observation after <u>each</u> response in the *Record of Responses*.

Assessment

1. Say: ***I am going to ask you to spell some words. Try to spell each word the best you can. Some words will be easy to spell; some words will be harder. When you don't know how to spell a word, say it slowly and write down all the sounds you hear.***

2. Say: ***Write your name on the line at the top of your paper.***

3. Then say: ***I will say each spelling word by itself and in a sentence. Then I will say the word again. Write each word by the number I say. Do you understand what to do?*** Repeat the directions if necessary.

4. Enunciate each spelling word clearly, and give student adequate time to respond. Say: ***Number 1. game*** (Pause) ***We won the soccer <u>game</u>.*** (Pause) ***game***

5. Continue the assessment using the remaining words and sentences; follow the same procedures as above.

2.	ride	We will <u>ride</u> our bikes to the park.	ride
3.	note	Her mother wrote a <u>note</u> to the teacher.	note
4.	vine	The <u>vine</u> grew up the side of the house.	vine
5.	ring	I found a pretty <u>ring</u> in the grass.	ring
6.	plant	We <u>plant</u> flowers each spring.	plant
7.	went	She <u>went</u> to the library.	went
8.	think	I <u>think</u> I will stay home tonight.	think
9.	then	We will get something to eat and <u>then</u> go home.	then
10.	shop	I like to go to the pet <u>shop</u>.	shop
11.	when	We'll begin <u>when</u> everyone gets here.	when
12.	chip	I like chocolate <u>chip</u> cookies.	chip
13.	eating	We are <u>eating</u> pizza for dinner.	eating
14.	stops	The bus <u>stops</u> in front of the school.	stops
15.	played	The children <u>played</u> kickball at recess.	played
16.	taller	The giraffe was <u>taller</u> than the tree.	taller

6. Say: **Now read each word to yourself. Place a check mark in the box after the word if you think the word looks right.** Give the student adequate time to respond.

7. Then say: **For each word that has no check mark, spell the word again so that it looks right. Write the word on the other side of the box.**
   [Note: The student's second attempt is to be written on the line to the right of the box.]

8. Collect the student's paper when he/she has completed the task.

After the Assessment

Scoring Guidelines

The words in Spelling Check III are grouped into four sets with common features.

- Set 1: Count each initial consonant and VCe rime spelled correctly as 1 point.
- Set 2: Count each initial consonant(s) and preconsonant-nasal rime spelled correctly as 1 point.
- Set 3: Count each initial digraph and short-vowel rime spelled correctly as 1 point.
- Set 4: Count each base word and each suffix spelled correctly as 1 point.
  [Note: (1) For words that the student did not check as correct, score the second spelling and <u>not</u> the first. (2) Correct responses must have the letters written in the correct sequential order to be counted as correct. Reversed letters, such as *b* for *d*, *t* for *f*, are not counted as correct. (3) Make note of the improper use of capital letters.

See an example of a completed *Record of Responses* for a spelling check on page 49.

Total score: 32

Determining Next Step

- Continue on to Task 28, "Using structural analysis to determine word meaning: suffixes I."
- STOP ASSESSING if the student (1) has demonstrated "no/little" or "some" control on any three tasks or (2) is becoming distracted.

Task 28

Using structural analysis to determine word meaning: suffixes I

Objective: To read aloud and use each word in a sentence to demonstrate an understanding of the word

Prior to the Assessment

Assemble the following materials:
- *Student Assessment Book:* Task 28
- *Record of Responses:* Task 28

Administering the Assessment

Use the *Recording Guidelines* provided in General Directions, page 18, to record your observation after <u>each</u> response in the *Record of Responses.*

Demonstration
1. Say: ***A suffix or ending has been added to these words. You are to read aloud each word and then use it in a sentence. I'll show you what to do.***
2. As you point to the starred example, say: ***Jumped.*** (Pause) ***The frog <u>jumped</u> into the pond.*** (Pause)
3. ***Do you understand what to do?*** Repeat directions if necessary. Then say: ***If you come to a word that you do not know and you cannot figure it out, or, if you do not know what it means, say "skip" and go on to the next word.***

Assessment
1. Say: ***You may begin with the first word now.*** If the student is uncertain, say: ***What is this word?*** Wait while the student responds.
2. Then say: ***Now, use that word in a sentence.***
   [<u>Note</u>: If the student's sentence does not clearly indicate an understanding of a word, ask him/her to tell you what the word means. For example, the sentences *It is cloudy.* or *It is broken.* do not demonstrate a clear understanding of either word.]
3. Continue the assessment; follow the same procedures as above.

After the Assessment

Scoring Guidelines

- Count each word read correctly or self-corrected as 1 point.
- Count each word that the student demonstrated understanding of as 1 point.

See an example of a completed *Record of Responses* for this task below.

Total score: 16

Determining Next Step

- Continue on to Task 29, "Recognizing high frequency words IV" (Timed).
- STOP ASSESSING if the student (1) has demonstrated "no/little" or "some" control on any three tasks or (2) is becoming distracted.

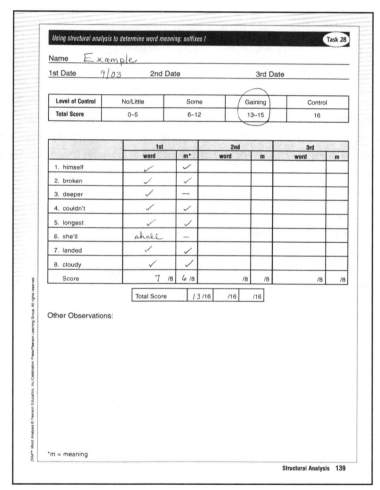

Using structural analysis to determine word meaning: suffixes I — Task 28

Name: Example

1st Date: 9/03   2nd Date: 3rd Date:

Level of Control	No/Little	Some	Gaining	Control
Total Score	0–5	6–12	13–15	16

	1st word	1st m*	2nd word	2nd m	3rd word	3rd m
1. himself	✓	✓				
2. broken	✓	✓				
3. deeper	✓	—				
4. couldn't	✓	✓				
5. longest	✓	✓				
6. she'll	shall	—				
7. landed	✓	✓				
8. cloudy	✓	✓				
Score	7 /8	6 /8	/8	/8	/8	/8

Total Score	13 /16	/16	/16

Other Observations:

*m = meaning

Structural Analysis 139

Task 29

Recognizing high frequency words IV

Objective: To quickly read aloud the words in each column within the specified time (1 minute 30 seconds)

Prior to the Assessment

Assemble the following materials:
- *Student Assessment Book:* Task 29
- *Record of Responses:* Task 29
- Stopwatch

Administering the Assessment

Use the *Recording Guidelines* provided in General Directions, page 18, to record your observation after <u>each</u> response in the *Record of Responses*.

Assessment
1. Say: **These are some words you will find in books. Please read each word. Begin by reading the words in the first column, then in the second, and so on. If you don't know a word, say "skip" and go on to the next word. Do you understand what to do?** Repeat directions if necessary.
2. Say: **You may begin now,** as you start the stopwatch.
   [<u>Note</u>: If the student hesitates after a 3-second wait time, tell her/him to read the next word or look for other known words in the column.
3. Stop the stopwatch when the student reads the last word or is unable to locate other known words; STOP this task when the maximum length of time has been reached.
   [<u>Note</u>: Maximum length of time is 1 minute 30 seconds.]

After the Assessment

Scoring Guidelines

Words confused with other words or words that are sounded out are not to be included in the total score.

- Place an X on top of the check mark of words that were sounded out and not quickly recognized.
- Place an X also on top of the check mark that indicated a correct response for all words that were confused with another word. For example, if the student identified *here* correctly and also said *here* for *her*, the word *here* would not be included in the total score.
- Count each word read correctly or self-corrected and not sounded out or confused with other words as 1 point.

See an example of a completed *Record of Responses* for this task below.

Total score: 50

Determining Next Step

- Continue on to Task 30, "Substituting rimes" (Timed).
- STOP ASSESSING if the student (1) has demonstrated "no/little" or "some" control on any three tasks or (2) is becoming distracted.

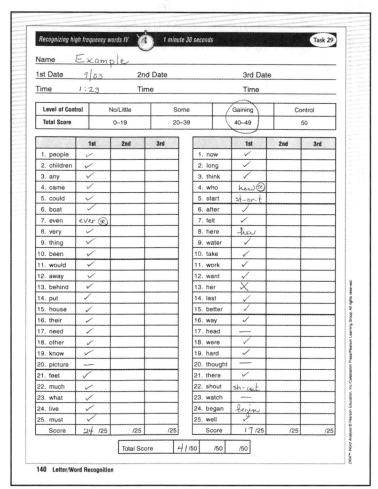

Task 30

Substituting rimes

Objective: To read six sets of words with different rimes within the specified length of time (2 minutes)

Prior to the Assessment

Assemble the following materials:
- *Student Assessment Book:* Task 30
- *Record of Responses:* Task 30
- Stopwatch

Administering the Assessment

Use the *Recording Guidelines* provided in General Directions, page 18, to record your observation after <u>each</u> response in the *Record of Responses.*

Assessment
1. Say: ***In this task you are to read each word in the six sets. Begin by reading the words in the first set, then the second, and so on. If you come to a word that you do not know and you cannot figure it out, say "skip" and go on to the next word. Do you understand what to do?*** Repeat directions if necessary.
2. Say: ***You may begin now,*** as you start the stopwatch.
3. Stop the stopwatch when the student completes the task; STOP this task when the maximum length of time has been reached.
   [<u>Note</u>: Maximum length of time is 2 minutes.]

After the Assessment

Scoring Guidelines

- Count each word read accurately or self-corrected as 1 point.

See an example of a completed *Record of Responses* for this task below.

Total score: 36

Determining Next Step

- Continue on to Task 31, "Using analogies to decode words."
- STOP ASSESSING if the student (1) has demonstrated "no/little" or "some" control on any three tasks or (2) is becoming distracted.

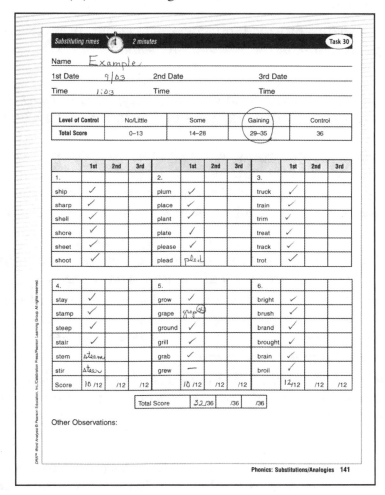

Substituting rimes — 2 minutes — Task 30

Name: Example

1st Date: 9/03 2nd Date: 3rd Date:

Time: 1:03 Time: Time:

Level of Control	No/Little	Some	Gaining	Control
Total Score	0–13	14–28	29–35	36

	1st	2nd	3rd		1st	2nd	3rd		1st	2nd	3rd
1.				**2.**				**3.**			
ship	✓			plum	✓			truck	✓		
sharp	✓			place	✓			train	✓		
shell	✓			plant	✓			trim	✓		
shore	✓			plate	✓			treat	✓		
sheet	✓			please	✓			track	✓		
shoot	✓			plead	pleld			trot	✓		
4.				**5.**				**6.**			
stay	✓			grow	✓			bright	✓		
stamp	✓			grape	grop (sc)			brush	✓		
steep	✓			ground	✓			brand	✓		
stair	✓			grill	✓			brought	✓		
stem	steem			grab	✓			brain	✓		
stir	steer			grew	—			broil	✓		
Score	10/12	/12	/12		10/12	/12	/12		12/12	/12	/12

Total Score: 32/36   /36   /36

Other Observations:

Phonics: Substitutions/Analogies   141

Task 31

Using analogies to decode words

Objective: To use parts of familiar words to problem-solve unknown words

Prior to the Assessment

Assemble the following materials:
- *Student Assessment Book:* Task 31
- *Record of Responses:* Task 31

Administering the Assessment

Use the *Recording Guidelines* provided in General Directions, page 18, to record your observation after <u>each</u> response in the *Record of Responses*.

Pre-Assessment

Point to the words in the upper left-hand corner and say: ***Please read these eight words. If you do not know a word and cannot figure it out, say "skip" and go on to the next word.***

- If the student <u>reads all eight words accurately</u>, this task is completed. Go to Task 32, "Identifying words with vowel patterns."
- If the student <u>reads fewer than eight words accurately</u>, have the student use only the sets of words below to problem-solve the word(s) he/she was unable to read initially.

Demonstration

1. Say: ***When reading, you can use parts of words you know to help you figure out words that you do not know. I'll show you what I mean.***
2. In the starred example point to the word *tree* and then to the word *made* as you say: ***Tree.*** (Pause) ***Made.***
3. Next, point to the word *trade* and say: ***I see that this word starts like* tree *and ends like* made. ***So I say /tr/ /ād/, trade.***
4. Say: ***Do you understand what to do?*** Repeat directions if necessary. Say: ***If you come to a word that you do not know and you cannot figure it out, say "skip" and go on to the next word.***

Assessment

1. Point to a set that includes a word that the student was unable to read in the pre-assessment and say: ***First, read the two words with underlined parts.*** Wait while the student responds.
   [<u>Note</u>: If the student is unable to read one or both words, say: ***Let's try another,*** and go on to another set of words.]
2. Say: ***Now, use what you know about these two words to read the third word.***
   [<u>Note</u>: Repeat these directions if the student has difficulty remembering the task.]
3. Continue assessing, using only the words the student did <u>not</u> read correctly in the pre-assessment.

After the Assessment

Scoring Guidelines

- Count each word read correctly or self-corrected in the pre-assessment as 1 point.
- Count each starred word read correctly or self-corrected in each set as 1 point.
  [Note: The student will receive credit for reading the word either in the pre-assessment or assessment sections of this task.]

See an example of a completed *Record of Responses* for this task below.

Total score: 8

Determining Next Step

- Continue on to Task 32, "Identifying words with vowel patterns."
- STOP ASSESSING if the student (1) has demonstrated "no/little" or "some" control on any three tasks or (2) is becoming distracted.

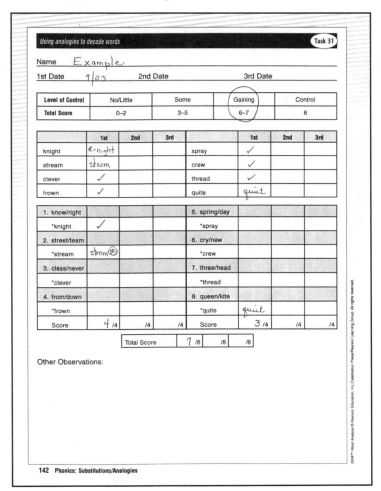

Task 32

Identifying words with vowel patterns

Objective: To (1) identify the vowel pattern in a set of words, and then (2) read aloud the words

Prior to the Assessment

Assemble the following materials:
- *Student Assessment Book:* Task 32
- *Record of Responses:* Task 32

Administering the Assessment

Use the *Recording Guidelines* provided in General Directions, page 18, to record your observation after <u>each</u> response in the *Record of Responses*.

Assessment
1. Say: **The words in each set have something in common. First, you are to tell me how the words are alike in the set and then read aloud words. If you come to a word that you do not know and you cannot figure it out, say "skip" and go on to the next word. Do you understand what to do?** Repeat directions if necessary.
2. Say: **We'll begin with the first set. How is this set of words alike?** Wait while the student responds.
3. Then say: **Now read aloud the words in this set.**
4. Continue the assessment for the remaining five sets of words; follow the same procedures as above.

After the Assessment

Scoring Guidelines

- Count each vowel pattern identified correctly as 1 point.
- Count each word read correctly or self-corrected response as 1 point.

See an example of a completed *Record of Responses* for this task below.

Total score: 36

Determining Next Step

- Continue on to Task 33, "Blending and using initial syllables."
- STOP ASSESSING if the student (1) has demonstrated "no/little" or "some" control on any three tasks or (2) is becoming distracted.

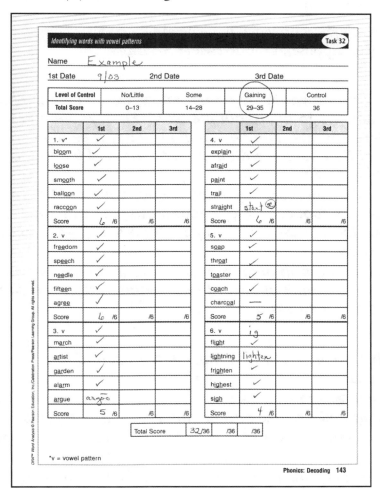

Identifying words with vowel patterns — Task 32

Name: Example

1st Date: 9/03   2nd Date: 3rd Date:

Level of Control	No/Little	Some	Gaining	Control
Total Score	0–13	14–28	29–35	36

	1st	2nd	3rd		1st	2nd	3rd
1. v*	✓			4. v	✓		
bloom	✓			explain	✓		
loose	✓			afraid	✓		
smooth	✓			paint	✓		
balloon	✓			trail	✓		
raccoon	✓			straight	start ⓐ		
Score	6 /6	/6	/6	Score	6 /6	/6	/6
2. v	✓			5. v	✓		
freedom	✓			soap	✓		
speech	✓			throat	✓		
needle	✓			toaster	✓		
fifteen	✓			coach	✓		
agree	✓			charcoal	—		
Score	6 /6	/6	/6	Score	5 /6	/6	/6
3. v	✓			6. v	i g		
march	✓			flight	✓		
artist	✓			lightning	lighten		
garden	✓			frighten	✓		
alarm	✓			highest	✓		
argue	argoo			sigh	✓		
Score	5 /6	/6	/6	Score	4 /6	/6	/6

	Total Score	32/36	/36	/36

*v = vowel pattern

Phonics: Decoding   143

Blending and using initial syllables

Objective: To (1) blend a group of letters, and then (2) give a word that begins with those blended sounds and makes sense

Prior to the Assessment

Assemble the following materials:
- *Student Assessment Book:* Task 33
- *Record of Responses:* Task 33

Administering the Assessment

Use the *Recording Guidelines* provided in General Directions, page 18, to record your observation after <u>each</u> response in the *Record of Responses*.

Demonstration
1. Say: **When we come to words we do not know, we sometimes have to blend the beginning sounds to figure out the word. First, you are to tell me how a group of letters sounds together. Then I will say a sentence, and you are to tell me a word that begins with those sounds and fits in the sentence. I'll show you what to do.**
2. Point to the starred example and say: **/rac/.** (Pause) **Last night down by the river I saw a ...** (Pause) **Raccoon.** (Pause) **Raccoon begins with /rac/ and raccoons often wash their food in the river. Do you understand what to do?** Repeat directions if necessary.
3. Say: **If you come to a group of letters you cannot figure out how they would sound or you cannot think of a word that begins with those sounds, say "skip" and go on to the next one.**

Assessment
1. Say: **Begin with number 1. How do these letters sound together?** Wait while the student responds.
2. Then say: **The man asked what is the ...** If the student is uncertain what to do, say: **What word would make sense and begins with these sounds?**
   [<u>Note</u>: If the student hesitates after an 8-second wait time, go to the next group of letters.]
3. Continue the assessment; follow the same procedures as above using the following sentences.
   - **2.** /min/ **I'll be back in a ...** (minute)
   - **3.** /prin/ **The story was about a ...** (prince, princess, principal)
   - **4.** /rab/ **Sam has a pet ...** (rabbit)
   - **5.** /soc/ **Our team won the ... game.** (soccer)
   - **6.** /cam/ **The reporter got his ... out of the bag.** (camera)
   - **7.** /bro/ **The glass was ...** (broken)

8. /oc/   **An** (pause) ***lives in the ocean.*** (octopus)
9. /thun/   **We heard** (pause) ***in the distance.*** (thunder)
10. /bas/   **Put the toys in the** ... (basket)

After the Assessment

Scoring Guidelines

- Count groups of letter/sounds blended together correctly or self-corrected as 1 point.
- Count each word that begins with the blended letter/sounds and fits in the sentence as 1 point.

See an example of a completed *Record of Responses* for this task below.

Total score: 20

Determining Next Step

- Continue on to Task 34, "Segmenting words into syllables II."
- STOP ASSESSING if the student (1) has demonstrated "no/little" or "some" control on any three tasks or (2) is becoming distracted.

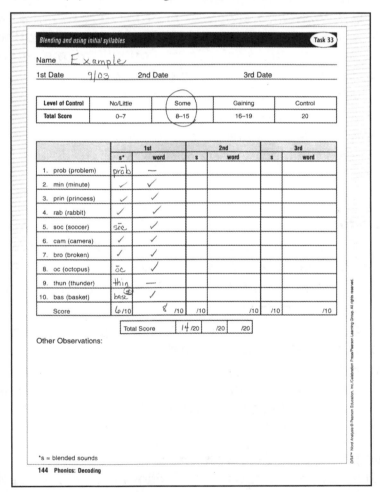

Blending and using initial syllables

Task 33

Name Example

1st Date 9/03   2nd Date   3rd Date

Level of Control	No/Little	Some	Gaining	Control
Total Score	0–7	8–15	16–19	20

	1st		2nd		3rd	
	s*	word	s	word	s	word
1. prob (problem)	prŏb	—				
2. min (minute)	✓	✓				
3. prin (princess)	✓	✓				
4. rab (rabbit)	✓	✓				
5. soc (soccer)	sŏc	✓				
6. cam (camera)	✓	✓				
7. bro (broken)	✓	✓				
8. oc (octopus)	ōc	✓				
9. thun (thunder)	thin	—				
10. bas (basket)	bāse	✓				
Score	6/10	8 /10	/10	/10	/10	/10

Total Score 14 /20   /20   /20

Other Observations:

*s = blended sounds

144 Phonics: Decoding

Task 34

Segmenting words into syllables II

Objective: To (1) say a word, (2) clap the syllables while saying the word, and (3) tell where to divide the word into syllables

Prior to the Assessment

Assemble the following materials:
- *Student Assessment Book:* Task 34
- *Record of Responses:* Task 34

Administering the Assessment

Use the *Recording Guidelines* provided in General Directions, page 18, to record your observation after <u>each</u> response in the *Record of Responses*.

Demonstration
1. Say: **Sometimes when we come to words we do not know, we have to take them apart or break them into syllables in order to read them. In this task you will do three things. First, you will read the word. Second, you will clap the syllables as you say the word again. Third, you will tell me where to divide that word into syllables. I'll show you what to do.**
2. Point to the first starred example *running* and say: **Running.**
3. Clap each syllable as you say: **Run·ning.** (2 claps)
4. Then say: **Running *is divided between the two* n's.**
   [<u>Note</u>: Use your finger, not a pen/pencil, to show where to divide a word into syllables.]

Shared Demonstration
1. Say: **Let's do one together.**
2. Point to the second starred example *blackberry* and say: **What is this word?**
3. Then say: **Clap each syllable as you say blackberry.**
4. Say: **Between what letters would this word be divided into syllables?**
   - If CORRECT, say: **That's right.**
   - If INCORRECT, point to the letters as you say: **Blackberry *is divided between the* k and b, *and also between the two* r's.**
5. **Do you understand what to do?** Repeat directions and/or demonstrations if necessary. **If you come to a word that you don't know and you cannot figure it out, say, "skip" and go on to the next word.**

Assessment
1. Say: **You may begin with the first word now.**
   [<u>Note</u>: If the student hesitates, use one of the following prompts: (1) **What is the word?** (2) **Now clap the syllables as you say the word again.** (3) **Between what letters would this word be divided into syllables?**]
2. Continue the assessment; follow the same procedures as above.

After the Assessment

Scoring Guidelines
- Count each word read correctly or self-corrected as 1 point.
- Count each word correctly segmented into syllables as 1 point.
- Count each word correctly divided into syllables as 1 point.

See an example of a completed *Record of Responses* for this task below.

Total score: 27

Determining Next Step
- Continue on to Task 35, "Using structural analysis to determine word meaning: suffixes II."
- STOP ASSESSING if the student (1) has demonstrated "no/little" or "some" control on any three tasks or (2) is becoming distracted.

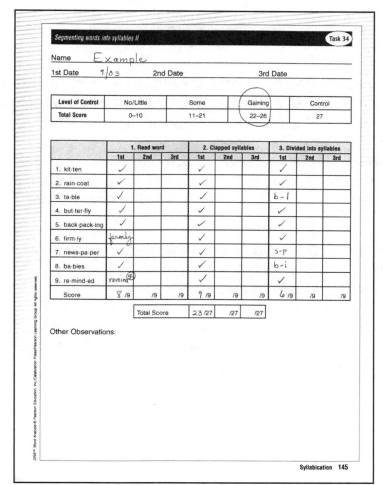

Segmenting words into syllables II — Task 34

Name: Example
1st Date 9/03   2nd Date   3rd Date

Level of Control	No/Little	Some	Gaining	Control
Total Score	0–10	11–21	22–26	27

	1. Read word			2. Clapped syllables			3. Divided into syllables		
	1st	2nd	3rd	1st	2nd	3rd	1st	2nd	3rd
1. kit·ten	✓			✓			✓		
2. rain·coat	✓			✓			✓		
3. ta·ble	✓			✓			b - l		
4. but·ter·fly	✓			✓			✓		
5. back·pack·ing	✓			✓			✓		
6. firm·ly	farmly			✓			✓		
7. news·pa·per	✓			✓			s-p		
8. ba·bies	✓			✓			b-i		
9. re·mind·ed	remind(sc)			✓			✓		
Score	8 /9	/9	/9	9 /9	/9	/9	6 /9	/9	/9

Total Score: 23 /27   /27   /27

Other Observations:

Syllabication 145

Using structural analysis to determine word meaning: suffixes II

Objective: To read aloud each word and use it in a sentence to demonstrate an understanding of the word

Prior to the Assessment

Assemble the following materials:
- *Student Assessment Book:* Task 35
- *Record of Responses:* Task 35

Administering the Assessment

Use the *Recording Guidelines* provided in General Directions, page 18, to record your observation after <u>each</u> response in the *Record of Responses*.

Demonstration
1. Say: ***A suffix or ending has been added to these words. You are to read aloud each word and then use it in a sentence. I'll show you what to do.***
2. As you point to the starred example, say: ***Reporter.*** (Pause) ***The <u>reporter</u> took notes during her interview with the mayor.***
3. Say: ***Do you understand what to do?*** Repeat directions if necessary. ***If you come to a word that you do not know and you cannot figure it out, or, if you do not know what it means, say "skip" and go on to the next word.***

Assessment
1. Say: ***You may begin with the first word now.*** If the student is uncertain, say: ***What is this word?*** Wait while the student responds.
2. Then say: ***Now, use that word in a sentence.***
   [<u>Note</u>: If the student's sentence does not clearly indicate an understanding of a word, ask him/her to tell you what the word means. For example, the sentences *He is helpless.* or *I like the motorcyclist.* do not demonstrate a clear understanding of either word.]
3. Continue the assessment; follow the same procedures as above.

After the Assessment

Scoring Guidelines

- Count each word read correctly or self-corrected as 1 point.
- Count each word that the student demonstrated understanding of as 1 point.

See an example of a completed *Record of Responses* for this task below.

> Total score: 16

Determining Next Step

- Continue on to Task 36, "Spelling Check IV."
- STOP ASSESSING if the student (1) has demonstrated "no/little" or "some" control on any three tasks or (2) is becoming distracted.

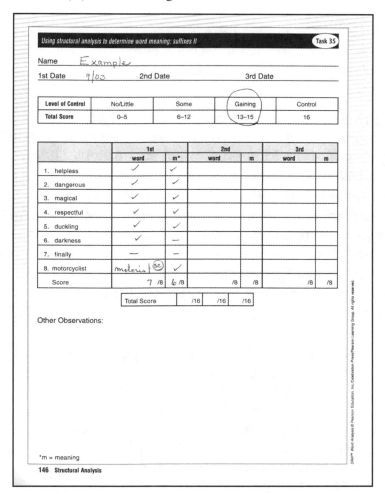

Using structural analysis to determine word meaning: suffixes II — Task 35

Name: Example

1st Date: 9/03   2nd Date: 3rd Date:

Level of Control	No/Little	Some	Gaining	Control
Total Score	0–5	6–12	13–15	16

	1st word	m*	2nd word	m	3rd word	m
1. helpless	✓	✓				
2. dangerous	✓	✓				
3. magical	✓	✓				
4. respectful	✓	✓				
5. duckling	✓	✓				
6. darkness	✓	—				
7. finally	—	—				
8. motorcyclist	motoris (sc)	✓				
Score	7 /8	6 /8	/8	/8	/8	/8

Total Score	/16	/16	/16

Other Observations:

*m = meaning

146   Structural Analysis

Spelling Check IV

Objective: To accurately spell each component of words with (1) r-controlled vowels, (2) suffixes, (3) VCe vowel patterns, (4) "ck" as final letters, and (5) an open first syllable

Prior to the Assessment

Assemble the following materials:
- *Student Assessment Book:* No accompanying page for this task
- *Record of Responses:* Task 36
- *Spell Check IV* form

Administering the Assessment

Use the *Recording Guidelines* provided in General Directions, page 18, to record your observation after <u>each</u> response in the *Record of Responses.*

Assessment

1. Say: ***I am going to ask you to spell some words. Try to spell each word the best you can. Some words will be easy to spell; some words will be harder. When you don't know how to spell a word, say it slowly and write down all the sounds you hear.*** Repeat the directions if necessary.
2. Say: ***Write your name on the line at the top of your paper.***
3. Then say: ***I will say each spelling word by itself and in a sentence. Then I will say the word again. Write each word by the number I say. Do you understand what to do?*** Repeat directions if necessary.
4. Enunciate each spelling word clearly, and give student adequate time to respond. Say: ***Number 1. card*** (Pause) ***I made a birthday <u>card</u> for my friend.*** (Pause) ***card***
5. Continue the assessment using the remaining words and sentences; follow the same procedures as above.

2.	dark	*We can see the stars when it gets <u>dark</u>.*	dark
3.	store	*I went to the <u>store</u> to buy some milk.*	store
4.	bird	*A <u>bird</u> is sitting on the tree branch.*	bird
5.	jumped	*The horse <u>jumped</u> over the fence*	jumped
6.	I've	*<u>I've</u> put my homework in my backpack.*	I've
7.	helpful	*The doorman was very <u>helpful</u>.*	helpful
8.	teacher	*The <u>teacher</u> read to the class after lunch.*	teacher
9.	wanted	*The people <u>wanted</u> their team to win.*	wanted
10.	didn't	*I <u>didn't</u> see you at recess.*	didn't
11.	skate	*I can <u>skate</u> around the rink.*	skate
12.	slide	*The children took turns going down the <u>slide</u>.*	slide
13.	smoke	*We saw the <u>smoke</u> from the campfire.*	smoke
14.	truck	*My brother has a red <u>truck</u>.*	truck
15.	clock	*The <u>clock</u> was on the wall by the door.*	clock
16.	snack	*We will have a <u>snack</u> after recess.*	snack

17.	table	*The book was on the <u>table</u> by the door.*	*table*
18.	spider	*The <u>spider</u> went up the spout.*	*spider*
19.	broken	*The leg on the chair was <u>broken</u>.*	*broken*
20.	student	*The <u>student</u> shared his project with the class.*	*student*

7. Say: **Now read each word to yourself. Place a check mark in the box after the word if you think the word looks right.** Give the student adequate time to respond.

8. Then say: **For each word that has no check mark, spell the word again so that it looks right. Write the word on the other side of the box.**
   [Note: The student's second attempt is to be written on the line to the right of the box.]

9. Collect the student's paper when he/she has completed the task.

After the Assessment

Scoring Guidelines

The words in Spelling Check IV are grouped into five sets with common features.

- Set 1: Count each group of initial consonant(s) and rime with r-controlled vowel spelled correctly as 1 point.
- Set 2: Count each base word and suffix spelled correctly as 1 point.
- Set 3: Count each initial consonant blend and VCe rime spelled correctly as 1 point.
- Set 4: Count each consonant blend and rime with *ck* spelled correctly as 1 point.
- Set 5: Count each syllable spelled correctly as 1 point.
  [Note: (1) For words that the student did not check as correct, score the second spelling and <u>not</u> the first. (2) Correct responses must have the letters written in the correct sequential order to be counted as correct. Reversed or inverted letters, such as *b* for *d*, *t* for *f*, are not counted as correct. (3) Make note of the improper use of capital letters.]

See an example of a completed *Record of Responses* for a spelling check on page 49.

Total score: 40

Determining Next Step

- Continue on to Task 37, "Using structural analysis to determine word meaning: prefixes."
- STOP ASSESSING if the student (1) has demonstrated "no/little" or "some" control on any three tasks or (2) is becoming distracted.

Task 37

Using structural analysis to determine word meaning: prefixes

Objective: To read aloud each word and tell what it means.

Prior to the Assessment

Assemble the following materials:
- *Student Assessment Book:* Task 37
- *Record of Responses:* Task 37

Administering the Assessment

Use the *Recording Guidelines* provided in General Directions, page 18, to record your observation after <u>each</u> response in the *Record of Responses*.

Demonstration

1. Say: ***A prefix has been added to these words. You are to read aloud each word and then tell me what the word means. I'll show you what to do.***

2. As you point to the starred example, say: ***Disobey.*** (Pause) **Disobey** *means not to obey or to do something you have been told not to do.*

3. Say: ***If you come to a word that you do not know and you cannot figure it out, or, if you do not know what it means, say "skip" and go on to the next word. Do you understand what to do?***

Assessment

1. Say: ***You may begin with the first word now.*** If the student is uncertain, say: ***What is this word?*** Wait while the student responds.

2. Then say: ***Now tell me what the word means.***

3. Continue the assessment; follow the same procedures as above.

After the Assessment

Scoring Guidelines
- Count each word read correctly or self-corrected as 1 point.
- Count each word that the student demonstrated understanding of as 1 point.

See an example of a completed *Record of Responses* for this task below.

Total score: 16

Determining Next Step
- Continue on to Task 38, "Using structural analysis to determine word meaning: suffixes III."
- STOP ASSESSING if the student (1) has demonstrated "no/little" or "some" control on any three tasks or (2) is becoming distracted.

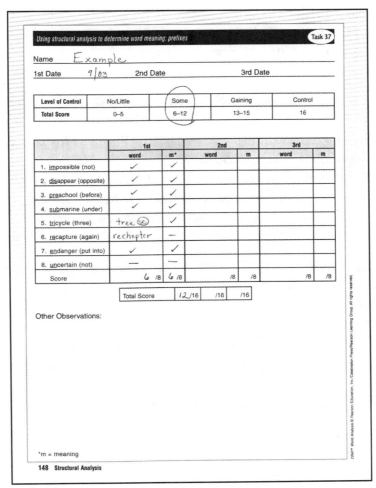

Using structural analysis to determine word meaning: prefixes — Task 37

Name: Example

1st Date: 9/03   2nd Date: 3rd Date:

Level of Control	No/Little	Some	Gaining	Control
Total Score	0–5	6–12	13–15	16

	1st word	m*	2nd word	m	3rd word	m
1. impossible (not)	✓	✓				
2. disappear (opposite)	✓	✓				
3. preschool (before)	✓	✓				
4. submarine (under)	✓	✓				
5. tricycle (three)	tree ⟨sc⟩	✓				
6. recapture (again)	rechapter	—				
7. endanger (put into)	✓	✓				
8. uncertain (not)	—	—				
Score	6 /8	6 /8	/8	/8	/8	/8

Total Score	12 /16	/16	/16

Other Observations:

*m = meaning

148 Structural Analysis

Task 38

Using structural analysis to determine word meaning: suffixes III

Objective: To read aloud each word and use it in a sentence to demonstrate an understanding of the word

Prior to the Assessment

Assemble the following materials:
- *Student Assessment Book:* Task 38
- *Record of Responses:* Task 38

Administering the Assessment

Use the *Recording Guidelines* provided in General Directions, page 18, to record your observation after <u>each</u> response in the *Record of Responses*.

Demonstration
1. Say: **A suffix or ending has been added to these words. You are to read aloud each word and then use it in a sentence. I'll show you what to do.**
2. As you point to the starred example, say: **Finalist.** (Pause) **The girl was surprised that she was a <u>finalist</u> in the competition.**
3. Say: **Do you understand what to do?** Repeat directions if necessary. **If you come to a word that you do not know and you cannot figure it out, or, if you don't know what it means, say "skip" and go on to the next word.**

Assessment
1. Say: **You may begin with the first word now.** If the student is uncertain, say: **What is this word?** Wait while the student responds.
2. Then say: **Now, use that word in a sentence.**
   [<u>Note</u>: If the student's sentence does <u>not</u> clearly indicate an understanding of a word, ask him/her to tell you what the word means. For example, the sentences *The photographer is here.* or *It is sinkable.* do not demonstrate a clear understanding of either word.]
3. Continue the assessment; follow the same procedures as above.

After the Assessment

Scoring Guidelines

- Count each word read correctly or self-corrected as 1 point.
- Count each word that the student demonstrated understanding of as 1 point.

See an example of a completed *Record of Responses* for this task below.

Total score: 16

Determining Next Step

- Continue on to Task 39, "Segmenting words into syllables III."
- STOP ASSESSING if the student (1) has demonstrated "no/little" or "some" control on any three tasks or (2) is becoming distracted.

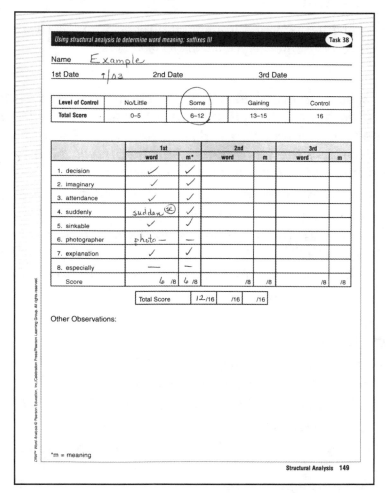

Segmenting words into syllables III

Objective: To (1) say a word, (2) clap the syllables while saying the word, and (3) tell where to divide that word into syllables

Prior to the Assessment

Assemble the following materials:
- *Student Assessment Book:* Task 39
- *Record of Responses:* Task 39

Administering the Assessment

Use the *Recording Guidelines* provided in general directions, page 18, to record your observation after each response in the *Record of Responses*.

Demonstration
1. Say: **Sometimes when we come to words we do not know, we have to take them apart or break them into syllables in order to read them. In this task you will do three things. First, you will read the word. Second, you will clap the syllables as you say the word again. Third, you will tell me where to divide that word into syllables. I'll show you what to do.**
2. Point to the first starred example *different* and say: **Different.**
3. Clap each syllable as you say: **Dif·fer·ent.** (3 claps)
4. Then point to the letters as you say: **Different *is divided between the two* f's *and between the* r *and* e.**
   [Note: Use your finger, <u>not</u> a pen/pencil, to show where to divide a word into syllables.]

Shared Demonstration
1. Say: **Let's do one together.**
2. Point to the second starred example *tomorrow* and say: **What is this word?**
3. Then say: **Clap each syllable as you say tomorrow.**
4. Say: **Between what letters would this word be divided into syllables?**
   - If CORRECT, say: **That's right.**
   - If INCORRECT, point to the letters as you say: **Tomorrow *is divided between the* o *and* m *and then between the two* r's.**
5. Say: **Do you understand what to do?** Repeat directions and/or demonstration if necessary. **If you come to a word that you do not know and you cannot figure it out, say "skip" and go on to the next word.**

Assessment
1. Say: **You may begin with the first word now.**
   [Note: If the student is hesitant, use one of the following prompts: (1) **What is that word?** (2) **Now clap the syllables as you say it again.** (3) **Between what letters would this word be divided into syllables?**]
2. Continue the assessment; follow the same procedures as above.

After the Assessment

Scoring Guidelines
- Count each word read correctly or self-corrected as 1 point.
- Count each word correctly segmented into syllables as 1 point.
- Count each word correctly divided into syllables as 1 point.

See an example of a completed *Record of Responses* for this task below.

Total score: 27

Determining Next Step
- Continue on to Task 40, "Spelling Check V."
- STOP ASSESSING if the student (1) has demonstrated "no/little" or "some" control on any three tasks or (2) is becoming distracted.

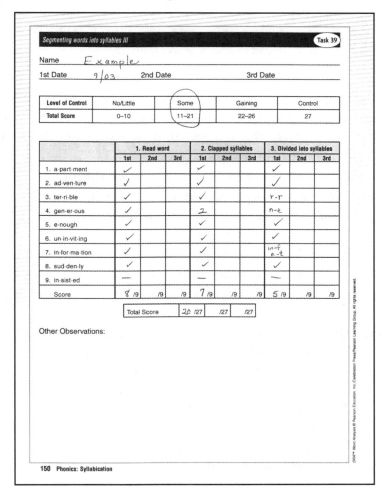

Spelling Check V

Objective: To accurately spell words with (1) prefixes, (2) closed first syllables, (3) suffixes, (4) 3-letter initial blends, (5) diphthongs, and (6) long vowel patterns

Prior to the Assessment

Assemble the following materials:
- *Student Assessment Book:* No accompanying page for this task
- *Record of Responses:* Task 40
- *Spelling Check V* form

Administering the Assessment

Use the *Recording Guidelines* provided in General Directions, page 18, to record your observation after <u>each</u> response in the *Record of Responses*.

Assessment

1. Say: ***I am going to ask you to spell some words. Try to spell each word the best you can. Some words will be easy to spell; some words will be harder. When you don't know how to spell a word, say it slowly and write down all the sounds you hear.*** Repeat the directions if necessary.
2. Say: ***Write your name on the line at the top of your paper.***
3. Then say: ***I will say each spelling word by itself and in a sentence. Then I will say the word again. Write each word by the number I say. Do you understand what to do?*** Repeat directions if necessary.
4. Enunciate each spelling word clearly, and give student adequate time to respond. Say: ***Number 1. unhappy*** (Pause) ***The baby was very <u>unhappy</u>.*** (Pause) ***unhappy***
5. Continue the assessment using the remaining words and sentences; follow the same procedures as above.

2.	preschool	His sister went to <u>preschool</u> each morning.	preschool
3.	rewrite	We will <u>rewrite</u> our reports tomorrow.	rewrite
4.	letter	The class wrote a <u>letter</u> to the president.	letter
5.	jacket	That man's <u>jacket</u> is red with black stripes.	jacket
6.	picture	The art teacher displayed each child's <u>picture</u>.	picture
7.	coming	A bus is <u>coming</u>.	coming
8.	wishes	He <u>wishes</u> he could go to camp.	wishes
9.	dresses	My sister gave four <u>dresses</u> away.	dresses
10.	biggest	The elephant was the <u>biggest</u> animal at the zoo.	biggest
11.	babies	Two <u>babies</u> were sleeping in their car seats.	babies
12.	spring	Flowers begin to grow in the <u>spring</u>.	spring
13.	strong	The weight lifters were very <u>strong</u>.	strong
14.	splash	A rock made a big <u>splash</u> when it hit the water.	splash
15.	scout	The girl <u>scout</u> had on her uniform.	scout
16.	ground	My friend found a quarter on the <u>ground</u>.	ground
17.	noise	The animals made a lot of <u>noise</u>.	noise

18.	point	<u>Point</u> to your favorite color.	*point*
19.	sweep	Please <u>sweep</u> the floor before you leave.	*sweep*
20.	train	The <u>train</u> made its way up the mountain.	*train*
21.	dream	I had a funny <u>dream</u> last night.	*dream*
22.	float	A boat will <u>float</u> in water.	*float*
23.	snail	A little <u>snail</u> was on the blade of grass.	*snail*
24.	bright	The sun was very <u>bright</u>.	*bright*

6. Say: **Now read each word to yourself. Place a check mark in the box after the word if you think the word looks right.** Give the student adequate time to respond.

7. Then say: **For each word that has no check mark, spell the word again so that it looks right. Write the word on the other side of the box.**
   [Note: The student's second attempt is to be written on the line to the right of the box.]
   See an example of a completed *Record of Responses* for a spelling check on page 49.

8. Collect the student's paper when he/she has completed the task.

After the Assessment

Scoring Guidelines
The words in Spelling Check V are grouped into six sets with common features.
- Set 1: Count each prefix and base word spelled correctly as 1 point.
- Set 2: Count each first and ending syllable spelled correctly as 1 point.
- Set 3: Count each base word and suffix spelled correctly as 1 point.
- Set 4: Count each three-letter blend and rime spelled correctly as 1 point.
- Set 5: Count each initial consonant(s) and rime with a diphthong spelled correctly as 1 point.
- Set 6: Count each consonant blend and long vowel rime spelled correctly as 1 point.
  [Note: Correct responses must have the letters written in the correct sequential order to be counted as correct. Reversed or inverted letters, such as *b* for *d, t* for *f,* are <u>not</u> counted as correct. Make note of the improper use of capital letters.]

Total score: 48

Record of Responses

There is a Record of Responses form for each task. Teachers are to follow the assessment guidelines to record student's responses as well as other behaviors or comments. The title of the task appears on the upper left side of the page, and the number of the task is in the upper right-hand side of the page. If the task is to be timed, an icon of a stopwatch and the maximum length of time are included between the task title and number.

Teachers are to write the student's name and then record the date in the designated space (1st, 2nd, or 3rd) each time the task is administrated.

The level of control is circled after the teacher calculates the student's total score on the task. For example, if the student's total score is 4 out of a possible 8, the teacher will circle "Some" because 4 falls within the range of 3–5 on this particular task, but if the total score is 6 out of a possible 8, the teacher will circle "Gaining."

Teachers record their observation of the student's responses to each task in the appropriate column as determined by whether or not it is the 1st, 2nd, or 3rd administration of the task. Teachers are to follow the assessment guidelines for recording student responses. Check marks indicate a <u>correct</u> response; written words, letters, sounds indicate an <u>incorrect</u> response; *sc* indicates a <u>self-corrected</u> response; and a dash indicates the item was <u>skipped</u> or <u>omitted</u>. Teachers are to make note of other observable behaviors, the student's attitude, pace, and/or comments in the section provided for other observations.

To determine the student's total score the teacher first counts the number of correct and self-corrected responses and places the number in each of the sections. Then he/she will add the two sections to obtain the total score for the particular task. The total score is then recorded in the appropriate space (1st, 2nd, or 3rd administration). A completed example of a Record of Responses is included in the teacher directions for most tasks.

Name

1st Date   2nd Date   3rd Date

Level of Control	No/Little	Some	Gaining	Control
Total Score	0–2	3–5	6–7	8

				1st	2nd	3rd
1. train	duck	wing	rain			
2. bat	sun	hat	cake			
3. man	fan	bed	chain			
4. boat	goat	cat	leaf			
5. snake	coat	pig	rake			
6. bee	tree	foot	log			
7. king	key	hand	ring			
8. dog	rake	frog	duck			
Total Score				/8	/8	/8

Other Observations:

Name

1st Date _____ 2nd Date _____ 3rd Date _____

Level of Control	No/Little	Some	Gaining	Control
Total Score	0–2	3–5	6–7	8

				1st	2nd	3rd
1. bike	bat	hand	scissors			
2. snake	yo-yo	sun	bee			
3. pig	shoe	car	pan			
4. cat	lock	cow	jet			
5. two	duck	tent	pear			
6. gum	toes	kite	game			
7. mat	moon	bed	goat			
8. log	pig	ring	lamp			
Total Score				/8	/8	/8

Other Observations:

Name _____

1st Date _____ 2nd Date _____ 3rd Date _____

Level of Control	No/Little	Some	Gaining	Control
Total Score	0–3	4–7	8–9	10

	1st Sound	2nd Sound	3rd Sound
1. pig /p/			
2. sun /s/			
3. tape /t/			
4. mice /m/			
5. van /v/			
6. duck /d/			
7. net /n/			
8. foot /f/			
9. cup /k/			
10. goat /g/			
Total Score	/10	/10	/10

Other Observations:

Name

1st Date _____ 2nd Date _____ 3rd Date _____

Level of Control	No/Little	Some	Gaining	Control
Total Score	0–2	3–5	6–7	8

	1st	2nd	3rd
1. Read first and last names			
2. Pointed to first name			
3. Pointed to last name			
4. Pointed to first letter in first name			
5. Pointed to last letter in first name			
6. Identified all letters in first name correctly			
7. Pointed to a capital or uppercase letter			
8. Identified all letters in last name correctly			
Total Score	/8	/8	/8

Write student's first and last names and check letters correctly named.

Other Observations:

Name _____

1st Date _____ 2nd Date _____ 3rd Date _____

Time _____ Time _____ Time _____

Level of Control	No/Little	Some	Gaining	Control
Total Score	0–9	10–20	21–25	26

	1st	2nd	3rd
1. O			
2. A			
3. X			
4. B			
5. S			
6. C			
7. E			
8. T			
9. K			
10. P			
11. I			
12. D			
13. M			
Score /13	/13	/13	

	1st	2nd	3rd
1. L			
2. R			
3. Z			
4. N			
5. F			
6. W			
7. H			
8. U			
9. G			
10. Y			
11. Q			
12. J			
13. V			
Score /13	/13	/13	

Total Score	/26	/26	/26

Other Observations:

| Recognizing lowercase letters 1 minute 30 seconds | Task 6 |

Name _____

| 1st Date _____ | 2nd Date _____ | 3rd Date _____ |
| Time _____ | Time _____ | Time _____ |

Level of Control	No/Little	Some	Gaining	Control
Total Score	0–9	10–20	21–25	26

	1st	2nd	3rd
1. o			
2. x			
3. s			
4. c			
5. e			
6. k			
7. r			
8. z			
9. m			
10. a			
11. w			
12. p			
13. t			
Score /13	/13	/13	

	1st	2nd	3rd
1. n			
2. y			
3. f			
4. h			
5. g			
6. v			
7. l			
8. u			
9. q			
10. i			
11. b			
12. j			
13. d			
Score /13	/13	/13	

Total Score	/26	/26	/26

Other Observations:

Name

1st Date   2nd Date   3rd Date

Level of Control	No/Little	Some	Gaining	Control
Total Score	0–2	3–5	6–7	8

	1st	2nd	3rd
1. One-to-one match with one-syllable words			
2. One-to-one match with one- and two-syllable words			
3. Pointed to the <u>word</u> "is"			
4. Identified the <u>letter</u> "is" <u>ends</u> with			
5. Identified the <u>letter</u> "playing" <u>begins</u> with			
6. Identified the <u>first letter</u> in "cat"			
7. Identified the <u>sound</u> "cat" <u>begins</u> with			
8. Identified the <u>sound</u> "cat" <u>ends</u> with			
Total Score	/8	/8	/8

Other Observations:

Task 8

Name

1st Date	2nd Date	3rd Date

Level of Control	No/Little	Some	Gaining	Control
Total Score	0–2	3–5	6	7

	1st	2nd	3rd
1. Dogs can run fast. (4 words)			
2. Apples are red. (3 words)			
3. Ducks swim in a pond. (5 words)			
4. Bears sleep in caves. (4 words)			
5. Some cats play with yarn. (5 words)			
6. I see a big red ball. (6 words)			
7. Jane likes to go fishing. (5 words)			
Total Score	/7	/7	/7

Other Observations:

Name

| 1st Date | 2nd Date | 3rd Date |

| Time | Time | Time |

Level of Control	No/Little	Some	Gaining	Control
Total Score	0–7	8–15	16–19	20

	1st	2nd	3rd
1. I			
2. the			
3. a			
4. go			
5. up			
6. in			
7. dog			
8. to			
9. see			
10. and			
Score	/10	/10	/10

	1st	2nd	3rd
1. is			
2. you			
3. can			
4. he			
5. it			
6. look			
7. my			
8. at			
9. on			
10. like			
Score	/10	/10	/10

Total Score	/20	/20	/20

Other Observations:

Name _____

1st Date _____ 2nd Date _____ 3rd Date _____

Level of Control	No/Little	Some	Gaining	Control
Total Score	0–9	10–18	19–23	24

Spelling Word	Initial Consonant	1st	2nd	3rd	Long/Open Vowel	1st	2nd	3rd
1. no	n				o			
2. go	g				o			
3. he	h				e			
4. we	w				e			
Score		/4	/4	/4		/4	/4	/4

Spelling Word	Short Vowel	1st	2nd	3rd	Final Consonant	1st	2nd	3rd
5. on	o				n			
6. at	a				t			
7. is	i				s			
8. up	u				p			
Score		/4	/4	/4		/4	/4	/4

Spelling Word	Initial Consonant(s)	1st	2nd	3rd	Final Vowel(s)	1st	2nd	3rd
9. my	m				y			
10. to	t				o			
11. the	th				e			
12. see	s				ee			
Score		/4	/4	/4		/4	/4	/4

Total Score	/24	/24	/24

Name _____

1st Date _____ 2nd Date _____ 3rd Date _____

Time _____ Time _____ Time _____

Level of Control	No/Little	Some	Gaining	Control
Total Score	0–18	19–37	38–47	48

	1st		2nd		3rd	
	s*	word	s	word	s	word
1. s						
2. p						
3. t						
4. m						
5. k						
6. f						
7. z						
8. r						
9. j						
10. v						
11. n						
12. c						
Score	/12	/12	/12	/12	/12	/12

	1st		2nd		3rd	
	s*	word	s	word	s	word
1. h						
2. l						
3. w						
4. a						
5. o						
6. d						
7. g						
8. i						
9. b						
10. y						
11. e						
12. u						
Score	/12	/12	/12	/12	/12	/12

Total Score	/48	/48	/48

Other Observations:

*s = sound

Blending phonemes into words (Auditory/Oral)

Name

1st Date _____ 2nd Date _____ 3rd Date _____

Level of Control	No/Little	Some	Gaining	Control
Total Score	0–2	3–5	6–7	8

	1st	2nd	3rd
1. /sh/ /o͞o/ (shoe)			
2. /l/ /ī/ /t/ (light)			
3. /m/ /ă/ /s/ /k/ (mask)			
4. /f/ /ĭ/ /sh/ (fish)			
5. /b/ /ŭ/ /t/ /ər/ (butter)			
6. /t/ /ō/ /d/ (toad)			
7. /s/ /ŭ/ /n/ (sun)			
8. /d/ /r/ /ĕ/ /s/ (dress)			
Total Score	/8	/8	/8

Other Observations:

Name _____

1st Date _____ 2nd Date _____ 3rd Date _____

Level of Control	No/Little	Some	Gaining	Control
Total Score	0–2	3–5	6–7	8

	1st	2nd	3rd
1. chair			
2. log			
3. lake			
4. man			
5. hat			
6. blue			
7. cook			
8. sing			
Total Score	/8	/8	/8

Other Observations:

Name

1st Date   2nd Date   3rd Date

Level of Control	No/Little	Some	Gaining	Control
Total Score	0–2	3–5	6–7	8

	1st	2nd	3rd
1. (chair) /ch/ /er/			
2. (nut) /n/ /ŭt/			
3. (night) /n/ /īt/			
4. (shop) /sh/ /äp/			
5. (grape) /gr/ /āp/			
6. (rock) /r/ /ök/			
7. (splash) /spl/ /ăsh/			
8. (street) /str/ /ēt/			
Total Score	/8	/8	/8

Other Observations:

Name _____

1st Date _____ 2nd Date _____ 3rd Date _____

Level of Control	No/Little	Some	Gaining	Control
Total Score	0–3	4–6	7–8	9

	1st	2nd	3rd
1. call (without /k/) /ôl/			
2. boat (without /b/) /ōt/			
3. date (without /d/) /āt/			
4. cap (without /k/) /ăp/			
5. kite (without /k/) /īt/			
6. went (without /wh/) /ĕnt/			
7. dark (without /d/) /ärk/			
8. scout (without /sk/) /out/			
9. grow (without /gr/) /ō/			
Total Score	/9	/9	/9

Other Observations:

Name

1st Date   2nd Date   3rd Date

Level of Control	No/Little	Some	Gaining	Control
Total Score	0–12	13–25	26–31	32

Spelling Word	Initial Consonant	1st	2nd	3rd	Short Vowel	1st	2nd	3rd	Final Consonant	1st	2nd	3rd
1. not	n				o				t			
2. can	c				a				n			
3. got	g				o				t			
4. had	h				a				d			
5. bus	b				u				s			
6. sit	s				i				t			
7. pet	p				e				t			
8. bug	b				u				g			
Score		/8	/8	/8		/8	/8	/8		/8	/8	/8

Spelling Word	Initial Consonant	1st	2nd	3rd	Spelling Pattern	1st	2nd	3rd
9. day	d				ay			
10. look	l				ook			
11. will	w				ill			
12. call	c				all			
Score		/4	/4	/4		/4	/4	/4

Total Score		/32	/32	/32

Other Observations:

Name

1st Date | 2nd Date | 3rd Date

Time | Time | Time

Level of Control	No/Little	Some	Gaining	Control
Total Score	0–11	12–23	24–29	30

	1st	2nd	3rd
1. big			
2. one			
3. play			
4. stop			
5. do			
6. she			
7. will			
8. are			
9. for			
10. little			
11. not			
12. by			
13. but			
14. all			
15. said			
Score	/15	/15	/15

	1st	2nd	3rd
1. eat			
2. home			
3. out			
4. help			
5. old			
6. get			
7. his			
8. was			
9. have			
10. did			
11. had			
12. they			
13. ask			
14. time			
15. him			
Score	/15	/15	/15

Total Score	/30	/30	/30

Other Observations:

Name

1st Date   2nd Date   3rd Date

Level of Control	No/Little	Some	Gaining	Control
Total Score	0–2	3–5	6–7	8

	1st	2nd	3rd
1. vol·ca·no (3 claps)			
2. ti·ger (2 claps)			
3. ba·na·na (3 claps)			
4. mo·tor·cy·cle (4 claps)			
5. grass·hop·per (3 claps)			
6. tel·e·vi·sion (4 claps)			
7. hip·po·pot·a·mus (5 claps)			
8. cat·er·pil·lar (4 claps)			
Total Score	/8	/8	/8

Other Observations:

Name

1st Date   2nd Date   3rd Date

Level of Control	No/Little	Some	Gaining	Control
Total Score	0–2	3–5	6–7	8

	1st	2nd	3rd
1. man			
2. top			
3. dog			
4. pig			
5. fish			
6. ball			
7. net			
8. sun			
Total Score	/8	/8	/8

Other Observations:

Deleting final sounds (Auditory/Oral)

Name _____

1st Date _____ 2nd Date _____ 3rd Date _____

Level of Control	No/Little	Some	Gaining	Control
Total Score	0–3	4–6	7–8	9

	1st	2nd	3rd
1. note (without /t/) /nō/			
2. moth (without /th/) /mŏ/			
3. bend (without /d/) /bĕn/			
4. grape (without /p/) /grā/			
5. first (without /st/) /fûr/			
6. huge (without /j/) /hyōō/			
7. seen (without /n/) /sē/			
8. crash (without /sh/) /kră/			
9. time (without /m/) /tī/			
Total Score	/9	/9	/9

Other Observations:

Name _____

1st Date _____ 2nd Date _____ 3rd Date _____

Level of Control	No/Little	Some	Gaining	Control
Total Score	0–2	3–5	6–7	8

	1st	2nd	3rd
1. lad (3)			
2. oak (2)			
3. chain (3)			
4. sled (4)			
5. ill (2)			
6. phone (3)			
7. new (2)			
8. treat (4)			
Total Score	/8	/8	/8

Other Observations:

Name _____

1st Date _____ 2nd Date _____ 3rd Date _____

Time _____ Time _____ Time _____

Level of Control	No/Little	Some	Gaining	Control
Total Score	0–19	20–39	40–49	50

	1st	2nd	3rd
1. first			
2. down			
3. under			
4. run			
5. each			
6. this			
7. only			
8. your			
9. before			
10. them			
11. went			
12. door			
13. because			
14. right			
15. again			
16. made			
17. year			
18. try			
19. around			
20. walk			
21. next			
22. some			
23. then			
24. girl			
25. about			
Score	/25	/25	/25

	1st	2nd	3rd
1. with			
2. tree			
3. man			
4. that			
5. good			
6. boy			
7. make			
8. tell			
9. more			
10. of			
11. when			
12. animal			
13. saw			
14. find			
15. most			
16. place			
17. great			
18. move			
19. just			
20. from			
21. back			
22. off			
23. over			
24. as			
25. call			
Score	/25	/25	/25

Total Score	/50	/50	/50

Name

1st Date   2nd Date   3rd Date

Level of Control	No/Little	Some	Gaining	Control
Total Score	0–17	18–35	36–44	45

	1st	2nd	3rd		1st	2nd	3rd		1st	2nd	3rd
1. i*				2. i				3. i			
s**				s				s			
will				can				then			
hill				fan				when			
still				plan				men			
4. i				5. i				6. i			
s				s				s			
my				mat				stop			
why				that				drop			
try				flat				plop			
7. i				8. i				9. i			
s				s				s			
know				gold				right			
snow				told				night			
slow				cold				bright			
Score	/15	/15	/15		/15	/15	/15		/15	/15	/15

Total Score	/45	/45	/45

Other Observations:

* i = identified how words are alike

** s = blended sounds or word minus onset

Name _____

1st Date _____ 2nd Date _____ 3rd Date _____

Level of Control	No/Little	Some	Gaining	Control
Total Score	0–17	18–35	36–44	45

	1st	2nd	3rd		1st	2nd	3rd		1st	2nd	3rd
1. i*				2. i				3. i			
s**				s				s			
will				him				bus			
win				his				bug			
with				hid				bump			

	1st	2nd	3rd		1st	2nd	3rd		1st	2nd	3rd
4. i				5. i				6. i			
s				s				s			
dog				must				had			
doll				mug				has			
dot				much				hand			

	1st	2nd	3rd		1st	2nd	3rd		1st	2nd	3rd
7. i				8. i				9. i			
s				s				s			
can				home				cake			
camp				hope				came			
cab				hose				cape			
Score	/15	/15	/15		/15	/15	/15		/15	/15	/15

Total Score	/45	/45	/45

Other Observations:

 * i = identified how words are alike

** s = blended first two letter sounds

Name

1st Date	2nd Date	3rd Date
Time	Time	Time

Level of Control	No/Little	Some	Gaining	Control
Total Score	0–9	10–18	19–23	24

	1st		2nd		3rd	
	s*	word	s	word	s	word
1. st						
2. pl						
3. tr						
4. dr						
5. bl						
6. fr						
7. sn						
8. sw						
9. sp						
10. gl						
11. sm						
12. str						
Score	/12	/12	/12	/12	/12	/12

Total Score	/24	/24	/24

Other Observations:

*s = blended sounds

Name

1st Date   2nd Date   3rd Date

Level of Control	No/Little	Some	Gaining	Control
Total Score	0–11	12–23	24–29	30

	1st	2nd	3rd		1st	2nd	3rd
1. short o				4. short i			
long o				long i			
lot				night			
know				kit			
boat				tie			
hope				wise			
Score	/6	/6	/6		/6	/6	/6
2. short a				5. short u			
long a				long u			
take				bug			
way				fruit			
rain				true			
mad				cube			
Score	/6	/6	/6		/6	/6	/6
3. short e							
long e							
bed							
feel							
beat							
Pete							
Score	/6	/6	/6				

Total Score	/30	/30	/30

Name _____

1st Date   2nd Date   3rd Date

Level of Control	No/Little	Some	Gaining	Control
Total Score	0–12	13–25	26–31	32

Spelling Word	Initial Consonant	1st	2nd	3rd	Rime/VCe Vowel Pattern	1st	2nd	3rd
1. game	g				ame			
2. ride	r				ide			
3. note	n				ote			
4. vine	v				ine			
Score		/4	/4	/4		/4	/4	/4

Spelling Word	Initial Consonant(s)	1st	2nd	3rd	Rime/ Pre-consonant Nasal	1st	2nd	3rd
5. ring	r				ing			
6. plant	pl				ant			
7. went	w				ent			
8. think	th				ink			
Score		/4	/4	/4		/4	/4	/4

Spelling Word	Initial Digraph	1st	2nd	3rd	Rime/ Short Vowel	1st	2nd	3rd
9. then	th				en			
10. shop	sh				op			
11. when	wh				en			
12. chip	ch				ip			
Score		/4	/4	/4		/4	/4	/4

Spelling Word	Base Word	1st	2nd	3rd	Suffix	1st	2nd	3rd
13. eating	eat				ing			
14. stops	stop				s			
15. played	play				ed			
16. taller	tall				er			
Score		/4	/4	/4		/4	/4	/4

Total Score	/32	/32	/32

Other Observations:

Name

1st Date   2nd Date   3rd Date

Level of Control	No/Little	Some	Gaining	Control
Total Score	0–5	6–12	13–15	16

	1st		2nd		3rd	
	word	m*	word	m	word	m
1. himself						
2. broken						
3. deeper						
4. couldn't						
5. longest						
6. she'll						
7. landed						
8. cloudy						
Score		/8	/8		/8	/8		/8	/8

Total Score	/16	/16	/16

Other Observations:

*m = meaning

Name _____

1st Date _____ 2nd Date _____ 3rd Date _____

Time _____ Time _____ Time _____

Level of Control	No/Little	Some	Gaining	Control
Total Score	0–19	20–39	40–49	50

	1st	2nd	3rd
1. people			
2. children			
3. any			
4. came			
5. could			
6. boat			
7. even			
8. very			
9. thing			
10. been			
11. would			
12. away			
13. behind			
14. put			
15. house			
16. their			
17. need			
18. other			
19. know			
20. picture			
21. feet			
22. much			
23. what			
24. live			
25. must			
Score	/25	/25	/25

	1st	2nd	3rd
1. now			
2. long			
3. think			
4. who			
5. start			
6. after			
7. felt			
8. here			
9. water			
10. take			
11. work			
12. want			
13. her			
14. last			
15. better			
16. way			
17. head			
18. were			
19. hard			
20. thought			
21. there			
22. shout			
23. watch			
24. began			
25. well			
Score	/25	/25	/25

Total Score	/50	/50	/50

Name _____

1st Date _____ 2nd Date _____ 3rd Date _____

Time _____ Time _____ Time _____

Level of Control	No/Little	Some	Gaining	Control
Total Score	0–13	14–28	29–35	36

	1st	2nd	3rd		1st	2nd	3rd		1st	2nd	3rd
1.				2.				3.			
ship				plum				truck			
sharp				place				train			
shell				plant				trim			
shore				plate				treat			
sheet				please				track			
shoot				plead				trot			

	1st	2nd	3rd		1st	2nd	3rd		1st	2nd	3rd
4.				5.				6.			
stay				grow				bright			
stamp				grape				brush			
steep				ground				brand			
stair				grill				brought			
stem				grab				brain			
stir				grew				broil			
Score	/12	/12	/12		/12	/12	/12		/12	/12	/12

Total Score	/36	/36	/36

Other Observations:

Name _____

1st Date _____ 2nd Date _____ 3rd Date _____

Level of Control	No/Little	Some	Gaining	Control
Total Score	0–2	3–5	6–7	8

	1st	2nd	3rd		1st	2nd	3rd
knight				spray			
stream				crew			
clever				thread			
frown				quite			

	1st	2nd	3rd		1st	2nd	3rd
1. know/right				5. spring/day			
*knight				*spray			
2. street/team				6. cry/new			
*stream				*crew			
3. class/never				7. three/head			
*clever				*thread			
4. from/down				8. queen/kite			
*frown				*quite			
Score	/4	/4	/4	Score	/4	/4	/4

Total Score	/8	/8	/8

Other Observations:

Name _____

1st Date _____ 2nd Date _____ 3rd Date _____

Level of Control	No/Little	Some	Gaining	Control
Total Score	0–13	14–28	29–35	36

	1st	2nd	3rd
1. v*			
bloom			
loose			
smooth			
balloon			
raccoon			
Score	/6	/6	/6
2. v			
freedom			
speech			
needle			
fifteen			
agree			
Score	/6	/6	/6
3. v			
march			
artist			
garden			
alarm			
argue			
Score	/6	/6	/6

	1st	2nd	3rd
4. v			
explain			
afraid			
paint			
trail			
straight			
Score	/6	/6	/6
5. v			
soap			
throat			
toaster			
coach			
charcoal			
Score	/6	/6	/6
6. v			
flight			
lightning			
frighten			
highest			
sigh			
Score	/6	/6	/6

Total Score	/36	/36	/36

*v = vowel pattern

Name

1st Date   2nd Date   3rd Date

Level of Control	No/Little	Some	Gaining	Control
Total Score	0–7	8–15	16–19	20

	1st		2nd		3rd	
	s*	word	s	word	s	word
1. prob (problem)						
2. min (minute)						
3. prin (princess)						
4. rab (rabbit)						
5. soc (soccer)						
6. cam (camera)						
7. bro (broken)						
8. oc (octopus)						
9. thun (thunder)						
10. bas (basket)						
Score	/10	/10	/10	/10	/10	/10

Total Score	/20	/20	/20

Other Observations:

*s = blended sounds

Name

1st Date   2nd Date   3rd Date

Level of Control	No/Little	Some	Gaining	Control
Total Score	0–10	11–21	22–26	27

	1. Read word			2. Clapped syllables			3. Divided into syllables		
	1st	2nd	3rd	1st	2nd	3rd	1st	2nd	3rd
1. kit·ten									
2. rain·coat									
3. ta·ble									
4. but·ter·fly									
5. back·pack·ing									
6. firm·ly									
7. news·pa·per									
8. ba·bies									
9. re·mind·ed									
Score	/9	/9	/9	/9	/9	/9	/9	/9	/9

Total Score	/27	/27	/27

Other Observations:

Name _____

1st Date _____ 2nd Date _____ 3rd Date _____

Level of Control	No/Little	Some	Gaining	Control
Total Score	0–5	6–12	13–15	16

	1st		2nd		3rd	
	word	m*	word	m	word	m
1. helpless						
2. dangerous						
3. magical						
4. respectful						
5. duckling						
6. darkness						
7. finally						
8. motorcyclist						
Score		/8	/8		/8	/8		/8	/8

Total Score	/16	/16	/16

Other Observations:

*m = meaning

Name _____

1st Date _____   2nd Date _____   3rd Date _____

Level of Control	No/Little	Some	Gaining	Control
Total Score	0–15	16–31	32–39	40

Spelling Word	Initial Consonant(s)	1st	2nd	3rd	Rime/r-controlled Vowel	1st	2nd	3rd
1. card	c				ard			
2. dark	d				ark			
3. store	st				ore			
4. bird	b				ird			
Score		/4	/4	/4		/4	/4	/4

Spelling Word	Base Word	1st	2nd	3rd	Suffix	1st	2nd	3rd
5. jumped	jump				ed			
6. I've	I				've			
7. helpful	help				ful			
8. teacher	teach				er			
9. wanted	want				ed			
10. didn't	did				n't			
Score		/6	/6	/6		/6	/6	/6

Spelling Word	Consonant Blend	1st	2nd	3rd	Rime/VCe Pattern	1st	2nd	3rd
11. skate	sk				ate			
12. slide	sl				ide			
13. smoke	sm				oke			
Score		/3	/3	/3		/3	/3	/3

Spelling Word	Consonant Blend	1st	2nd	3rd	Rime ending with *ck*	1st	2nd	3rd
14. truck	tr				uck			
15. clock	cl				ock			
16. snack	sn				ack			
Score		/3	/3	/3		/3	/3	/3

Spelling Word	First/Open Syllable	1st	2nd	3rd	Last Syllable	1st	2nd	3rd
17. table	ta				ble			
18. spider	spi				der			
19. broken	bro				ken			
20. student	stu				dent			
Score		/4	/4	/4		/4	/4	/4

Total Score	/40	/40	/40

Name

1st Date   2nd Date   3rd Date

Level of Control	No/Little	Some	Gaining	Control
Total Score	0–5	6–12	13–15	16

	1st		2nd		3rd	
	word	m*	word	m	word	m
1. <u>im</u>possible (not)						
2. <u>dis</u>appear (opposite)						
3. <u>pre</u>school (before)						
4. <u>sub</u>marine (under)						
5. <u>tri</u>cycle (three)						
6. <u>re</u>capture (again)						
7. <u>en</u>danger (put into)						
8. <u>un</u>certain (not)						
Score	/8	/8	/8	/8	/8	/8

Total Score	/16	/16	/16

Other Observations:

*m = meaning

Name _____

1st Date _____ 2nd Date _____ 3rd Date _____

Level of Control	No/Little	Some	Gaining	Control
Total Score	0–5	6–12	13–15	16

	1st		2nd		3rd	
	word	m*	word	m	word	m
1. decision						
2. imaginary						
3. attendance						
4. suddenly						
5. sinkable						
6. photographer						
7. explanation						
8. especially						
Score		/8	/8		/8	/8	/8	/8

Total Score	/16	/16	/16

Other Observations:

*m = meaning

Name _____

1st Date _____ 2nd Date _____ 3rd Date _____

Level of Control	No/Little	Some	Gaining	Control
Total Score	0–10	11–21	22–26	27

	1. Read word			2. Clapped syllables			3. Divided into syllables		
	1st	2nd	3rd	1st	2nd	3rd	1st	2nd	3rd
1. a·part·ment									
2. ad·ven·ture									
3. ter·ri·ble									
4. gen·er·ous									
5. e·nough									
6. un·in·vit·ing									
7. in·for·ma·tion									
8. sud·den·ly									
9. in·sist·ed									
Score	/9	/9	/9	/9	/9	/9	/9	/9	/9

Total Score	/27	/27	/27

Other Observations:

Name _____

1st Date _____ 2nd Date _____ 3rd Date _____

Level of Control	No/Little	Some	Gaining	Control
Total Score	0–18	19–37	38–47	48

Spelling Word	Prefix	1st	2nd	3rd	Base Word	1st	2nd	3rd
1. unhappy	un				happy			
2. preschool	pre				school			
3. rewrite	re				write			
Score		/3	/3	/3		/3	/3	/3
Spelling Word	First/Closed Syllable	1st	2nd	3rd	Last Syllable	1st	2nd	3rd
4. letter	let				ter			
5. jacket	jac				ket			
6. picture	pic				ture			
Score		/3	/3	/3		/3	/3	/3
Spelling Word	Base Word	1st	2nd	3rd	Suffix	1st	2nd	3rd
7. coming	com(e)				ing			
8. wishes	wish				es			
9. dresses	dress				es			
10. biggest	big				est			
11. babies	bab(y)				ies			
Score		/5	/5	/5		/5	/5	/5
Spelling Word	3-Letter Consonant Blend	1st	2nd	3rd	Rime	1st	2nd	3rd
12. spring	spr				ing			
13. strong	str				ong			
14. splash	spl				ash			
Score		/3	/3	/3		/3	/3	/3
Spelling Word	Initial Consonant(s)	1st	2nd	3rd	Rime with Diphthong	1st	2nd	3rd
15. scout	sc				out			
16. ground	gr				ound			
17. noise	n				oise			
18. point	p				oint			
Score		/4	/4	/4		/4	/4	/4
Spelling Word	Consonant Blend	1st	2nd	3rd	Rime/Long Vowel w/ Silent Letter(s)	1st	2nd	3rd
19. sweep	sw				eep			
20. train	tr				ain			
21. dream	dr				eam			
22. float	fl				oat			
23. snail	sn				ail			
24. bright	br				ight			
Score		/6	/6	/6		/6	/6	/6

	Total Score	/48	/48	/48

DRA™ *Word Analysis* Spelling Sheets

The *DRA Word Analysis* spelling sheets are to be used for the five spelling tasks (Tasks 10, 16, 27, 36, and 40) in this assessment. The form is slightly different for Tasks 27, 36, and 40. In these three spelling tasks the student, after he/she has written the dictated spelling words, is asked to place a check mark in the box after each word he/she thinks looks right. For each word that has no check mark, the student is then directed to spell the word again so that it looks right. The student's second attempt is to be written on the line to the right of the box. See a completed example below.

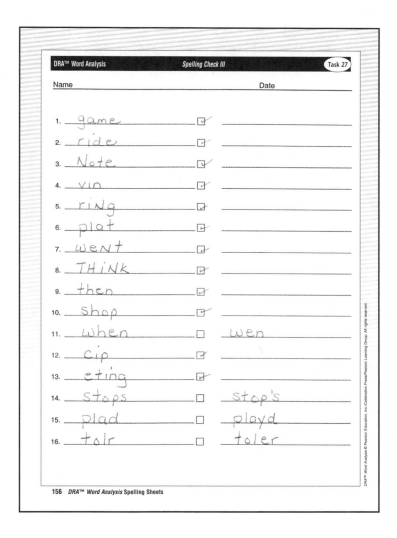

Name _____   Date _____

1. _____

2. _____

3. _____

4. _____

5. _____

6. _____

7. _____

8. _____

9. _____

10. _____

11. _____

12. _____

Name _____   Date _____

1. _____

2. _____

3. _____

4. _____

5. _____

6. _____

7. _____

8. _____

9. _____

10. _____

11. _____

12. _____

Name _____   Date _____

1. _____ ☐ _____

2. _____ ☐ _____

3. _____ ☐ _____

4. _____ ☐ _____

5. _____ ☐ _____

6. _____ ☐ _____

7. _____ ☐ _____

8. _____ ☐ _____

9. _____ ☐ _____

10. _____ ☐ _____

11. _____ ☐ _____

12. _____ ☐ _____

13. _____ ☐ _____

14. _____ ☐ _____

15. _____ ☐ _____

16. _____ ☐ _____

Name _____   Date _____

1. _____ ☐ _____
2. _____ ☐ _____
3. _____ ☐ _____
4. _____ ☐ _____
5. _____ ☐ _____
6. _____ ☐ _____
7. _____ ☐ _____
8. _____ ☐ _____
9. _____ ☐ _____
10. _____ ☐ _____
11. _____ ☐ _____
12. _____ ☐ _____
13. _____ ☐ _____
14. _____ ☐ _____
15. _____ ☐ _____
16. _____ ☐ _____
17. _____ ☐ _____
18. _____ ☐ _____
19. _____ ☐ _____
20. _____ ☐ _____

Name _____   Date _____

1. _____ ☐ _____

2. _____ ☐ _____

3. _____ ☐ _____

4. _____ ☐ _____

5. _____ ☐ _____

6. _____ ☐ _____

7. _____ ☐ _____

8. _____ ☐ _____

9. _____ ☐ _____

10. _____ ☐ _____

11. _____ ☐ _____

12. _____ ☐ _____

13. _____ ☐ _____

14. _____ ☐ _____

15. _____ ☐ _____

16. _____ ☐ _____

17. _____ ☐ _____

18. _____ ☐ _____

19. _____ ☐ _____

20. _____ ☐ _____

21. _____ ☐ _____

22. _____ ☐ _____

23. _____ ☐ _____

24. _____ ☐ _____

Spelling and Oral Reading Miscues Analysis

In the *DRA™ Word Analysis* teachers observe how students identify and spell words in isolation, but it is critical that teachers also observe how students identify and spell unknown or less familiar words in context while independently reading and/or writing for meaningful purposes. The Spelling and Oral Reading Miscues Analysis form is included so that teachers may observe more closely how students work with words while reading and writing texts.

It is strongly recommended that teachers use this form with struggling readers. It is beneficial for teachers to be cognizant of what struggling readers attend to and control as well as what they do not attend to and/or control when reading and spelling. The information teachers gather will help them plan more effectively and implement developmentally appropriate instruction.

What students control changes over time with instruction and multiple opportunities to independently read easy and engaging texts; therefore it is recommended that this analysis be done periodically throughout the school year.

See a completed example of the Spelling and Oral Reading Miscues Analysis on page 163.

Name _____ Grade _____ Date _____

PART 1

Conventionally Spelled Words

On the lines below, record up to 12 different words consistently spelled conventionally in the student's independent writing sample, excluding names of people or characters. Begin by recording the longest words spelled conventionally first.

1.		5.		9.	
2.		6.		10.	
3.		7.		11.	
4.		8.		12.	

Spelling Approximations

Record up to 12 different spelling approximations included in the student's independent writing sample. Exclude names of people and characters.

Approximation	1.	2.	3.
Intended Word			
Approximation	4.	5.	6.
Intended Word			
Approximation	7.	8.	9.
Intended Word			
Approximation	10.	11.	12.
Intended Word			

Observations _____

_____

_____

What does the student need to learn next? _____

_____

_____

_____

Name _____ DRA Text Level(s) _____

PART 2

Self-corrected Miscues

Record up to 12 different self-corrected miscues included in the student's records of oral reading.

Self-corrected Miscue	1.	2.	3.
Word in Text			
Self-corrected Miscue	4.	5.	6.
Word in Text			
Self-corrected Miscue	7.	8.	9.
Word in Text			
Self-corrected Miscue	10.	11.	12.
Word in Text			

Miscues

Record up to 12 different miscues included in the student's records of oral reading.

Miscue	1.	2.	3.
Word in Text			
Miscue	4.	5.	6.
Word in Text			
Miscue	7.	8.	9.
Word in Text			
Miscue	10.	11.	12.
Word in Text			

Observations _____

_____

_____

What does the student need to learn next? _____

_____

Name _Example_   Grade 1   Date 2/03

PART 1

Conventionally Spelled Words

On the lines below, record up to 12 different words consistently spelled conventionally in the student's independent writing sample, excluding names of people or characters. Begin by recording the longest words spelled conventionally first.

1.	went	5.	eat	9.	a
2.	one	6.	to	10.	
3.	the	7.	he	11.	
4.	get	8.	as	12.	

Spelling Approximations

Record up to 12 different spelling approximations included in the student's independent writing sample. Exclude names of people and characters.

Approximation	1. bay/boy	2. fir	3. bg/big
Intended Word	day	flower	dog
Approximation	4. Aafing	5. nadrs	6. hous
Intended Word	something	neighbors	house
Approximation	7. a	8. kudo	9. uf
Intended Word	ate	couple	of
Approximation	10. cut	11. ran	12. fas
Intended Word	caught	run	fast

Observations _control some one syllable words (2-3 letters)_ _b/d and possibly d/p confusion; beginning sound_ _controlled most of the time_

What does the student need to learn next? _distinguish between d/b/p_ _high-frequency words_

Name _Example_   DRA Text Level(s) 4, 6

PART 2

Self-corrected Miscues

Record up to 12 different self-corrected miscues included in the student's records of oral reading.

Self-corrected Miscue	1. went	2. said	3.
Word in Text	were	she	
Self-corrected Miscue	4.	5.	6.
Word in Text			
Self-corrected Miscue	7.	8.	9.
Word in Text			
Self-corrected Miscue	10.	11.	12.
Word in Text			

Miscues

Record up to 12 different miscues included in the student's records of oral reading.

Miscue	1. Kate	2. up	3. the
Word in Text	Kim	out	her
Miscue	4. called	5. for	6. Grandmother's
Word in Text	class	after	Grandma's
Miscue	7. Tuesday	8.	9.
Word in Text	Thursday		
Miscue	10.	11.	12.
Word in Text			

Observations _some control of initial letter/sounds;_ _neglects endings; some miscues interfere with_ _meaning_

What does the student need to learn next? _monitor to check if word_ _choice makes sense and looks right; check endings of words_

DRA™ *Word Analysis* Group Profiles

The *DRA™ Word Analysis* Group Profiles enable teachers to compile each student's levels of control for the tasks he/she completed in order to group the students according to instructional needs and plan more effectively for their instruction. These profiles include the tasks that students reading specific *DRA* text levels are most likely to complete. Group profiles are provided for

- Emerging Readers (DRA text level 3 or less)

- Early Readers (DRA text levels 4–8)

- Early Transitional Readers (DRA text levels 10–12)

- Mid-Transitional Readers (DRA text levels 14–18)

- Late Transitional Readers (DRA text levels 20–24)

- Extending Readers (DRA text levels 28–38)

Teachers record students' first names and last initials in the designated spaces at the top of the form. For each task completed, the teacher records the student's level of control: *C* for Controls, *G* for Gaining Control, *S* for Some Control, and *N* or *L* for No or Little Control. Highlighting or circling the *S*'s, *L*'s, and *N*'s reinforces the identified areas of instructional need. Teachers may use the information on the completed Group Profile form to organize flexible groups for targeted instruction.

Please note that the *DRA Word Analysis* not only reflects a student's strengths and weaknesses, but, also reflects instructional opportunities. For example, if students have not been taught how to distinguish initial sounds and have not had multiple opportunities to sort and/or identify words that begin with the same sound, their responses to that particular task will reflect a lack of instruction and possibly <u>not</u> a lack of ability.

See a completed example of a *DRA Word Analysis* Group Profile on the next page.

Teacher *Sample*   Grade *2*   Date *Beginning of Year*

DRA Word Analysis Tasks	Student Names	Britanny S.	Hakeem R.	Daniel H.	Justin B.	Taneica J.	John L.		
DRA Level		4	4	4	4	8	8		
		Level of Control (N, L, S, G, C)							
Phonological Awareness									
Rhyming									
13. Provides words that rhyme		C	C	G	G	G	G		
Alliteration									
19. Provides words that begin with the same sound			G	Ⓢ	Ⓢ	G	Ⓝ		
Phonemic awareness									
12. Blends phonemes into words		Ⓢ	C	Ⓢ	C	C	C		
15. Deletes onsets		Ⓝ	C	C	C	C	C		
20. Deletes final sounds			G			Ⓝ	G		
21. Segments words into phonemes			Ⓢ			Ⓢ	Ⓢ		
Segmentation									
8. Segments sentences into words		C	C	Ⓢ	G	C	C		
14. Segments words into onsets and rimes		G	C	G	Ⓢ	G	G		
18. Segments words into syllables I			Ⓢ			G	C		
Letter/Word Recognition									
9. Recognizes high frequency words I		G	C	G	G	C	C		
17. Recognizes high frequency words II		Ⓢ	G	Ⓢ	G	G	G		
22. Recognizes high frequency words III						Ⓢ	Ⓢ		
Phonics									
Encoding									
10. Spells 2–3 letter high frequency words		G	C	C	C	G	C		
16. Spells words with short vowels, high frequency words with common spelling patterns		G	Ⓢ	G	Ⓢ	G	G		
Decoding									
11. Identifies and uses initial sounds		C	G	G	C	C	C		
Substitutions/Analogies									
23. Substitutes onsets: rhyming words									
24. Substitutes final sounds									

DRA™ Word Analysis Group Profiles **167**

Teacher _____ Grade _____ Date _____

	Student Names						
DRA Level							
DRA Word Analysis Tasks	**Level of Control (N, L, S, G, C)**						
Phonological Awareness							
Rhyming							
1. Distinguishes pictured rhyming words							
13. Provides words that rhyme							
Alliteration							
2. Distinguishes initial sounds of pictured words							
Phonemic awareness							
3. Isolates the initial sound of a word							
12. Blends phonemes into words							
15. Deletes onsets							
Segmentation							
8. Segments sentences into words							
14. Segments words into onsets and rimes							
Metalanguage							
4. Understands words used to talk about printed language concepts I							
7. Understands words used to talk about printed language concepts II							
Letter/Word Recognition							
5. Names capital letters							
6. Names lowercase letters							
9. Recognized high frequency words I							
Phonics							
Encoding							
10. Spells 2–3 letter high frequency words							
16. Spells words with short vowels, high frequency words with common spelling patterns							
Decoding							
11. Identifies and uses initial sounds							

Teacher _____   Grade _____   Date _____

Student Names								
DRA Level								
DRA Word Analysis Tasks	**Level of Control (N, L, S, G, C)**							
Phonological Awareness								
Rhyming								
13. Provides words that rhyme								
Alliteration								
19. Provides words that begin with the same sound								
Phonemic awareness								
12. Blends phonemes into words								
15. Deletes onsets								
20. Deletes final sounds								
21. Segments words into phonemes								
Segmentation								
8. Segments sentences into words								
14. Segments words into onsets and rimes								
18. Segments words into syllables I								
Letter/Word Recognition								
9. Recognizes high frequency words I								
17. Recognizes high frequency words II								
22. Recognizes high frequency words III								
Phonics								
Encoding								
10. Spells 2–3 letter high frequency words								
16. Spells words with short vowels, high frequency words with common spelling patterns								
Decoding								
11. Identifies and uses initial sounds								
Substitutions/Analogies								
23. Substitutes onsets: rhyming words								
24. Substitutes final sounds								

Teacher _____ Grade _____ Date _____

	Student Names							
DRA Level								
***DRA Word Analysis* Tasks**	**Level of Control (N, L, S, G, C)**							
Phonological Awareness								
Rhyming								
13. Provides words that rhyme								
Alliteration								
19. Provides words that begin with the same sound								
Phonemic awareness								
12. Blends phonemes into words								
15. Deletes onsets								
20. Deletes final sounds								
21. Segments words into phonemes								
Segmentation								
14. Segments words into onsets and rimes								
18. Segments words into syllables I								
Letter/Word Recognition								
17. Recognizes high frequency words II								
22. Recognizes high frequency words III								
Phonics								
Encoding								
16. Spells words with short vowels, high frequency words with common spelling patterns								
27. Spells words with VCe, initial digraphs, preconsonant nasals, suffixes								
Decoding								
25. Blends and uses initial consonant sounds								
26. Identifies words with long/short vowels								
Substitutions/Analogies								
23. Substitutes onsets: rhyming words								
24. Substitutes final sounds								
Structural Analysis								
28. Uses structural analysis to determine word meanings: suffixes I								

Teacher   Grade   Date

	Student Names							
DRA Level								
DRA Word Analysis Tasks	**Level of Control (N, L, S, G, C)**							
Phonological Awareness								
Alliteration								
19. Provides words that begin with the same sound								
Phonemic awareness								
20. Deletes final sounds								
21. Segments words into phonemes								
Segmentation								
18. Segments words into syllables I								
Letter/Word Recognition								
17. Recognizes high frequency words II								
22. Recognizes high frequency words III								
29. Recognizes high frequency words IV								
Phonics								
Encoding								
16. Spells words with short vowels, common spelling patterns								
27. Spells words with VCe, initial digraphs, preconsonant nasals, suffixes								
Decoding								
25. Blends and uses initial consonant sounds								
26. Identifies words with long/short vowels								
32. Identifies words with vowel patterns								
33. Blends and uses initial syllables								
Substitutions/Analogies								
23. Substitutes onsets: rhyming words								
24. Substitutes final sounds								
30. Substitutes rimes								
31. Uses analogies to decode words								
Structural Analysis								
28. Uses structural analysis to determine word meanings: suffixes I								

Teacher _____   Grade _____   Date _____

	Student Names							
DRA Level								
DRA Word Analysis Tasks	**Level of Control (N, L, S, G, C)**							
Phonological Awareness								
Phonemic awareness								
20. Deletes final sounds								
21. Segments words into phonemes								
Letter/Word Recognition								
22. Recognizes high frequency words III								
29. Recognizes high frequency words IV								
Phonics								
Encoding								
27. Spells words with VCe, initial digraphs, preconsonant nasals, suffixes								
36. Spells words with r-controlled vowels, suffixes, initial blends, ck, open 1st syllable								
Decoding								
25. Blends and uses initial consonant sounds								
26. Identifies words with long/short vowels								
32. Identifies words with vowel patterns								
33. Blends and uses initial syllables								
Substitutions/Analogies								
23. Substitutes onsets: rhyming words								
24. Substitutes final sounds								
30. Substitutes rimes								
31. Uses analogies to decode words								
Structural Analysis and Syllabication								
28. Uses structural analysis to determine word meanings: suffixes I								
34. Segments words into syllables II								
35. Uses structural analysis to determine word meanings: suffixes II								
37. Uses structural analysis to determine word meanings: prefixes								

Teacher _____　Grade _____　Date _____

	Student Names							
DRA Level								
DRA Word Analysis Tasks	**Level of Control (N, L, S, G, C)**							
Letter/Word Recognition								
29. Recognizes high frequency words IV								
Phonics								
Encoding								
27. Spells words with VCe, initial digraphs, preconsonant nasals, suffixes								
36. Spells words with r-controlled vowels, suffixes, initial blends, ck, open first syllable								
40. Spells words with prefixes, closed first syllables, suffixes, 3-letter initial blends, diphthongs, long vowel patterns								
Decoding								
25. Blends and uses initial consonant sounds								
26. Identifies words with long/short vowels								
32. Identifies words with vowel patterns								
33. Blends and uses initial syllables								
Substitutions/Analogies								
24. Substitutes final sounds								
30. Substitutes rimes								
31. Uses analogies to decode words								
Structural Analysis and Syllabication								
28. Uses structural analysis to determine word meanings: suffixes I								
34. Segments words into syllables II								
35. Uses structural analysis to determine word meanings: suffixes II								
37. Uses structural analysis to determine word meanings: prefixes								
38. Uses structural analysis to determine word meanings: suffixes III								
39. Segments words into syllables III								

DRA™ Word Analysis
Mini-Lessons/Learning Activities

What teachers do with the information after assessing students directly affects how the students perform on subsequent assessments. If teachers will identify students' instructional needs, develop a thoughtful plan of action, and implement developmentally appropriate learning experiences, there should be observable shifts in how students respond.

Students who find learning to read challenging need to have numerous repeated learning experiences before they truly understand and control a concept, strategy, and/or skill. Two or three experiences are not enough. It is important that teachers teach, reteach, review, and reassess until the students demonstrate control of the various word analysis tasks. At the same time, teachers should provide students with ample developmentally appropriate texts to read. In the context of reading connected text for meaningful purposes, developing readers not only become more proficient in using what they learned but also are in a position to extend their own learning.

This section, *"DRA™ Word Analysis* Mini-Lessons/Learning Activities," is designed to assist teachers in planning for instruction based on the students' needs. It includes a brief introduction to each of the five strands: Phonological Awareness, Metalanguage, Letter/High Frequency Word Recognition, Phonics, and Structural Analysis/Syllabication. General implications for supportive learning activities as well as recommended teacher references are provided in the introduction of each strand to help teachers gain a better understanding of what and how to effectively teach and scaffold students' learning. For the various tasks within the strands, there are a few specific examples of how to introduce, scaffold, and reinforce the students' learning.

When planning for instruction, it is important for teachers to remember that the five strands, Phonological Awareness, Metalanguage, Letter/High Frequency Word Recognition, Phonics, and Structural Analysis/Syllabication, like fibers within a fabric, are an inter-related part of the reading and writing process. Mini-lessons should be well planned, take ten to fifteen minutes, and show students how to use the information and/or skill in the context of real reading and writing. Providing students time as well as a variety of developmentally appropriate materials to read daily is essential for students to become proficient readers.

In recent years, the insights gained from ongoing brain research as well as research documenting effective teaching practices have clarified and extended teachers' understanding of how people learn and how to more effectively teach/reteach, scaffold, and reinforce student learning. The following recommended references focus on teaching and supporting struggling readers.

Allington, Richard L. *What Really Matters for Struggling Readers: Designing Research-Based Programs.*

Armstrong, Thomas. *The Multiple Intelligences of Reading and Writing: Making the Words Come Alive.*

Dahl, Karin, Patricia Scharer, Lora Lawson, and Patricia Grogan. "Help for Children Who Struggle With Phonics," Chapter 3 in *Rethinking Phonics: Making the Best Teaching Decisions.*

Fountas, Irene C., and Gay Su Pinnell. "Struggling Readers and Writers: Teaching That Makes a Difference," pp. 386–388 in *Guiding Readers and Writers Grades 3–6: Teaching Comprehension, Genre, and Content Literacy.*

Lyons, Carol. *Teaching Struggling Readers: How to Use Brain-Based Research to Maximize Learning.*

Strickland, Dorothy, Kathy Ganske, and Joanne Monroe. *Supporting Struggling Readers and Writers: Strategies for Classroom Intervention 3–6.*

Strand 1: Phonological Awareness

Purpose: To help students develop phonological awareness: the ability to hear and explicitly attend to sounds in (not the meaning of) spoken words and manipulate the sounds in spoken words.

Rationale: In learning to read and spell, it is important that developing readers/writers understand that spoken words are made up of components (syllables, onsets, rimes, and phonemes) and that these components can be manipulated (segmented, blended, substituted, and/or deleted). This understanding later supports their learning and use of phonics knowledge to decode and encode words.

Supportive Learning Activities

Immersing students in oral language throughout the school day in a variety of meaningful learning activities enables them to enjoy as well as develop an awareness of and the ability to attend to and "play" with the sounds in words. It is important that kindergarten and first-grade teachers provide a variety of oral language learning activities that are engaging and age-appropriate on a daily basis. Teachers need to read aloud engaging books, poetry, and rhymes, as well as sing nursery rhymes and songs that students enjoy. Teachers can also take advantage of instructional "down time" and encourage children to identify or generate words that rhyme or begin with the same sound; segment words into syllables, onsets and rimes, or phonemes; and blend phonemes into words. For example, students could be asked to give a word that rhymes with a given word as they are getting into and/or standing in line.

Recommended References

Booth, David. "Language Delights and Word Play: The Foundation to Literacy Learning" in *Voices on Word Matters: Learning About Phonics and Spelling in the Literacy Classroom*.

Chapman, Marilyn. "Phonemic Awareness: Clarifying What We Know" in *Literacy Teaching and Learning: An International Journal of Early Reading and Writing*.

Cunningham, Patricia, M. "The Foundation for Phonics They Can Use," Chapter 1 in *Phonics They Use: Words for Reading and Writing*, Third Edition.

Fountas, Irene C., and Gay Su Pinnell. *Sing a Song of Poetry: A Teaching Resource for Phonics, Word Study, and Fluency*.

Honig, Bill, Linda Diamond, and Linda Gutlohn. "Phonemic Awareness," Chapter 7 in *Teaching Reading Sourcebook: For Kindergarten Through Eighth Grade*.

Prelutsky, Jack. *Read-Aloud Rhymes for the Very Young*.

Rasinski, Timothy V., and Nancy D. Padak. "Teaching Phonemic Awareness," Chapter 4 in *From Phonics to Fluency: Effective Teaching of Decoding and Reading Fluency in the Elementary School*.

Rasinski, Timothy V., and Belinda S. Zimmerman. *Phonics Poetry: Teaching Word Families*.

Phonological Awareness: Mini-Lessons/Learning Activities

The *DRA™ Word Analysis* suggested mini-lessons/learning activities for the phonological awareness tasks include rhyming, alliteration, segmentation, and phonemic awareness.

Phonological Awareness: Rhyming

Purpose: To teach students to recognize spoken words that rhyme and orally generate rhyming words

Rationale: The ability to recognize and orally generate rhymes prepares developing readers to eventually attend to and use phonograms/rimes within written words. Rhyming also creates a basis for using analogies to decode and/or spell words with common rimes. For example, the student can assume if two words rhyme, both words will probably end with the same letters.

Task 1: Distinguishing pictured rhyming words (Auditory/Oral)

OBJECTIVE

The student will be able to identify a picture in a set that rhymes with the first picture.

MATERIALS

* picture cards that include words that rhyme and do not rhyme, such as *cat, mat, hand, cap*

TEACH/RETEACH

1. Select two picture cards whose names rhyme and two picture cards whose names do not rhyme, such as picture cards for *cat, mat, hand,* and *cap.*

2. Point to and say the names of the pictures and have the student repeat. [Note: Do <u>not</u> use the same set of pictures included in the assessment task.]

3. Give the picture of the cat to the student and explain: **Cat *ends with /at/. Say* cat, /at/.**

4. Point to the picture of the mat and say: ***This is a mat.* Mat *ends with /at/.* Cat *ends with /at/.* Cat, mat *have the same ending.* Cat, mat *rhyme. Now you say* cat, mat.** Then give the picture of the mat to the student.

5. Point to the hand and say: ***This is a hand.* Hand *ends with /and/.* Cat *ends with /at/.* Hand, cat *have different endings.* Hand, cat *do not rhyme. Now you say* hand, cat.** Turn over the picture of the hand.

6. Point to the cap and say: ***This is a cap.* Cap *ends with /ap/.* Cat *ends with /at/.* Cap, cat *do not have the same ending.* Cap, cat *do not rhyme. Now you say* cap, cat.** Turn over the picture of the cap.

SCAFFOLD

- Continue in a similar manner with new sets of picture cards. Have students (1) name the four pictures, (2) identify the pictures whose names rhyme, and (3) turn over the pictures that do not rhyme.

- Teach students a silly rhyme or song, such as the following:

  A-hunting we will go!

  A-hunting we will go!

  We'll catch a <u>fox</u> and put him in a <u>box</u>.

  And then we'll let him go.

  Use picture pairs of an animal and an item whose name rhymes (*bug, mug; cat, hat; frog, log; hen, pen; mouse, house; pig, wig; skunk, trunk*), have students sing new verses by changing line three.

REINFORCE

- Gather three to four sets of rhyming picture cards. Have student partners sort the picture cards into sets of words that rhyme.

- Ask each student to tell you a word that rhymes with a given word as he/she lines up to go to lunch or recess.

Task 13: Providing words that rhyme (Auditory/Oral)

OBJECTIVE

The student will be able to provide a word that rhymes with each word given by the teacher.

MATERIALS

- simple poems, rhymes, and/or jingles

TEACH/RETEACH

1. Say: **Jack and Jill went up the hill. Now you say, "Jack and Jill went up the hill."**

2. Say: **In this rhyme the words** Jill **and** hill **rhyme. Words that have the same ending sounds are called rhyming words.** Jill **ends with /il/.** Hill **ends with /il/.** Jill, hill **rhyme.** Jill, hill **rhyme with** Bill. Jill, hill, Bill **are words that rhyme because all three words end with the sounds /il/. Now you say** Jill, hill, Bill **and listen to the sounds at the end of each word.** Wait while the students repeat the words.

3. Say: **Now we could say, "Jack and Jill went up the hill. On the way they met Bill and Ph___."** Give students time to say *Phil*. If necessary, say *Phil*.

4. Ask students to repeat the rhyme with you.

SCAFFOLD

1. Say: **Today I am going to say a rhyme, and I want you to help me finish it. Little Bo Peep can't find her sh_____.** Give students time to say *sheep*. If necessary, say *sheep* and have students repeat the rhyme.

2. **What word rhymes with Peep?** Reinforce correct response. If incorrect, repeat the rhyme emphasizing the rime /ēp/.

3. **What is another word that rhymes with Peep, sheep?** (*leap, sleep, creep, deep*, etc.)

4. Reinforce by explaining: **The words peep, sheep, _____** (insert rhyming word) **rhyme because they end with the same sounds /eep/.**

5. Repeat using one or more of the following examples, such as:

   "Up in the <u>tree</u> I <u>see</u> a bird looking at <u>me</u>."

   "Hey, <u>diddle</u>, <u>diddle</u>. The cat and the <u>fiddle</u>."

   "Teddy Bear, Teddy Bear, turn out the <u>light</u>. Teddy Bear, Teddy Bear, say good <u>night</u>."

   "Cock-a-doodle-<u>doo</u>! I lost my <u>shoe</u>. <u>Boo-hoo</u>, <u>boo-hoo</u>."

   "Hickory, dickory, <u>dare</u>. The pig flew up in the <u>air</u>."

REINFORCE

- Read or recite a simple poem or jingle. Have students identify words that rhyme and then give other words that rhyme. [See *Sing a Song of Poetry*, *Phonics Poetry*, *Read Aloud Rhymes*, as well as other poetry anthologies.]

- Before lunch or recess, create a rhyming-word train. The first person, the engine, gives the initial word, such as *bee*. To become a part of the train, each child must provide a word that rhymes, such as *he, tree, see, we, me, flee*. (Words may be real or nonsense.) Once the train is formed, the children holding on to the person in front of them walk around the room or out the door. Each child, starting with the engine, says his/her rhyming word, one after another, (*bee, he, tea, see, we, ...*) faster and/or slower, depending upon the speed of the train.

Phonological Awareness: Alliteration

Purpose: To teach students to recognize spoken words with the same onset and orally generate words that begin with the same sound(s)

Rationale: The ability to recognize and orally generate words that begin with the same sound(s) enables developing readers to eventually attend to and use initial onsets within written words. Alliteration also creates a basis for using analogies to decode and/or spell words with common onsets.

Task 2: Distinguishing initial sounds of pictured words

OBJECTIVE

The student will be able to identify a picture in a set that begins with the same sound as the first picture.

MATERIALS

- picture cards, such as bat, wall, bike, house
- construction paper
- magazines, catalogs, newspaper ads
- scissors
- glue

TEACH/RETEACH

1. Display four picture cards including two with names that begin with the same consonant sound, such as *bat, wall, bike,* and *house.*
   [Note: Do not use the same set of pictures included in the assessment task.]

2. Point to each picture as you say its name, and have the students repeat.

3. Point to the bat and say: **Bat *begins with /b/. Say /b/* bat.** Wait for students to respond.

4. Point to the bike and say: **Bike *begins with /b/. Say /b/* bike.** Wait for students to respond. **Bat, bike *begin with the same sound, /b/. Say* bat, bike.**

5. Then say: **House *begins with /h/. Say /h/* house.** Wait for students to respond. **Bat *begins with /b/.* House begins with /h/. Bat *and* house *do not begin the same.*** Turn over the picture of the house.

6. Follow the same procedure with *wall.*

7. Have the students say the names of the pictured words that begin with the same onset once again and tell you the beginning sound(s).

8. Ask: **What other words or names do you know that begin with the sound /b/?** If students do not respond, provide several examples, such as *Bill, Bob, Brenda, baby, basket,* etc.

SCAFFOLD

1. Continue the same activity with another set of five picture cards. (Include three words with the same onset and two words with a different onset, but do not use the same set of pictures included in the assessment task.)

2. Turn over the cards that do not begin with the same onset.

3. Ask students to say the names of the pictures with the same onset and tell you the beginning sound(s).

4. Ask students to tell you other words or names that begin with that sound.

REINFORCE

- Have students work in small groups. Give each group a set of ten to twelve picture cards whose names begin with two or three different consonant sounds. Have the group members say the picture names and sort them into sets of words with the same onset.

- Have students work independently or in pairs to cut five to six pictures from old magazines, catalogs, and/or newspaper ads whose names begin with a given sound and glue them onto construction paper. When finished, ask students to share their beginning sound and the names of the pictures that they found with the group.

- As students leave for the day, ask each one to tell a word that begins with the same sound as a given word. If students are uncertain, give them a clue. For example, if you give the word ten, you might say, "Your foot has *ten* /t/___" (toes).

Task 19: Providing words that begin with the same sound (Auditory/Oral)

OBJECTIVE

The student will be able to provide a word that begins with the same sound as the word given by the teacher.

MATERIALS

- picture cards, such as ball, bed, box

TEACH/RETEACH

1. Show three picture cards whose names begin with the same consonant sound, such as pictures for ball, bed, box.
   [Note: Do <u>not</u> use the same set of pictures included in the assessment task.]

2. Say the name of each picture, and have the students repeat the names of the pictures as you point to them.

3. Point to the ball and say: **Ball *begins with /b/. Say /b/* ball.** Wait for students to respond.

4. Point to the bat and say: **Bed *begins with /b/. Say /b/* bed.** Wait for students to respond.

5. Point to the box and say: **Box *begins with /b/. Say /b/* box.** Wait for students to respond. **Ball, bat, box *begin with the same sound, /b/. Say* ball, bed, box.**

6. Then say: ***Now I am going to think of another word that begins with same sound as* ball, bed, box*, /b/.*** Pause. **Bob *begins with /b/.* Ball, bed, box, Bob *begin with /b/.***

SCAFFOLD

1. Have the student repeat the /b/ sound and think of another word that begins with the same sound. Give clues if necessary:

   Name something you read that begins with /b/. (*book*)

   Name a long, yellow fruit that begins with /b/. (*banana*)

   Name an animal that builds dams and begins with /b/. (*beaver*)

   Name a game that begins with /b/. (*baseball* or *basketball*)

2. Continue in a similar manner with other consonant sounds.

REINFORCE

- Form a circle of students to play an adapted version of "Duck, Duck, Goose." One child will walk outside the circle. The child walking outside the circle must say a word that begins with the same sound as his/her first name as he/she touches each child's shoulder. For example, a child named Sara could say the word *see* as she touches Jim's shoulder, *sat* as she touches Jamie's shoulder, and *sun* as she touches Billy's shoulder. When she cannot think of another word that begins with the same sound as her name, she is to say the next child's name, Brittany. Both children, Sara and Brittany walk quickly around the circle. Then Sara takes Brittany's place in the circle, and Brittany begins to say words that begin with the sound /b/. To make the game easier, you may have students in the circle also give words that begin with the designated sound.

- As each child leaves group time, have him or her say a word that begins with the same sound as his/her first name or a word given by the teacher.

Phonological Awareness: Phonemic Awareness

Purpose: To help students develop phonemic awareness, the understanding that spoken words are composed of speech sounds (phonemes), and to teach students how to explicitly attend to, blend, segment, and manipulate the phonemes in spoken words

Rationale: Although phonemic awareness begins as an auditory skill, it continues to develop as students learn to connect sounds with print while learning to read. Phonemic awareness helps emerging and early readers to understand the alphabetic principle (letter/sound correspondences), observe the ways that letter sequences represent the sounds in written words, learn how to decode (convert and blend letter sequences into their spoken form), and segment one-syllable words into phonemes in order to write them.

Task 3: Isolating the initial sound of a word (Auditory/Oral)

OBJECTIVE

The student will be able to repeat a word given and provide the onset of the word.

MATERIALS

- picture cards, such as sun, scissors, socks, bug, bird, book

TEACH/RETEACH

1. Identify initial consonant sounds you wish to focus on and select several picture cards for each sound. For example, for the sound /s/ you could have pictures of the Sun, scissors, socks; for /b/ you could have pictures of a bug, bird, book.

2. Hold up the picture of the Sun and say: **This is a picture of the Sun. The first sound that I hear in Sun is /s/. You say Sun.** Wait for students to respond. **The first sound in Sun is /s/. You say /s/.**

3. Hold up the picture of the scissors and say: **This is a picture of scissors. The first sound that I hear in scissors is /s/. You say scissors.** Wait for students to respond. **The first sound in scissors is /s/. You say /s/.**

4. Repeat using the picture card for socks.

5. Review by having the group say with you each picture's name and the first sound.

SCAFFOLD

1. Hold up the picture of the bug and say: **What is this?** Say *bug* if students are uncertain.

2. Ask: **What is the first sound you hear in bug?** Wait for students to respond. If the students respond correctly, say: **That's right. The first sound in bug is /b/.** If not, say: **Listen as I say the word bug in parts /b/ /ug/. The first sound in bug is /b/. You say bug /b/.**

3. Repeat using the picture cards for bird and book.

4. Review by having the group say with you each picture's name and the first sound for both sets of pictures.

5. At another time, continue with other initial consonant sounds.

REINFORCE

- Interactive/Shared Writing

  1. While co-writing, ask the students to tell you the first sound of each word you plan to write before actually writing the word.

  2. After rereading the co-constructed story, cover one or two words, say the word, and ask the students to tell you the first sound in the word. Uncover the word, and help students confirm their response.

- During indoor recess, play a game of "I Spy." Model by saying: **I spy something in the room that begins with /d/. What is it?** (*desk*) Then have students continue by thinking of the name of an object, isolating the initial sound in the name and giving the sound as a clue.

Task 12: Blending phonemes into words (Auditory/Oral)

OBJECTIVE
The student will be able to listen to the individual phonemes in a word and then say the word.

MATERIALS
- none

TEACH/RETEACH
1. Say: **Today we are going to play a word game. I am going to say the sounds in a word that you know. You are to listen carefully so you can tell me the word that the sounds make. I'll show you what to do. /c/ /a/ /t/.** Be sure to segment the sounds and then slowly blend the sounds together. **/c/ /a/ /t/. Cat. /c/ /a/ /t/ is cat. The <u>cat</u> is sleeping on the mat.** [Note: Do <u>not</u> use the same set of words included in the assessment task.]

2. Say: **Listen as I do another word. /d/ /ô/ /g/. /d/ /ô/ /g/. Dog. Now you say /d/ /ô/ /g/ dog.** Wait while students respond. **The <u>dog</u> chased the rabbit.**

SCAFFOLD
1. Give a clue to describe a one-syllable word that is a familiar concept. The clue should consist of a description and the individual phonemes in the word, such as: **I'm thinking of something you wear on your foot. It is a /s/ /ä/ /k/. What am I thinking of?**

2. If the students have difficulty answering, slowly repeat the phonemes and then blend them to say the word: **/s/ /ä/ /k/, /s/ /ä/ /k/, sock.** [Note: Slowly blend the second time you say the phonemes in the word.] Have the student repeat the segmented phonemes and the word.

3. Continue in the same manner with other familiar objects, such as coat, hat, shirt, glove, shoe, dress.

REINFORCE
- "Simon Says"

  1. Tell students they are going to play "Simon Says" but they need to listen carefully because Simon is going to say the sounds in the words.

  2. Say: **When Simon says touch your /l/ /e/ /g/, you are to touch your /l/_____.** Give students time to respond. If correct, say: **That's right. /l/ /e/ /g/ is leg. Do you understand?**

  3. Continue with one-syllable words for different parts of their bodies, such as /l/ /i/ /p/ /s/ (*lips*), /n/ /ō/ /z/ (*nose*), etc.

Task 15: Deleting onsets (Auditory/Oral)

OBJECTIVE

The student will be able to (1) repeat a word given by the teacher and then (2) say the same word without the first sound or sounds.

MATERIALS

- picture cards with one-syllable names, such as moon, star, sun, cloud
- picture cards or objects from the play corner, such as pan, spoon, dish, lid, knife, cup, glass
- picture cards of a cat, fox, mouse, duck, bird, frog, goat, hen, cow, snake, fish, spider, snail, bug, sheep, and chick
- square pieces of different colored paper such as green, red, blue, brown, gray, black, white, pink, yellow, purple

TEACH/RETEACH

1. Say: **Today I am going to show you one way to play with words.** Hold up a picture of a moon. **Listen as I say a word and then separate the first sound from the rest of the word. Moon. Now I will say moon without the first sound /m/.** Pause. **/o͞on/. Now you say moon.** Wait while students respond, then say: **Now you say moon without /m/.**

2. Say: **Listen as I do another one.** Hold up a picture of a star. **Star. Star without the first sound is /tär/. You say star, tar.**

3. Then say: **Star without /st/ is /är/. You say star, /är/.**

4. Repeat the demonstration using one or two other examples, such as *Sun* and/or *cloud.*

SCAFFOLD

1. Hold up a picture card or object from the play corner, such as a pan. Say: **Now you try one. Say pan.** Wait for students to respond. **Now say pan without the first sound /p/.** (/an/)

2. Say: **Let's do another one. Say spoon.** Wait for students to respond. **Now say spoon without the first sounds /sp/.** (/o͞on/)

3. Then say: **Now say spoon without the first sound /s/.** (/o͞on/) If the students do not respond, segment the /s/ /po͞on/.

4. Continue in a similar manner with other words, such as *fork, lid, dish, knife, cup, glass,* etc.
   [Note: Do <u>not</u> use the same set of words included in the assessment task.]

REINFORCE

- Deleting Onset Card Game
   1. Display picture cards with one-syllable names, such as *cat, fox, mouse, duck, bird, frog, goat, hen, cow, snake, fish, spider, snail, bug, sheep,* and *chick* on the table or in a pocket chart. Have the students sit in a semicircle facing the cards.

2. Say: ***In this game, you are to see how many cards you can win. You will win a card each time it is your turn if you say the name of the picture and then repeat the name without the first sound. I'll show you what to do. You'll say, "Please give me the cat, /at/," and I'll give the picture of the cat. We will keep going around the circle until all the cards are gone. Do you understand what to do?***

[Note: Accept as correct if the student deletes either the blend or only the first letter of the blend in words like *frog*. So, /rog/ or /og/ is acceptable.]

3. Repeat the game at another time using different picture cards.

Task 20: Deleting final sounds (Auditory/Oral)

OBJECTIVE

The student will be able to (1) repeat a word given by the teacher and (2) say the same word without the last sound(s).

MATERIALS

* pictured word cards, such as coat, hat, dog, cat, bird, fish, pig, duck, chick, frog
* sets of four different colored blocks or counters

TEACH/RETEACH

1. Say: ***Today we are to play with words by taking off the last sound. I'll show you what to do.***

2. Hold up the picture of a coat and say: ***Listen as I say each sound in the word*** coat. ***/k/ /ō/ /t/. Now you say the sounds for*** coat ***with me. /k/ /ō/ /t/.***

3. Put down a colored block to represent each of the three sounds in the word *coat*. Touch each block as you segment the sounds in *coat* a second time.

4. Then say: ***If I take away the last sound in*** coat, ***two sounds will be left.*** Remove the final block in the group of three as you say: ***I will take away the last block. Now I'll say*** coat ***without the last sound /t/.*** Touch the blocks as you say: ***/k/ /ō/. Coat without /t/ is /kō/. Now you say*** coat, ***/kō/.***

5. Say: ***Let's do another one.*** Hold up the picture of a hat and say: ***Hat.*** Put down a block for each sound as you segment the sounds in hat. ***/h/ /a/ /t/. Hat.*** Remove the last block and say: ***Hat without the last sound /t/ is /ha/. Now you say*** hat, ***/ha/.***

SCAFFOLD

1. Give each student a set of colored blocks. Hold up a picture of a dog and say: ***You say*** dog. ***Touch a block for each sound you hear in*** dog. Model the task again, if needed.

2. Have the student remove the last block and say dog without the /g/. Assist students who are unable to delete the last sound.

3. Reinforce by saying: **Dog** *without /g/ is /dô/.*

4. Continue in a similar manner with other pictured words, such as *cat, bird, fish, pig, duck, chick, frog*.
   [Note: Do <u>not</u> use the same set of words included in the assessment task. After students understand the task, do the task orally without the blocks.]

REINFORCE
- As the students gain proficiency with sound deletion, ask:

  What word do I have if I take the last sound /t/ away from seat? (*sea*)

  What word do I have if I take the last sound /n/ away from plane? (*play*)

  What word do I have if I take the last sound /t/ away from paint? (*pain*)

  What word do I have if I take the last sound /k/ away from fork? (*for*)

  What word do I have if I take the last sound /p/ away from soap? (*so*)

  What word do I have if I take the last sound /t/ away from beet? (*bee*)

Task 21: Segmenting words into phonemes (Auditory/Oral)

OBJECTIVE
The student will be able to segment a given word into phonemes.

MATERIALS
- picture cards, such as car, dog, cat, frog, bird, hen, snake
- self-stick notes
- tokens or coins
- chart paper

TEACH/RETEACH
1. Say: ***Today I am going to show you how to hear the sounds in words.***

2. Show a picture of a word with two to three phonemes, such as *car*. Say: **Car.** Place a plain self-stick note on the board for each segmented sound. ***/k/ /är/.*** **Car** *has 2 sounds /k/ /är/.*

3. Have the students say each sound in *car* as you point to the self-stick notes.

4. Show another picture, such as a dog. Say: **Dog.** Place a self-stick note on the board for each segmented sound. ***/d/ /ô/ /g/. Say the sounds with me /d/ /ô/ /g/. Dog has three sounds.***

5. Draw four boxes (large enough that a self-stick will fit) on the board or chart paper. Repeat the process with the words *car* and *dog* but this time place a self-stick note in each box for each segmented sound in the word.

SCAFFOLD

1. Give the students four counters and a sheet of paper with four small boxes (big enough for a counter to fit).

2. Display a pictured word with three or four phonemes, such as *cat, frog, bird, hen, snake.*

3. Ask the students to say the name of the picture. Then have the students segment each sound in the word as they push up a counter into each box to show the number of sounds they hear in the word.

4. Repeat demonstration if students are unable to respond correctly.

5. Continue with the other pictured words.

6. If needed, repeat this task at another time. Continue to do so until the students demonstrate that they understand the process.
   [<u>Note</u>: Do <u>not</u> use the same set of words included in the assessment task.]

REINFORCE

- Interactive/Shared Writing

  1. Have students draw a short line for each sound they hear in the word you are planning to write on their individual dry-erase board. For example, the student would draw three disconnected lines (__ __ __) for the word, *had.*

  2. Ask them to show you their board before you actually write the word.

- Ask students to draw short lines in their writing journal to help them think about the sounds in unfamiliar words.
  [<u>Note</u>: This activity should be discontinued once the student demonstrates that he/she no longer needs this kind of help.]

Phonological Awareness: Segmentation

Purpose: To teach students how to segment sentences into words and words into syllables, onsets, and/or rimes

Rationale: The ability to segment spoken sentences into words helps prepare emerging and early readers to attend to word boundaries when learning to match one-to-one in reading and leave space between words when writing. Segmenting spoken words into syllables, onsets, and/or rimes enables developing readers to use their knowledge of these components to break written words into more manageable chunks as well as identify parts of words that are similar to other known words. For example, knowing the sounds /st/ in *stop* and /ā/ in *day* will enable a student to figure out and spell the word *stay.*

Task 8: Segmenting sentences into words

OBJECTIVE
The student will be able to use a number line to show the number of words in a given sentence.

MATERIALS
- action picture cards, such as a child jumping rope, swinging on a swing, playing soccer, riding a bike, reading a book
- dry-erase boards and markers
- chart paper

TEACH/RETEACH
1. Say: **When we want to tell other people something, we put what we want to say in a sentence. A sentence can have a few words or many words. "I like apples" is a short sentence. "Jack and Jill went up the hill" is a longer sentence.**
2. Say: **I like apples.** Repeat the sentence. Draw a line on the board or chart paper for each word as you say it in the sentence. ___ ___ ___.
3. Tap each line as you and the students repeat: **I like apples.**
4. Explain: **This sentence tells what I like. The sentence has three words.**
5. Touch each line as you say each word again: **I like apples.**
6. Repeat the activity, for the sentence "Jack and Jill went up the hill."
7. Explain: **This sentence tells what Jack and Jill did. It has seven words.**
8. Touch each line as you say each word again: **Jack and Jill went up the hill.**
9. Then ask one student what he/she likes to eat.
10. Say: **To help me think about this sentence, I will draw a line for each word I say. "____(insert child's name) likes to eat ____(insert food item)."**

SCAFFOLD
1. Display a simple action picture card, such as a child jumping rope.
2. Have the students plan a sentence, such as "The girl is jumping rope."
3. Ask each child to draw a line on his/her dry-erase board for each word in the sentence. For example, they would draw ___ ___ ___ ___ ___ to represent the words in "The girl is jumping rope."

4. Ask students to hold up their dry-erase board so you are able to see them. Note which students need more help.

5. Draw a line on the board as the students repeat the sentence word by word to reinforce the process.

REINFORCE
- Interactive Shared/Writing
  1. Have the students draw a short line on their individual dry-erase board for each word they hear in the sentence you are planning to write.

  2. Ask them to show you their dry-erase board before you actually co-write the sentence.

- Independent Writing
  1. Have the students draw a short line on their paper or in their journal for each word they hear in the sentence they plan to write.

  2. Then write the words on lines.
  [Note: This activity should be discontinued once the student demonstrates that he/she no longer needs this kind of help.]

Task 14: Segmenting words into onsets and rimes (Auditory/Oral)

OBJECTIVE
The student will be able to segment a given word by separating the onset from the rime.

MATERIALS
- picture cards, such as bear, bird, bat, deer, fox, pig, dog, cat, mouse, fish
- string

TEACH/RETEACH
1. Display picture cards of familiar animals. Choose names that are one-syllable words, such as a *bear, bird, bat, deer, fox, pig, dog, cat, mouse, fish*. Ask the student to name the animals. Offer help if needed.

2. Say: ***I'm going to choose one animal and say its name in two parts.*** Hold up a picture of a pig and say: ***pig. I will separate the first part of the word from the last part like this: /p/ /ig/; pig, /p/ /ig/. Now you say the two parts in the word*** pig.

3. Hold up the picture of the cat and say: ***Now I will separate the word*** cat ***in two parts. I will separate the first part of the word from the last part like this: /k/ /at/; cat, /k/ /at/. Now you say the two parts in the word*** cat.

SCAFFOLD

1. Continue by having a student select one of the remaining animals.

2. Ask: **What is the name of your animal?** Give the student time to respond.

3. Then say: **Now separate the first part of the word _____ (insert animal name) from the last part.** Give the student assistance if needed.

4. Continue until all animal names have been segmented into onsets and rimes. [Note: Do <u>not</u> use the same set of words included in the assessment task.]

REINFORCE

- "Come, Have Tea"

    1. Give each student in the group a picture card of an animal, such as a fox, cat, fish, mouse, bat, pig, hen. [You could tie a string to the picture card so the student could wear it like a necklace.]

    2. Say: **We are going to play a game called "Come, Have Tea." I will be the fox. The fox will ask each animal to come to tea. When you hear the fox say the first and last part of your animal's name, such as /m/ /ouse/, and ask you to come to tea, you are to say: "No, no, /f/ /ox/, no tea for me." Then you will walk quickly around behind the circle of chairs while the rest of the group says: "No, no, /f/ /ox/, /m/ /ouse/ wants no tea." Then you will stand behind your chair while fox asks the other animals to come to tea. Do you understand what to do?**

    3. Begin the game by saying: **/m/ /ouse/. /m/ /ouse/, come, have tea with me.**

    4. Prompt the student holding the mouse picture card to say: **"No, no, /f/ /ox/, no tea for me."** Then walk quickly around behind the circle of chairs and remain standing behind his/her chair.

    5. As mouse walks around the circle, prompt the other students to say: **"No, no, /f/ /ox/, /m/ /ouse/ wants no tea."**

    6. Fox continues to ask each animal until everyone in the group is standing behind his/her chair. When everyone is standing, fox walks quickly around behind the children and taps the next person to be the fox.

- After read-alouds and during interactive writing, ask students to segment selected words into onsets and rimes.

Task 18: Segmenting words into syllables I

OBJECTIVE
The student will be able to (1) say the name of a pictured object, and (2) clap the syllables as he/she says the word again.

MATERIALS
- picture cards of animals whose names are one or more syllables, such as lion, elephant, snake, turtle, duck, giraffe, kangaroo, monkey
- three large index cards with one large dot on the first card, two large dots on second, and three large dots on the third card. [Other index cards with four or more dots may be needed when you have students segment their names into syllables.]

TEACH/RETEACH
1. Say: **We can hear the parts of a word when we say words slowly. Some words have one part. Other words have two or more parts. These parts are called syllables.**

2. Show a picture of an animal, such as a lion. Point to the picture and say: **Listen as I say the parts of the word** lion**: /lī/ /on/. This time I'll clap as I say the parts of the word: /lī/ /on** (clap twice). **Lion has two parts or syllables. Now you say** lion **as you clap each syllable.**

3. Continue with an animal picture whose name has three syllables. Say each name and clap the syllables. Have the students repeat.

SCAFFOLD
1. On the board draw a box for each set of dots (one, two, and three) or place three cards with one, two, or three dots in a pocket chart.

2. Show the students a picture of an animal from the same set as above. If the students are uncertain of the name, say the word without emphasizing the syllables.

3. Have the students say and clap each syllable in the name. Then place the picture on the chalk ledge or in a pocket chart under the number of dots that corresponds with the number of syllables in the picture name.

4. If an incorrect response is given, say: **Let's do it together.** Clap the word with the students, and have them repeat it before placing the picture in the appropriate set.

5. When all the picture cards are sorted, review by saying and clapping the syllables for each animal name in the three sets.

6. After many successful attempts with one-, two-, and three-syllable words, picture names with four and five syllables, such as *rhinoceros* or *hippopotamus,* or pictures of other common foods, such as *apple, banana, pizza, grapes, oranges,* may be added.
[Note: Do not use the same set of pictured words included in the assessment task.]

REINFORCE

- Clap Syllables in Students' Names

    1. Have large index cards with sets of dots to represent the number of syllables in the students' first names and/or last names.

    2. Ask students to stand up when you hold up a card with the number of dots (syllables) in their first name. To get in line each child must say and clap the syllables in his/her name.

    3. At another time, use the students' last names.

- After read-alouds and during interactive writing, ask students to say and clap the syllables in selected words.

Strand 2: Metalanguage

Purpose: To teach students the words/terms used to talk about and analyze language

Rationale: In order for emerging and early readers to benefit from instruction about early concepts of print, they must understand the terms that teachers use, i.e., *word, sentence, letter, sound, first, last,* etc.

Supportive Learning Activities

As teachers teach and/or call students' attention to various features of words, they often assume that the students know what they are talking about. It is important for teachers to clearly identify the word component(s) they are discussing. For example, using a frame or highlighting in some way the part of the word the students are to attend to is essential especially for emerging and early readers. Asking students to later frame the same part in different words during the shared reading of a big book or interactive writing and/or highlight a specific feature, such as first letter of all words or capital letters in a short rhyme or poem, reinforces their understanding of the term. Shared writing and reading experiences give teachers many opportunities to explain, call attention to, demonstrate, and informally assess student's understanding of the language used to talk about printed language concepts.

It must be noted that even though *DRA™ Word Analysis* includes only the language used to talk about basic concepts of print, students must continue to learn the vocabulary used by teachers to discuss word components, i.e., *consonant, vowel, prefix, ending/suffix, syllable,* etc., in order to attend to and understand what is being taught.

Recommended References

Fisher, Bobbi, and Emily Fisher Medvic. "Preparation and Materials," Chapter 4, and "Methods and Strategies," Chapter 5 in *Perspectives on Shared Reading: Planning and Practice.*

Harris, Theodore, and Richard Hodges. *The Literacy Dictionary: The Vocabulary of Reading and Writing.*

McCarrier, Andrea, Gay Su Pinnell, and Irene C. Fountas. "Constructing a Text: Learning About Letters and How Print Works," Chapter 7 in *Interactive Writing: How Language and Literacy Come Together, K/2.*

Parkes, Brenda. "Using Shared Reading for Implicit and Explicit Instruction," Chapter 3 in *Read It Again! Revisiting Shared Reading.*

Metalanguage: Mini-Lessons/Learning Activities

Task 4: Understanding words used to talk about printed language concepts I

OBJECTIVE

The student will be able to demonstrate an understanding of words used to talk about printed language concepts, such as *name, first, last, letter,* and *capital* or *uppercase letter.*

MATERIALS

- paper
- large letter cards
- highlighters
- marker

TEACH/RETEACH

1. Have the student watch as you write his or her first name in fairly large manuscript letters on a sheet of paper. Say the letters as you write them.

2. Then say: **This is your name. Your name is a word. Every word has its own special letters. The letters in your name are …** (Point and say each letter name.)

3. Ask the student to name the letters in his or her name. Give support as needed.

4. Say: **The first letter in your name is a capital letter. Point to the first letter in your name. What is that letter called?**

5. Continue: **The other letters in your name are lowercase letters. Point to each lowercase letter as you say its name. What is the last letter in your name?**

SCAFFOLD

1. Repeat the steps above using one student's first and last names.

2. Write the student's first and last name in fairly large manuscript letters on a sheet of paper.

3. Ask the students or a student to:

   - **Name the letters in _____ (insert student's name) <u>first</u> name.**
   - **Name just the <u>lowercase letters</u>.**
   - **Point to the <u>first letter</u>.**
   - **Point to the <u>last letter</u>.**
   - **Name the letters in _____ (insert student's name) last name.**
   - **Name just the <u>lowercase letters</u>.**
   - **Point to the <u>first letter</u>.**

- *Point to the <u>last letter</u>.*
- *Point to a <u>capital letter</u> in _____(insert student's name) <u>first</u> name and <u>last</u> name.*

REINFORCE

- Have student volunteers stand at the front of the room holding large letter cards to form the name of one of the students. Ask the remaining students to identify the letters in the name, both capital and lowercase, as well as the first and last letter. Read the name together. Continue with new student volunteers, forming other students' names. After students are comfortable with the task, you may also include the name of your school, city, state, street, etc.

- Have students highlight the feature you want them to attend to, such as the first letter of each word or each capital letter, in a copy of a short rhyme or poem that they are familiar with.
[Note: Asking students to highlight whatever word feature you wish them to attend to reinforces as well as verifies their understanding of the concept.]

Task 7: Understanding words used to talk about printed language concepts II

OBJECTIVE

The student will be able to demonstrate an understanding of words used to talk about printed language concepts, such as *word, letter, first, last, begin, end,* and *sound*.

MATERIALS

- chart paper
- marker

TEACH/RETEACH

1. Co-write with a group of students a short story or rhyme consisting of two to three sentences on chart paper.
[Note: You could model writing the sentence *"Run, run as fast as you can," said the gingerbread man.* after reading the story of the gingerbread man. You could also write about a special activity, such as We have art today. We will paint pictures.]

2. Think aloud and demonstrate how to plan what you will write, say the first word slowly, identify the first sound, and form the letter that represents the sound you hear. Continue the process with the other sounds in the word. Reread, think aloud, and model writing the remaining words in the first sentence or phrase. Use the terms, *word, letter, first, last, begin, end,* and *sound* as you write the first sentence.

SCAFFOLD

1. Continue to reinforce the terms, *word, letter, first, last, begin, end,* and *sound* as you co-construct and write the remainder of story.

2. Point to each word as you reread what you and the students have written so the group can tell you what the next word is to be. Ask: **What is the first sound in ___? What letter(s) make that sound?** and so on until the word is written.

3. Ask a student to point and reread what has been written and to show you where the next word is to be written. Continue with the process until the short story is completed.

4. After the story is completed, frame one of the words in the story and say:

   This is the word ___. Say it with me.

   Let's read the letters in ___: _-_-_ (insert letter names).

   What letter does the word ___ begin with?

   Tell me the sound the letter ___ makes.

   What letter does the word ___ end with?

   What sound does the letter ___ make?

5. On the following day, ask a student to point to
   a. the words as the group rereads the story
   b. the first word and the last word in the story
   c. a word that begins and/or ends with __ (specify a letter or sound)

6. Say to another student: **Frame the word ___ (a common two to three letter word in the story).**

7. Ask the group to name the letters in selected words. Then ask:

   What letter does ___ begin with?

   What sound does ___ begin with?

   What letter does ___ end with?

   What sound does ___ end with?

   Help the group to segment the sounds if necessary.

REINFORCE
   - During shared reading sessions after reading a big book, a rhyme, or story written by the group, ask students to (1) find the first and last word on a page, (2) frame and name the first or last letter in a specified word, (3) say the beginning or ending sound of a specified word.

   - During shared/interactive writing, ask students to:

     1. Show you where to:
        a. Begin a new sentence
        b. Write the next word (leaving a space between the words)
        c. Add a period to end a sentence

     2. Segment the sounds in words and tell you what letter(s) make each sound

     3. Write the letter(s) that represents the designated sound

Strand 3:
Letter/High Frequency Word Recognition

Letter Recognition

Purpose: To teach students to quickly recognize capital and lowercase letters of the alphabet, and name the letters in different contexts and forms

Rationale: Letter recognition forms the foundation for the understanding of the alphabetic principle that letters of the alphabet represent the sounds of spoken language. Knowing the names of the letters of the alphabet makes learning the sounds for the letters easier for emerging and early readers. Automatic recognition of letters enables developing readers to quickly access and use what they know about the letter(s) as one source of information when problem-solving unknown words in context and/or decoding isolated words.

Supportive Learning Activities

Teachers are encouraged to involve students in a variety of activities that support students' learning of the letters of the alphabet. They include listening to ABC books read aloud, singing alphabet songs, making individual alphabet charts or books, working with magnetic letters, forming letters out of clay or in a sand tray, and sorting letter cards into sets of letters with common features or capital and lowercase letters. For students who have limited literacy experiences, teaching them to recognize and name the letters in their first name is a good place to begin.

It is also important to use multiple modalities when teaching students how to attend to the distinctive features of and form different letters. For example, when demonstrating how to form the letter *a*, the teacher should say in coordination with forming the letter, "over, around and down," so the action and spoken words are completed at the same time. Teaching students to do the same helps them to consistently and correctly form and recognize the letter(s). The correct formation of letters enables students to quickly distinguish between similar letters such as *h* and *n* or *c* and *e* when they appear in written words.

Recommended References

Dorn, Linda, and Carla Soffos. Table 4.1 "Language Prompts for Movement Patterns to Form Letters," page 57 in *Shaping Literate Minds: Developing Self-Regulated Learners.*

Dufresne, Michèle. "Learning About Letters," Chapter 2 in *Word Solvers: Making Sense of Letters and Sounds.*

Honig, Bill, Linda Diamond, and Linda Gutlohn. "Alphabet Recognition," Chapter 6 in *Teaching Reading Sourcebook: For Kindergarten Through Eighth Grade.*

McCarrier, Andrea, and Ida Patacca. "Kindergarten Explorations of Letters, Sounds, and Words" Chapter 5 in *Voices on Word Matters: Learning About Phonics and Spelling in the Literacy Classroom.*

Letter Recognition: Mini-Lessons/Learning Activities

Task 5: Recognizing capital letters *(Timed)*

OBJECTIVE
The student will be able to recognize and name capital letters within the specified time (1 minute 30 seconds).

MATERIALS
- alphabet chart
- set of capital (uppercase) letter cards
- alphabet books
- short story, poem, or rhyme, such as "Jump or Jiggle"
- highlighters
- dry-erase boards and markers

TEACH/RETEACH
1. Recite or sing "The Alphabet Song," inviting the student to join in.

2. Point to each letter on an alphabet chart as it is named, saying: ***Capital or uppercase A, lowercase a, _____(insert the name of the object associated with the letter, such as apple).***

3. Point to *Aa* on the alphabet chart and explain: ***Each letter of the alphabet can be written in two ways.*** Point to the capital letter *A* and say: ***This is a capital or uppercase letter A. The names Adam or Amanda begin with a capital or uppercase A.***
   [Note: Use students' names whenever possible and use the terms *uppercase* and *capital* together so students become familiar with both.]

4. Point to other capital or uppercase letters and give students names that begin with the selected letter.

5. Next, teach how to form a selected group of capital letters that include common features, such as *B, D, P, R.*
   [Note: See "Language Prompts for Movement Patterns to Form Letters," on page 57 in *Shaping Literate Minds: Developing Self-Regulated Learners.*]

6. Have students form the letters in the air and then on their dry-erase board. Continue the process, eventually introducing all the capital/uppercase letters over time.

SCAFFOLD
1. Write each student's first and last names in large manuscript letters on a chart. Highlight the first letter of each name.

2. Read the students' names together.

3. Have individual students locate the names that begin with a specified letter, such as capital or uppercase letter *S* or *D.*

REINFORCE

- Periodically distribute capital letter cards to students. Sing together "The Alphabet Song," and have students hold up the corresponding letter as it is named in the song.

- Collect a wide range of alphabet books to use as shared reading with students to provide practice in using letter names, recognizing letter forms, and developing new concepts.

- Emphasize the use of capital letters during morning message or shared/interactive writing experiences (to begin the name of a person or place, names of days and months, to begin a sentence).

- Have the student find and name capital letters in print around the classroom.

- Have students find and highlight the capital letters on a copy of a short story, poem, and/or rhyme, such as "Jump or Jiggle" on page 7 in *Read-Aloud Rhymes for the Very Young* by Jack Prelutsky.
  [Note: You could also copy this poem onto chart paper or an overhead transparency. Then give students a capital letter card and ask them to find the word that begins with that letter.]

- Have students sort their names into sets containing the same initial capital letter.

Task 6: Recognizing lowercase letters *(Timed)*

OBJECTIVE

The student will be able to recognize and name lowercase letters within the specified time (1 minute 30 seconds).

MATERIALS

- alphabet chart
- lowercase letter cards
- dry-erase boards and markers
- chart paper or blank overhead transparency
- short story, poem, or rhyme, such as "Higglety, Pigglety, Pop"
- paper
- colored markers or crayons

TEACH/RETEACH

1. Use an alphabet chart and ask the students to say the letter names with you, as you point to each letter.
   [Note: This should be done daily in kindergarten and first-grade classrooms.]

2. Point to *Aa* on the alphabet chart and remind the student: **Each letter of the alphabet can be written in two ways. Today we will talk about the lowercase letters of the alphabet.**

3. Distribute selected lowercase letter alphabet cards, such as *a, c, o, g, d*.

4. Ask the students to say the letter name when given a card. If the student cannot name the letter, say its name for the student to repeat.

5. Then have the students take turns finding their letter on the alphabet chart.

6. Next, teach how to form a selected group of lowercase letters that include common features, such as *o, a, c, d, g*. Have the students practice forming the letter in the air and on a dry-erase board.
[Note: See "Language Prompts for Movement Patterns to Form Letters," on page 57 in *Shaping Literate Minds: Developing Self-Regulated Learners*.]

SCAFFOLD

- Help students make their own alphabet chart or book.

- Have students work in pairs and read/reread early primary and their own alphabet books.

- Spread a complete set of alphabet cards in random order on a table. As you slowly recite the alphabet together, have the students find the corresponding card and place them in order. Once arranged, have the students say each letter name as someone points to each letter.

- Have students sort letters of the alphabet into sets with similar shapes. Ask them to explain how they decided which letters should be grouped together.

- Tell students to form a selected letter(s) on their dry-erase board, show you, and then erase.

REINFORCE

- Have students find and highlight a specific lowercase letter on a copy of a short story, poem, and/or rhyme. For example, students could highlight the letter *p* in a copy of "Higglety, Pigglety, Pop!"
[Note: See page 5 in *Read-Aloud Rhymes for the Very Young* by Jack Prelutsky.]

- Provide capital and lowercase magnetic letters and magnetic boards in your word-and-letter center for students to form their names and those of classmates. Encourage students to identify each letter in the names they make.

- Reread the alphabet chart daily. Over time vary how you have the students read the chart so that they become fluent and flexible in identifying letters and their relationships to sounds. Some possible alternatives are:

  Say just the letter names.

  Say the letter names and a word that begins with that letter.

  Say the letter names and give a sound the letter makes.

  Start with the letter *z* and go backward.

  Go down the columns (*Aa, Ee, Ii, Mm*) instead of across the rows (*Aa, Bb, Cc, Dd*)

  Give the sound(s) that each letter makes (e.g., two sounds for the letters *a, c, e, g, i, o, s, u*).

High Frequency Word Recognition

Purpose: To foster the students' automatic recognition and understanding of high frequency words encountered in developmentally appropriate reading materials

Rationale: The automatic recognition and understanding of many high frequency words enables developing readers to focus on the construction of meaning in texts that are "just right" (not too difficult). This growing core of known words supports reading fluency as well as provides a basis for using analogies to quickly problem-solve words with similar spelling patterns and/or meanings.

Supportive Learning Activities

Helping students attend to the spelling patterns in high frequency words through a variety of activities reinforces and extends their control of the words they frequently encounter when reading. These activities may include

1. making words with magnetic letters
2. writing the same word multiple times using different-colored markers
3. sorting sets of words according to common features
4. highlighting high frequency words in copies of poems or short stories
5. going on a word hunt around the room to find how many times a specific word has been used

One of the most effective ways to increase the number of words automatically recognized and understood is to provide developing readers multiple opportunities daily to read and reread a great number of texts independently. Making choral and partner reading as well as home reading an integral part of the school's reading program supports the rereading of texts for meaningful purposes. Repeated readings also foster students' reading fluency (reading rate, phrasing, and intonation) when teachers model and support what fluent reading sounds like.
[Note: The high frequency word lists in the *DRA™ Word Analysis* include words ranked in order of their frequency of occurrence as calculated from the *DRA* and other similarly leveled texts.]

Recommended References

Cunningham, Patricia M. "Reading and Spelling High Frequency Words," Chapter 2 in *Phonics They Use: Words for Reading and Writing*, Third Edition.

Dufresne, Michèle. "Learning Words," Chapter 3 in *Word Solvers: Making Sense of Letters and Sounds*.

Fountas, Irene C., and Gay Su Pinnell. *Sing a Song of Poetry: A Teaching Resource for Phonics, Word Study, and Fluency.*

Fry, Edward, Jacqueline Kress, and Dona Lee Fountoukidis. "Instant Words," pages 47–53, in *The Reading Teacher's Book of Lists*, Fourth Edition.

Hundley, Susan, and Diane Powell. "Investigating Letters and Words Through Shared Reading" in *Voices on Word Matters: Learning About Phonics and Spelling in the Literacy Classroom.*

Martinez, Miriam, Nancy L. Roser, and Susan Strecker. "I Never Thought I Could Be a Star: Readers Theatre Ticket to Fluency." *The Reading Teacher* 52, 4: 326–334.

Opitz, Michael F., and Timothy V. Rasinski. "Sharing and Performing," Chapter 3 in *Good-Bye Round Robin: 25 Effective Oral Reading Strategies*.

Routman, Regie. "Plan for and Monitor Independent Reading," Chapter 6 in *Reading Essentials: The Specifics You Need to Teach Reading Well*.

Tiberski, Sharon. "Matching Children With Books for Independent Reading," Chapter 11 in *On Solid Ground: Strategies for Teaching Reading K–3*.

High Frequency Word Recognition: Mini-Lessons/ Learning Activities

Tasks 9, 17, 22, 29: Identify high frequency words *(Timed)*

OBJECTIVE

The student will be able to quickly read aloud the words in each column within the specified time (1 minute 30 seconds).

MATERIALS

- magnetic board and letters or letter cards
- index cards
- dry-erase boards and markers
- highlighters
- short story, poem, rhyme, such as "Out"

TEACH/RETEACH

1. Select the high frequency word that you wish to teach.

2. Form the word with magnetic letters on a magnetic board.

3. First have the students
   a. look at the word; say the names of the letters in sequence
   b. listen to the word in a sentence
      [Note: Use context sentences that relate to the student to help students build meaning for high frequency words, such as: *I like the shoes Pedro is wearing. Syrena's birthday is in October. Nick, where do you like to go after school? This cookie is for Ashley.*]
   c. hear the word segmented into onset and rime and phonemes

4. Then have the students
   a. say the word
   b. use the word in a sentence
   c. segment the word into onset and rime and phonemes
   d. think of other words that begin and/or end with the same sounds and letters
   e. make the word several times with magnetic letters or letter cards
   f. write the word several times on their dry-erase board

g. locate and frame or highlight the word in a text
[Note: For irregular high frequency words, such as *the, to, of, is, said, were, come,* etc., present each word as a whole. Have the students (1) name the letters in sequence and then say the word, (2) practice writing it multiple times on a small dry-erase board, and (3) review these words frequently until they are able to recognize and write them correctly and quickly.]

SCAFFOLD

- Add each high frequency word to the classroom word wall and review on a regular basis. See "Doing a Word Wall" pages 58–64 in *Phonics They Use: Words for Reading and Writing,* Third Edition by Pat Cunningham.

- Have students locate and frame or highlight the word after a shared reading of a big book, at the end of an interactive writing lesson, and in copies of short stories, poems, and/or rhymes. For example, either the word *the* or *out* could be highlighted in a copy of the jump-rope rhyme "Out," on page 204 in *Sing a Song of Poetry: A Teaching Resource for Phonics, Word Study, and Fluency* by Irene Fountas and Gay Su Pinnell.

REINFORCE

- Provide lots of easy texts for students to read/reread with a partner and independently. This is the most effective way to reinforce and extend students' control of high frequency words.

- Present a number of high frequency words on index cards and have the student read the words as quickly as possible.

Strand 4: Phonics

Purpose: To teach students the relationships between letters/graphemes and sounds/phonemes, and how to use their understanding of grapheme/phoneme relationships to encode and decode words

Rationale: The study of phonics helps developing readers learn how to analyze and work with words. In reading, developing readers use what they know about grapheme/phoneme relationships to help them identify and pronounce new words while constructing meaning. In writing they use what they know about phoneme/grapheme relationships to record the sounds they hear in words and then check to see that the words look right. The ability to substitute onsets and rimes greatly expands the number of words developing readers are able to identify and spell. It also supports the use of analogies when words cannot be sounded out letter by letter. Developing readers/writers' understanding of how words work continues to evolve over time as they encounter and work with more complex vowel patterns within words. As students gain skill in using phonics knowledge, they become increasingly more independent in achieving their own purposes and more confident as readers and writers.

Supportive Learning Activities

It is important that students learn early on letter sound correspondences and decoding strategies in order to become effective in problem-solving unknown words in context as well as identifying isolated words. As students participate in teacher-directed word studies, shared or guided reading groups, and mini-lessons that are developmentally appropriate, they learn how to

1. attend to various features of words
2. search through words in a left-to-right sequence
3. blend letter sounds
4. take apart words
5. use analogies

Activities such as sorting words with common spelling patterns, segmenting printed words into onsets and rimes, and substituting onsets and rimes help developing readers to (1) attend to letter sequences and vowel patterns within words and (2) use portions of known words to spell or decode unknown words as needed. Encouraging students to closely examine the letter combinations and vowel patterns in words after they have identified them in reading and/or spelled them will increase their proficiency in using these spelling patterns later on to identify unfamiliar words.

Shared and interactive writing lessons provide students with opportunities to learn how to attend to various components of spoken words, segment words into manageable units, and record the sounds heard. As teachers demonstrate and rehearse each step of the process when spelling a less familiar word, students observe and learn how it is done. Developmentally appropriate instruction and frequent opportunities to write independently strengthen developing readers/writers' understanding of sound/spelling pattern relationships and how words are constructed. Over time developing writers extend the number of words they are able to spell conventionally. They also become more skillful in using their knowledge of sound letter relationships and analogies to write at least an approximation, if not the conventional spelling, of many one-syllable words.

Developing readers become more efficient in attending to and using their knowledge of letter sound relationships and vowel patterns to identify new words as they extensively read and/or reread texts on their independent level. Providing developing readers with (1) time daily to read independently and (2) a variety of engaging texts from which to choose is essential if these readers are to become fluent and flexible in applying what they know about phonics.

Recommended References

Askew, Billie. "Helping Young Readers Learn How to Problem Solve Words While Reading," Chapter 12 in *Voices on Word Matters: Learning About Phonics and Spelling in the Literacy Classroom.*

Bear, Donald R., Marcia Invernizzi, Shane Templeton, and Francine Johnston. "Word Study for Beginners in the Letter Name-Alphabetic Stage," Chapter 6, and "Word Study for Transitional Learners in the Within Word Pattern Stage," Chapter 7 in *Words Their Way: Word Study for Phonics, Vocabulary, and Spelling Instruction*, Second Edition.

Cunningham, Patricia M., "Using Phonics and Spelling Patterns," Chapter 3 in *Phonics They Use: Words for Reading and Writing*, Third Edition.

Cunningham, Patricia M. and Richard Allington. "Developing Decoding and Spelling Fluency (Commonly Called 'Phonics'!)," Chapter 5 in *Classrooms That Work: They Can All Read and Write*, Second Edition.

Dahl, Karin L., et al. "Writing to Share the Pen and Phonics Knowledge," Chapter 9 in *Rethinking Phonics: Making the Best Teaching Decisions.*

Dufresne, Michèle. "Problem-Solving New Words," Chapter 4 in *Word Solvers: Making Sense of Letters and Sounds.*

Fresch, Mary Jo, and Aileen Ford Wheaton. "Organized Word Lists: A Handy Resource for Spelling Instruction," Chapter 4 in *The Spelling List and Word Study Resource Book.*

Fresch, Mary Jo, and Aileen Ford Wheaton. "How to Plan and Manage Spelling Instruction," Chapter 6 in *Teaching and Assessing Spelling: A Practical Approach That Strikes the Balance Between Whole-Group and Individualized Instruction.*

Fountas, Irene C., and Gay Su Pinnell. *Sing a Song of Poetry: A Teaching Resource for Phonics, Word Study, and Fluency.*

Fry, Edward, Jacqueline Kress, and Dona Lee Fountoukidis. "Phonics," Section 1 in *The Reading Teacher's Book of Lists*, Fourth Edition.

Fry, Edward. *Phonics Patterns: Onset and Rhyme Word Lists*, Fourth Edition.

Ganske, Kathy. "Planning Appropriate Instruction," Chapter 3 in *Word Journeys: Assessment-Guided Phonics, Spelling, and Vocabulary Instruction.*

Honig, Bill, Linda Diamond, and Linda Gutlohn. "Phonics," Chapter 8 in *Teaching Reading Sourcebook: For Kindergarten Through Eighth Grade.*

Marten, Cindy. "Essential Classroom Practices," Chapter 4 in *Word Crafting: Teaching Spelling, Grades K-6.*

Moustafa, Margaret. "How Children Use Their Knowledge of Spoken Sounds to Pronounce Unfamiliar Print," Chapter 5 in *Beyond Traditional Phonics: Research Discoveries and Reading Instruction.*

Rasinski, Timothy V., and Nancy D. Padak. "Onsets, Rimes, and Basic Phonics Patterns," Chapter 5 in *From Phonics to Fluency: Effective Teaching of Decoding and Reading Fluency in the Elementary School.*

Rasinski, Timothy V. and Belinda S. Zimmerman. *Phonics Poetry: Teaching Word Families.*

Routman, Regie. "Spelling and Word Study in the Reading-Writing Classroom," Chapter 10 in *Conversations: Strategies for Teaching, Learning, and Evaluating.*

Wilde, Sandra. "How Children Learn to Spell: Evidence From Decades of Research," Chapter 14 in *Voices on Word Matters: Learning About Phonics and Spelling in the Literacy Classroom.*

Phonics: Mini-Lessons/Learning Activities

The *DRA™ Word Analysis* suggested mini-lessons/learning activities for phonics are subdivided into encoding, decoding, and substitutions/analogies.

Encoding

Purpose: To teach students the relationship between sounds/phonemes and letters/graphemes, how to segment spoken words into syllables, onsets, rimes, and phonemes as needed, and how to use what they know about phoneme/grapheme relationships, spelling patterns, and analogies to spell and check the spelling of unfamiliar words

Rationale: In order for developing writers to communicate their thoughts and ideas in writing, they must initially learn how to segment sounds in two or three letter words, identify the individual sounds and the letter(s) that represent each sound, and form the identified letters in the correct sequence.

This process enables them to build a core of known words and gain a preliminary understanding of how to spell phonetically regular words. At the same time they must also learn how to spell some key irregular high frequency words, such as *the, to, of, were, said, come,* so they are able to write these words quickly and not rely on sounding them out. As students' core of known spelling words increases in number and complexity, learning how to use analogies enables them to spell a variety of words with various vowel patterns. With experience they become skilled in knowing when to (1) segment a word into syllables, onsets, rimes, and/or phonemes, (2) use analogies, and/or (3) use a combination of sounding out and analogies to spell and check the spelling of less familiar words. The ultimate goal for students is not to learn/memorize how to spell a set of words but to gain the knowledge, concepts, strategies, and confidence to construct and check the spelling of whatever word is needed at the time.

Tasks 10 and 16: Spelling Checks I and II

OBJECTIVE

The student will be able to segment words into phonemes and write two to three letter words phonetically spelled and some high frequency words.

MATERIALS

- word cards for sorting activities
- small dry-erase boards and markers
- magnetic letters or letter cards
- small magnetic boards
- highlighters
- short stories, poems, and/or rhymes

TEACH/RETEACH

1. Select a two or three letter word that can be spelled phonetically, such as *can, dad, at*.

2. Say: **Listen for the sounds in the word.** Then say the word slowly and have the student repeat the sounds in the word slowly.

3. Say: **Now you say the word slowly.**

4. Link sounds and letters by saying:

   What is the first sound?

   What letter makes that sound?

   Put that letter on your magnetic board.

   Continue the process until the remaining sounds/letters in the word have been identified and formed with magnetic letters or letter cards.

5. Have students make the word several times using magnetic letters or letter cards and check the word by saying the word slowly as he/she slides his/her finger under each letter, matching the letter(s) with the sound.

6. Have the student say the letter names in sequence and then say the word several times.

7. Ask: **What other words do you know that begin and/or end with the same letters?** Suggest words if students are unable to respond.

8. Have the students write the word several times on their dry-erase board.

9. Have several students use the word in a sentence.

SCAFFOLD

1. Repeat the steps above until the students demonstrate that they are able to quickly and accurately write each word.

2. Periodically review by asking students to write several words with spelling patterns previously studied.
   [Note: For irregular high frequency words, such as *the, to, of, is, said,* etc., present each word as a whole. Have the students (1) name the letters in sequence and then say the word, (2) practice writing it several times on a small dry-erase board, and (3) review these words frequently until they are able to write them correctly and quickly.

REINFORCE

- Provide partners or small groups with a set of word cards. Have students sort the words by a common feature that they share, such as words with two letters, words with the same initial consonant or vowel, words with the same short vowel or a long vowel, etc.

- Establish how new words can be made by constructing CVC words using letter cards or magnetic letters *n, o, t, g, h, i, s, a.* For example,

  1. Ask the students to make *not.*

  2. Have them check the word by saying the word slowly as they run their finger under each letter.

  3. Tell them to write the word on a sheet of paper or in their word study journal.

  4. Then have them change *not* to *got.*

  5. Continue this process until they have made and written *hot, hit, his, has, hat, sat, sit.*

  6. Have them read the list of words they made and review what they did to make new words.

[Note: See "Changing a Hen to a Fox" on pages 92–93 in *Phonics They Use: Words for Reading and Writing,* Third Edition, for other examples.]

Tasks 27, 36, 40: Spelling Checks III, IV, and V

OBJECTIVE

The student will be able to accurately spell words with increasingly more complex spelling patterns, such as consonant blends, digraphs, long vowel patterns, pre-consonant nasals, polysyllabic words including some prefixes and/or suffixes.

MATERIALS

- letter cards or magnetic letters
- dry-erase boards and markers
- word cards for sorting

TEACH/RETEACH

1. Identify the spelling pattern you wish to focus on. Select two or three words as examples. Say the words aloud as the students listen. For example, to focus on words with the VCe pattern, select words with which the students are familiar to present the spelling pattern: *name, like, note*.

2. Write the words on the board as you repeat them. Ask: **How are these words alike? Say the words with me.**

3. Segment the onset and rime in each word and then ask: **What vowel sounds do you hear?** (Establish that the words have a long vowel sound and follow the VCe spelling pattern.)

4. Underline the long vowel pattern (*name, like, note*).

5. Have students make the words several times using magnetic letters or letter cards and check by saying the words slowly as they slide their finger under each letter matching the letter(s) with the sound.

6. Ask: **What other words do you know that have the same spelling patterns?** Suggest words if students are unable to respond.

7. Cover the words on the board. Have the students close their eyes and picture each word as you say each one aloud.

8. Ask the students to write each word on a dry-erase board and then check the spelling using the words on the board.

SCAFFOLD

1. Ask the students to search for and record new words with the same spelling pattern over the next couple of days. With the help of students write all the words with the same spelling pattern on a chart for future reference.
   [Note: You may also make a list of exceptions, e.g., *have, were, love.*]

2. Ask students to locate and frame or highlight words with the identified spelling pattern in copies of poems, rhymes, short stories, and in their own writing.

3. Include two to three words with the identified spelling pattern in your weekly spelling test.

4. Have student select two or three words from the list as exemplars to include in their word study journal.

Use the same procedure to teach words with other spelling patterns, such as: (1) initial digraphs as in *thing, chip*; (2) blends as in *green, street*; (3) rhyming patterns as in *rain, skate, play, store*; (4) pre-consonant nasal rime as in *sing, went*; (5) an *r*-controlled vowel rime as in *barn, bird*; and (6) base words with affixes as in *helpful, unable, slowly, rewinding*.

REINFORCE

- Use index cards to make sets of word cards for sorting words with different spelling patterns, e.g., with the VCe pattern (*like, made, shade, strike*), initial digraph and short vowel rime (*then, when, chat, ship*), pre-consonant nasal rime (*bent, find, stand, string*), and *r*-controlled vowel rime (*farm, fern, more, bird*). Have partners read the words and sort them into patterns. Ask students to explain their sorts.

- Create a poster showing six steps to better spelling. Include:
  - **Look** at the word.
  - **Say** the word.
  - **Link** letters and sounds and **search** for spelling patterns.
  - **Think** of other known words with the same spelling patterns.
  - **Write** the word.
  - **Check** the word.

  Encourage students to follow the steps with spelling words that are introduced.

- When a new spelling pattern is introduced, add two to three exemplar words to the classroom word wall and have students add several examples in their word study journals.

Decoding

Purpose: To teach students the relationship between letters/graphemes and sounds/phonemes, how to search through words in a left-to-right sequence attending to letter information, to recognize letter combinations and/or spelling patterns in words, and how to blend letter sounds and use analogies to problem-solve words in context and/or decode isolated words

Rationale: In order for developing readers to focus their attention on constructing meaning while reading, it is important that they learn how to quickly and efficiently identify unknown or less familiar words. Initially they must learn letter/sound correspondences and how to sequentially blend two or three letter sounds. This process enables them to gain a basic understanding of how to decode many predictable one-syllable words.

As developing readers encounter more words while reading texts at an appropriate level of difficulty and have opportunities to analyze and sort words by various features, their skill in identifying words with a variety of letter sequences and vowel patterns will continue to evolve. Once again, the ultimate goal for students is not to learn/memorize a set of words but to gain the knowledge, strategies, and confidence to problem-solve/decode whatever unknown word is encountered.

Task 11: Identifying and using initial sounds *(Timed)*

OBJECTIVE
The student will be able to provide the phoneme for each letter and give a word or name that begins with that phoneme within the specified time (4 minutes).

MATERIALS
- letter cards
- paper

TEACH/RETEACH
1. Identify one letter sound you wish to focus on, for example, the letter *t*.

2. Begin with phonemic awareness by having the students listen as you say a tongue twister, such as: **Turtle talks to toad.**

3. Have the students repeat the sentence and tell how the words are alike. If necessary, repeat each word emphasizing the initial sound: **/t/, turtle, /t/, talks, /t/, to, /t/, toad.** Point out that all the words begin with the sound /t/.

4. Introduce the letter *t* by showing a letter card. Explain: **This is the letter t. T stands for the /t/ sound at the beginning of each word in "Turtle talks to toad."** Ask the students to repeat the letter sound and the sentence.

SCAFFOLD
1. Give each student a letter *t* card.

2. To reinforce sound discrimination, say: **I am going to say some words. When you hear a word that begins with the /t/ sound, hold up the letter card. Say: turkey, panda, lion, tiger, toad, frog, elephant, tuna, giraffe, bird, toucan, parrot, zebra, turtle.**

3. Ask the students to repeat the sound of the letter *t* and think of other words or names that begin with the /t/ sound.

4. Have students cut out pictures of items that begin with the /t/ sound out of old magazines, flyers, and catalogues to make a poster of words that begin the letter *t*.

Teach and scaffold students' learning of the other letter sounds. Once they learn the process, they will begin to learn letter sounds on their own.

REINFORCE
- Provide materials for students to make their own alphabet books or charts. Encourage students to read/reread these at home and during independent reading time.

- Provide materials in the classroom word-and-letter center for students to create individual letter books. Using blank books with six or eight pages, students can write the letter on the left-hand page and draw or paste a picture of an object beginning with the letter on the right-hand page. Encourage students to read/reread their letter books at home and during independent reading time.

- Provide partners or small groups of students with sets of 10–12 letter cards. Have them turn the cards face down and take turns to select a card, identify the letter, give the sound, and then name a word that begins with the letter sound.

- Ask students to frame or circle words that begin with the designated letter in shared reading and/or interactive writing.

- Hold up a letter card, and ask students to quickly tell you the sound and then a word that starts with that sound before sitting down, getting into line, or while waiting in line.

Task 25: Blending and using initial consonant sounds *(Timed)*

OBJECTIVE
The student will be able to (1) blend two or three consonant letter sounds, and (2) say a word or name that begins with the consonant blend within the specified time (2 minutes 30 seconds).

MATERIALS
- word cards
- chart paper
- letter cards/magnetic letters, such as *s, t, f, r, b, l, m, w*
- short stories, poems, and rhymes
- markers
- highlighters

TEACH/RETEACH
1. Introduce the students to a blend by writing a two-letter blend, such as *st,* on the board.

2. Demonstrate how to blend the two letter sounds, and then ask students if they know any words or names that begin with those sounds. Write the suggested words and names on chart paper for future reference.

3. Reread the initial list of words together.

4. Select two or three of the words given by the students to function as key words in helping the students remember the letter-sound associations. These words should be added to the classroom word wall and the students' word study journals.

SCAFFOLD
1. Read a poem or short story containing words with the identified consonant blend.

2. After reading the poem or short story, reread it and have the students raise their hand when they hear a word beginning with the blend. Stop and add these words to your original list.

3. Over the next couple of days, ask students to find other words to add to the list.

4. Give the students a copy of the poem or short story, and ask them to highlight the blend each time it is used. For example, you could use the following short story for the blend *st*.

> Stan bought a pet hamster at the pet store. When he got home, the first thing he did was put his hamster in a cage and give him some water. Then Stan stood and thought about a name for his hamster. He wanted a name that started with the same letters as Stan. So he thought about Steve, Stella, Stacy, and Star. At last he decided that Star was the best name for his hamster.

[Note: *St* can be located at the beginning, in the middle, and at the end of words.]

Follow the same procedures for other consonant blends that need to be taught or reinforced.

REINFORCE

- Have students read and sort words that begin with the common letters, i.e., *s* (*sand, sun, sit, soon, Sara*), *t* (*ten, Tom, tan, too, Ted*), and *st* (*stand, store, story, stay, Steven*) into three sets.

- Provide materials in the classroom word-and-letter center for students to create individual blend books. Using blank books with six or eight pages, students can write the blend on the left-hand page and draw or paste a picture of an object beginning with the letter on the right-hand page. Encourage students to read/reread these books at home and during independent reading time. [Note: See pictures of words beginning with blends in the Appendix of *Words Their Way: Word Study for Phonics, Vocabulary, and Spelling Instruction*.]

- Dictate five or six words beginning with the letters *s*, *t*, and *st*, such as *sand, stop, ten, stand, stone*, and *same* for students to spell on their dry-erase board. Have them check to see if the words look right before showing you.

- Write four or five words on the board, such as *fly, play, ball, cool*, and *keep*. Tell the students to change these words so they begin with *st* (*sty, stay, stall, stool*, and *steep*). After the making the new words, have the students read them and use them in a sentence.

- Assign an action word to each consonant blend you wish to reinforce, such as *stand, frown, blink, smile, swing, stretch*. Provide students with letter cards (*s, t, f, r, b, l, m*, and *w*) to spell the blends *st, fr, bl, sm, sw, str*. Begin an action game by saying: *Who can smile?* The students will hold up the letter cards *sm*, repeat the word, and demonstrate the action. Continue with another action word until each consonant blend is identified.

Task 26: Identifying words with long and short vowels

OBJECTIVE

The student will be able to (1) tell how the words are alike in each set, (2) say the long and short sounds of the designated vowel, and (3) read the words in the set.

MATERIALS

- picture cards
- word cards
- dry-erase boards and markers
- short story, poem, and rhyme
- highlighters

TEACH/RETEACH

1. Select the vowel sound to teach, such as /e/.

2. Display three or four picture cards whose names have the sound, such as *bed, leg, nest,* and *pen.* Say each picture name and have the students repeat the words.

3. Ask the students to tell you how the words are alike. Say the words again slowly if the students are uncertain.

4. Write the picture names on the board. Say: **Tell me how the words are alike.** Underline the vowel and read the words together.

5. Say: **Listen as I read each word.** Track the letters as you slowly read the words. Then ask: **What is the sound for letter e?** Verify and identify the sound as a "short vowel *e* sound."

6. Cover up the words and dictate each of the words for the students to spell. Be sure to use the each word in a sentence as well.

7. Have the students repeat each word slowly and write it on a dry-erase board.

8. Ask students to underline the letter that represents the common vowel sound.

SCAFFOLD

1. Have students look for and write down other words containing the identified short vowel for several days.

2. Compile a group list of words containing the identified short vowel for future reference.

3. Have students highlight the words that include the designated vowel sound in copies of short poems, rhymes, and in their own writing.

4. Select two or three words to serve as an exemplar on the classroom word wall and in each student's word study journal.

Repeat the steps for other long and short vowel sounds.

REINFORCE

- Word Sort

    1. Write 12 to 16 words containing the long and short sounds for a designated vowel, such as *deck, red, left, peg, stem, when, send, step, she, knee, heat, leave, dream, seed, green, sweep,* on index cards and place them in random order.

    2. Have partners or a small group of students read the words out loud and sort them into two groups. One group with the short vowel sound and the other with the long vowel sound. Have the students read aloud the words in each set as a check.

- Dictate a sentence using words that have both the long and short sound of the same vowel letter. If possible use one of the students' names, such as *Steve fed his pet hen seeds. Nick and Mike did not like to fight. Kate made a mask for Dan.* Have the students write the dictated sentences then underline the vowel or vowel pattern in each word.

Task 32: Identifying words with vowel patterns

OBJECTIVE

The student will be able to identify the vowel pattern in a set of words and read aloud the words.

MATERIALS

- index cards
- chart paper
- dry-erase boards and markers
- short stories, poems, rhymes
- highlighters

TEACH/RETEACH

1. Select a vowel pattern, such as *ea, ee, ou, oa, oo,* etc., to teach.

2. Select three or four words with the identified vowel pattern, such as *out, sound, mouse,* and *proud.*

3. Say the selected words, and ask students to tell you how the words are alike. Repeat the words slowly if students are uncertain.

4. Write the selected words on the board or chart paper. Say each word slowly as you write it.

5. Ask students to tell you how the words are alike. Underline the vowel pattern, and read the words together.

6. Ask: **What is the sound for the letters** ou?

7. Cover up the words and dictate each of the words. Be sure to use the each word in a sentence as well.

8. Have the students repeat word slowly and write it on a dry-erase board.

9. Ask students to underline the letters that represent the common vowel sound.

SCAFFOLD

1. Have students look for and write down words containing the identified vowel pattern /ou/ over the next couple of days.

2. Compile a list of words containing the identified vowel pattern on chart paper for future reference.

3. Have students highlight the words that include the designated vowel pattern in a copy of a short story, poem, rhyme, or in their writing.

4. Select two or three words to serve as an exemplar on the classroom word wall and in each student's word study journal.

Repeat the steps for other vowel patterns.

[Note: Do not use the same set of words included in the assessment task. See lists of words with a variety of vowel patterns in *The Spelling List and Word Study Resource Book* and *Phonics Patterns: Onset and Rhyme Word Lists,* Fourth Edition.]

REINFORCE

- Write several words on index cards with vowel patterns you wish to review, such as *ou, ea, ai, igh.* Word cards could include *about, count, aloud, found, mouse, mail, main, paint, train, easy, beast, beach, teach, speak, light, might, high, fright.* Have partners or small groups of students sort the cards into vowel patterns and read the words in each set. Ask students to add other words they know that fit into the categories.

- Give groups of students the letters *a, e, i, b, l, m, n, p, r, s, t.* Have them use the letters to build as many words as possible with different vowel patterns. (*short a, e, i; long vowels ai, ea, aCe*). Have each group create their own list of words on chart paper. The list might include the following words:

bat	met	sit	trail	meat	same
mat	set	lip	train	team	tame
sat	bet	nip	paint	steam	mate
last	stem	trip	rain	beast	lame
blast	best	pin	mail	stream	blames
mast	step	trim	pail	meal	stale

Task 33: Blending and using initial syllables

OBJECTIVE

The student will be able to blend a group of letters and give a word that makes sense and begins with those blended sounds.

MATERIALS

- index cards
- self-stick notes
- highlighter
- overhead transparencies

TEACH/RETEACH

1. Write a sentence that contains a polysyllabic word, such as "We will go to the park and have a picnic."

2. Use several self-stick notes to cover the second syllable in the word.

3. Say: **When I am reading and come to a longer word that I don't know, sometimes I blend the letter sounds in the first part of the word and then think what would make sense. Let me show you.**

4. Read aloud the sentence and pause after blending the letters in the first syllable: **We will go to the park and have a /pic/ picnic.**

5. Uncover the rest of the word and say *picnic* as you run your finger under it. Say: **The word** picnic **makes sense and these are the letters I would expect to see in** picnic.

SCAFFOLD

1. Write another sentence on the board, such as "You may not go out," Dad said firmly.
   [Note: Do not use the same set of words and sentences included in the assessment task.]

2. Ask the students to read aloud the sentence and to use what they know to identify the first syllable of the word. Give the students time to respond.

3. If students are uncertain, help them blend the letter sounds or look for chunks and think what might make sense.

4. Remove the self-stick notes and confirm by rereading the sentence and running your finger under the word firmly as you say it. Ask: **Does the word** firmly **make sense in the sentence and look right. Are these the letters you expect to see in the word** firmly?

5. Use other words that the students have difficulty problem-solving in shared and/or guided reading. Help the students look at the first part of the word and think of a known word that looks similar or sound out the letters, and then suggest a word that begins with the blended sounds and makes sense in the story.

REINFORCE

- Problem-Solve Polysyllabic Words
  1. Tell students to be on the lookout for two- or three-syllable words in their reading.
  2. Have the students select a two- or three-syllable word that they think would be a new word for most students in the class and copy the sentence in which they found the word onto an index card.
  3. Ask them to highlight or underline the polysyllabic word.
  4. Transfer the sentences selected by the students onto an overhead transparency and over the next couple of days have one or two students read their sentences and ask the group to do a think-aloud demonstrating how to figure out the word.

Substitutions/Analogies

Purpose: To teach students how to (1) identify and divide written words into onsets and rimes and (2) use components of known words to problem-solve words in context and/or decode isolated words

Rationale: The ability to substitute onsets and rimes greatly expands the number of words developing readers are able to quickly identify. It also supports their use of analogies when words cannot be sounded out letter by letter. Over time as students' core of known words increases in number and complexity, learning how to use analogies enables them to problem-solve a variety of words with various vowel patterns. With experience they become skilled in knowing how and when to divide a word into onset and rime, use analogies, and/or use a combination of sounding out and analogies to identify unknown or less familiar words.

Task 23: Substituting onsets: rhyming words

OBJECTIVE

The student will be able to tell how each set of words is alike and read aloud the rhyming words in each set.

MATERIALS

- letter cards or magnetic letters
- word cards
- chart paper
- strips of paper

TEACH/RETEACH

1. Have the following magnetic letters on the board: *t, e, n, h, p, d.*
2. Say: ***I am going to make the word* ten.** Say each phoneme in the word as you pull down the letters in the word. **/t/ /e/ /n/**

3. Say the word slowly once more as run your finger under it. Write the word on the board or chart paper.

4. Segment the word *ten* into onset and rime. /t/ /en/

5. Say: If I remove the **/t/, I have /en/ left.**

6. Place the letter *p* in front of the letters *en* and say: **If I add the letter p the word will be pen. /p/ /en/**

7. Say the word slowly once more as you run your finger under it. Write the word on the board or chart paper.

8. Repeat the process with *h* and *d*.

9. Say: **I was able to make different words today by changing the first letter in the word** ten. **I made** (point as you read the words) **ten, pen, hen, den. These words rhyme. These words end with the letters** e, n **and say /en/ but each word begins with a different letter and sound.**

SCAFFOLD

1. Select the rime you want to teach, such as *an*.

2. Provide the students with the necessary letter cards or magnetic letters (e.g., *c, a, n, t, p, l*).

3. Explain: **You are going to build some words using these letter cards or magnetic letters. First, build the word** can. **What letters will you use to make** can? If the student has difficulty, segment the phonemes in the word *can*.

4. After students have made the word *can*, have them run their finger under it as they say it slowly and then copy the word onto a sheet of paper or in their word study journal.

5. Then say: **Now change** can **to** tan.
   What letter will you take away?
   What letter will you add?

6. After students have made the word *tan*, have them run their finger under it as they say it slowly and then copy the word onto their sheet of paper or in their word study journal.

7. Repeat the process with *p* (*pan*) and *pl* (*plan*).

8. Have the students read aloud the words on their paper and tell you how the words are alike and why these words rhyme. Help students if they are uncertain.

9. Continue in a similar manner with other phonograms/word families.
   [Note: See *Phonics Patterns: Onset and Rhyme Word Lists* and *The Spelling List and Word Study Resource Book*. Do <u>not</u> use the same set of words included in the assessment task.]

REINFORCE

- Have small group of students create word chains by listing all of the words they know with the same spelling pattern (same rime) on strips of paper. Students may connect paper strips if they need more paper.

- Word Sort
  1. Give students 18 to 20 word cards with several different phonograms. Word cards could include: *hit, lit, sit, quit, mice, rice, price, slice, went, bent, tent, Kent, date, Kate, late, plate, long, song, wrong, strong.*
  2. Ask the students to sort the word cards into sets of rhyming words.
  3. Have students read aloud the words in each set and tell you how the words in each set are alike (letters and sounds).

- Have students highlight the words that include the designated vowel pattern in a copy of a short story, poem, rhyme, or in their writing. [Note: See *Phonics Poetry: Teaching Word Families* by Timothy Rasinski and Belinda S. Zimmerman.]

Task 24: Substituting final sounds

OBJECTIVE

The student will be able to tell how each set of words is alike and read aloud the words in each set.

MATERIALS

- letter cards or magnetic letters
- word cards
- chart paper

TEACH/RETEACH

1. Have the following magnetic letters on the board: *t, m, a, n, p, h.*

2. Say: **I am going to make the word** man. Say each phoneme in word as you pull down the letters in the word. **/m/ /a/ /n/ man.**

3. Say the word slowly once more as you run your finger under it. Write the word on the board or chart paper.

4. Say: **If I remove the /n/, I have /ma/ left.**

5. Place the letter *p* after the letters *m a* and say: **If I put the letter p after the letters, I will make the word** map. **/ma/ /p/.**

6. Say the word slowly once more as you run your finger under it. Write the word on the board or chart paper.

7. Repeat the process with *t* (*mat*) and *th* (*math*).

8. Say: **I was able to make different words today by changing the last letter in the word** man. **I made** (point as you read the words) **man, map, mat, math. These words have the same beginning letters m a and the same sounds /ma/ but each word ends with a different letter and sound.**

SCAFFOLD

1. Select a word that can be easily changed by substituting the last letter(s), such as *bat, bag, bad, band*.
   [Note: Do not use the same set of words included in the assessment task.]

2. Provide the students with the necessary letter cards or magnetic letters (e.g., *b, a, n, t, g, d*).

3. Explain: **You are going to build some words using these letter cards or magnetic letters. First, build the word** bat. **What letters will you use to make** bat? If the student has difficulty, segment the phonemes in *bat*.

4. After students have made the word *bat*, have them run their finger under it as they say it slowly and then copy the word onto a sheet of paper or in their word study journal.

5. Then say: **Now change** bat **to** bag.
   What letter will you take away?
   What letter will you add?

6. After students have made the word *bag*, have them run their finger under it as they say it slowly and then copy the word onto their sheet of paper or in their word study journal.

7. Repeat the process with *d* (*bad*) and *nd* (*band*).

8. Have the students read aloud the words on their paper and tell you how the words are alike and what is different. Help students if they are uncertain.

REINFORCE

- Have students go on a word search and collect as many words as possible that begin with the identified consonant(s) and vowel. Then have a small group of students create word chains by listing all of the words they know and can find that begin with the same consonant(s) and vowel pattern on strips of paper. Students may connect paper strips if they need more paper.

- Word Sort
  1. Give students 18 to 20 word cards with several different phonograms but with the same initial consonant and vowel. Word cards could include: *band, back, bath, bat, bag, ball, bang, sat, sand, Sam, sang, sad, kid, kick, king, kiss, Kim, kit*.
  2. Ask the students to sort the word cards into sets of words with common features.
  3. Have students read aloud the words in each set and tell you how the words in each set are alike (letters and sounds).

Task 30: Substituting rimes *(Timed)*

OBJECTIVE
The student will be able to read the words in each set within the recommended length of time (2 minutes).

MATERIALS
- chart paper
- word cards

TEACH/RETEACH
1. Identify three examples of one-syllable words that have the same onset (consonant blends), such as *string, street, strike*.
   [<u>Note</u>: For suggestions of words to use, see *The Reading Teacher's Book of Lists*. Do <u>not</u> use the same set of words included in the assessment task.]

2. Begin by writing two of the words with the same onset but different rimes on chart paper, such as *string* and *street*.

3. Model observations that can be made about the two words. Say: ***I see that both words begin with the same letters* s, t, r, *and those letters together say /str/. The other letters in the words are different. The first word ends with* i, n, g *like in the word* sing.** Write the word *sing* beside the word *string*. ***So this word is /str/ /ing/,* string. *The kite was tied to a very long <u>string</u>.***

4. Then point to the word *street*. ***This word has the same beginning sound letters as* string, */str/ but it ends with the letters* eet *like in the word* meet.** Write the word *meet* beside the word *street*. ***So this word is /str/ /eet/,* street. *It is not safe to play in the <u>street</u>.***

5. Review the process by saying: ***I used what I knew about other words to help me figure out these words. You can do the same thing when you come to words you do not know in reading.***

SCAFFOLD
1. Add the third word to the chart. Ask the students to analyze all three words and explain how this word is similar to the first two words but different.

2. Say: ***What is this word?*** If the students are uncertain, ask: ***Do you know another word that ends with the letters* i, k, e?** (*like*). ***How do the letters* i, k, e *sound?***

3. Ask several students to use the word *strike* in a sentence.

4. Then say: ***Now read all three words.***

5. Cover up the words on the chart, and have the students write the words (*strike, string,* and *street*) on their dry-erase board as you dictate and use each word in a sentence. Ask them to underline the part that is different. Uncover the words on the chart so the students may check their spelling of the dictated words.

6. Ask the students to think of other words that begin with the same initial sounds. Record them on the chart.

7. Over the next couple of days, ask students to find other examples to add to your initial list.

8. Repeat the procedure with another onset and different set of rimes at another time.

REINFORCE
- Word Sort
  1. Provide students with word cards for sorting words with common onsets, such as: *snake, snow, snack, snap, snail, sneeze; string, strip, strand, strap, strike, strong; dry, dream, dress, drive, drift, dress, drank.*
  2. Have students read aloud the words in each set and tell you how the words in each set are alike.

Task 31: Using analogies to decode words

OBJECTIVE
The student will be able to use parts of familiar words to problem-solve unknown words.

MATERIALS
- chart paper
- markers

TEACH/RETEACH
1. Select a word with a vowel pattern, such as VVC or VCe, or includes silent letters like *igh*.
   [Note: For suggestions of words to use, see *The Reading Teacher's Book of Lists*. Do <u>not</u> use the same set of words included in the assessment task.]

2. Next, select two words that students are likely to know to help them figure out a less familiar word. For example, knowing the words *from* and *name* will enable students to figure out *frame*.

3. Say: **When I come to a word that I don't know, sometimes I find that it is helpful to think about other words that I know that are similar. I'll show you what I mean.**

4. Write the word *frame* on the board or chart paper and say: **I see that this word begins with the letters f, r like in the word from.** Write the word *from* beside the word *frame* and say: **From. The first part of the word from is /fr/.** Point to the word *frame* as you say: **The last part of this word is a, m, e like in the word name. Name without /n/ is /ām/.** Point to the word *frame* once again as you say **I can put together the two parts to read the word. /fr/ /ām/, frame. I put your picture in a red <u>frame</u>.**

SCAFFOLD

1. Select another word with a vowel pattern. For example, to problem-solve the word *crown* use the more familiar words *cry* and *down*.

2. Write the words *cry* and *down* on the board, and ask the students to read the two words.

3. Say: **Now separate the first part of cry from the last part. /cr/ /ī/.** If the students hesitate, cover up the rime and ask them how the two letters would sound together. Repeat with the word *down*.

4. Write the word *crown* on the board and say: **Use what you know about the first two words to figure out this word.** If the students hesitate, cover up the rime and ask them how the two letters would sound together. Then uncover the *own*.

5. Tell students to record in their word study journal what they can do when they come to an unknown word in reading. Ask them to use one of the words in the lesson as an example.

6. Repeat the steps for other words that (1) the students do not know and (2) cannot be sounded out letter by letter.

REINFORCE

- In shared and/or guided reading, help students use analogies to problem-solve less familiar words with vowel patterns that cannot be sounded out.

- Prepare several word cards with familiar sight words. Write and underscore the letters in the onset, such as: <u>cr</u>y, <u>gr</u>een, <u>pl</u>ay, <u>sk</u>y, and <u>st</u>op. Next, write and underscore the letters in a rime that can be combined with the underlined onsets, such as <u>late</u>. Distribute the cards to students and ask them to form new words using the onsets from five words and the rime in the word *late*. Have the students record the new words on the board or a sheet of paper and be prepared to use each new word in a sentence. Read the list together following the activity and ask several students to use each word in a sentence.

Strand 5: Syllabication/Structural Analysis

Purpose: To teach students how to use syllabication to pronounce unfamiliar polysyllabic words and structural analysis to help determine the meaning of words

Rationale: Extending readers (*DRA* text levels 28–38) will encounter more and more polysyllabic words while reading increasingly more challenging texts. As developing readers become more skilled in recognizing and using likely letter combinations in onsets and rimes to identify single-syllable words, they are able to use this knowledge to divide longer words into manageable chunks. Knowing how and where to divide words into either syllables, as in the word *in/ter/est/ing* or manageable chunks, as in the words *under/stand/ing* or *news/paper*, enables readers to quickly figure out the pronunciation of novel polysyllabic words.

In addition, learning how to use structural analysis in conjunction with context clues helps readers to construct at least a preliminary understanding of unfamiliar modified words while reading. Understanding what common prefixes and suffixes mean and how affixes modify or create new words when they are combined with base/root words will enable developing readers to be more independent in their analysis of unknown words.

Supportive Learning Activities

Late transitional and extending readers are in the early stages of learning how to identify syllable patterns and use structural analysis to determine word meanings. Teachers must use opportunities to show how to decode and analyze two or more syllable words in shared/guided reading and interactive writing lessons. It is important in the context of reading and writing real text to demonstrate how to take polysyllabic words apart in order to pronounce or write them, identify meaning units (base words and affixes) to establish the meaning of words, and use examples, synonyms, and/or antonyms to reinforce the meaning of words.

In mini-lessons teachers should help students look sequentially through two- or three-syllable words, identify familiar spelling patterns/letter combinations, and break the words into manageable chunks. A list of key known words representing initial consonants and common vowel patterns needs to be established and used as a reference to support the students' use of known words to problem-solve unknown words. Extending readers will become more efficient in figuring out the pronunciation and the meaning of unknown polysyllabic words when they are encouraged to use analogies, parts of known "big" words, to help them.
[Note: Patricia Cunningham has compiled a list of fifty polysyllabic words for intermediate students to use when problem-solving big words with similar parts. See pages 166–167 in *Phonics They Use: Words for Reading and Writing*, Third Edition. Also see suggested steps to help students read big words on pages 10–11 in *Teaching Reading Sourcebook: For Kindergarten Through Eighth Grade* by Bill Honig, Linda Diamond, and Linda Gutlohn.]

It is important when teaching new concepts, such as syllabication, to use known words, make sure students can hear and segment words orally into syllables, and work with the largest units first. For example, teach students how to divide compound words (*mailman, bookcase*) into syllables, then words with inflectional endings that require no spelling changes (*raining, shouted*), and then words with a double consonant (*rabbit, happy, swimming*). Teachers should also plan for and use word sorts to support and reinforce students' analysis of words with common features, such as number of syllables, words with common syllable junctures (*jump/ing, hop/ping, hop/ing, rain/ing*), prefixes and/or suffixes. Segmenting printed words into syllables as well as sorting words with common syllable patterns, prefixes, base words, and/or suffixes help developing readers to attend to letter sequences, vowel patterns, and meaning units within words. These activities will foster their proficiency in using spelling and syllable patterns to identify novel polysyllabic words in the future.

It is essential that teachers provide a variety of developmentally appropriate and engaging texts as well as time for students to read independently on a daily basis. Developing readers become more efficient in attending to and using their knowledge of spelling and syllable patterns as well as affixes and base words to identify new words as they extensively read texts on their independent level. If students are to gain fluency and flexibility in applying what they know about syllabication and structural analysis, they must be encouraged and given the time to read.

Recommended References

Bear, Donald, Marcia Invernizzi, Shane Templeton, and Francine Johnston. "Word Study for Intermediate Readers and Writers: The Syllables and Affixes Stage," Chapter 8 in *Words Their Way: Word Study for Phonics, Vocabulary, and Spelling Instruction*.

Cunningham, Patricia M. "Big Words," Chapter 4 in *Phonics They Use: Words for Reading and Writing*, Third Edition.

Fountas, Irene C., and Gay Su Pinnell. "Teaching for Word-Solving: Phonics, Spelling, and Vocabulary," Chapter 22 in *Guiding Readers and Writers Grades 3–6: Teaching Comprehension, Genre, and Content Literacy*.

Fresch, Mary Jo, and Aileen Ford Wheaton. "Organized Word Lists: A Handy Resource for Spelling Instruction," Chapter 4 in *The Spelling List and Word Study Resource Book*.

Fry, Edward, Jacqueline Kress, and Dona Lee Fountoukidis. "Vocabulary," Section 3 in *The Reading Teacher's Book of Lists*, Fourth Edition.

Ganske, Kathy. "Syllable Juncture Word Study," Chapter 6 in *Word Journeys: Assessment-Guided Phonics, Spelling, and Vocabulary Instruction*.

Honig, Bill, Linda Diamond, and Linda Gutlohn. "Multisyllabic Words," Chapter 10, and "Word-Learning Strategies," Chapter 15 in *Teaching Reading Sourcebook: For Kindergarten Through Eighth Grade*.

Rasinski, Timothy V., and Nancy D. Padak. "Teaching Advanced Word Patterns," Chapter 6 in *From Phonics to Fluency: Effective Teaching of Decoding and Reading Fluency in the Elementary School*.

Syllabication and Structural Analysis: Mini-Lessons/Learning Activities

Syllabication

Purpose: To teach students the concept of a syllable, to attend to letter combinations and syllable patterns within polysyllabic words, to recognize syllable boundaries and familiar chunks within polysyllabic words, and to identify common affixes as whole units in order to pronounce polysyllabic words

Rationale: For late transitional and extending readers in second grade and beyond, it is important that they learn how to chunk or divide longer words into manageable parts in order to quickly problem-solve polysyllabic words while reading. Students' core of known single-syllable words, hopefully including a variety of words with various vowel patterns, becomes a basis for identifying familiar spelling patterns first in simple two- or three-syllable words and later on in more complex polysyllabic words.

Learning how to look for familiar consonant and vowel patterns within polysyllabic words and use what they know about sounding out and analogies enables these readers to problem-solve many two- or three-syllable words independently while reading. Becoming aware of base words and common affixes as whole units further enables students to quickly divide and pronounce common polysyllabic words that have been modified by the addition of a prefix and/or suffix.

Tasks 34 and 39: Segmenting words into syllables II and III

OBJECTIVE
The student will be able to say a word, clap the syllables while saying the word, and tell where to divide the word into syllables.

MATERIALS
- chart paper
- dry-erase boards and markers

TEACH/RETEACH
1. To determine whether the student is able to think about words as having separate parts or syllables, begin with an oral activity. Say: **I will say two words. Then you are to repeat each word and clap the number of parts or syllables in the word. Say the word** bedroom **as you clap the syllables.** Give students time to respond. **Say the word** grasshopper **as you clap the syllables.**

2. Then write the word *bedroom* on the board or chart paper and say: **Let's clap the syllables once more and I'll show how to divide the word** bedroom **into syllables. I know that every syllable, or word part, has just one vowel sound.**

3. Say the word slowly and underline the vowel sound in *bed* and then in *room*. Then say: ***I also see that this word is a compound word. It is made up of two words,*** **bed** ***and*** **room.** ***Both*** **bed** ***and*** **room** ***have one vowel sound, so the word*** **bedroom** ***is divided into syllables between*** **bed** ***and*** **room,** ***between the letters*** **d** ***and*** **r.** Draw a line between the letters *d* and *r*.

4. Next say: ***Let's say*** **grasshopper** ***as you clap the syllables.*** Give students time to respond. ***Now I'll show you how to divide the word*** **grasshopper** ***into syllables. First, I must remember that every syllable, or word part, has just one vowel sound.***

5. Say the word slowly and underline the vowel sounds in *grass* and then in *hopper*. Then say: ***I also see that this word is made up of two words*** **grass** ***and*** **hopper. Grass** ***has one vowel sound but*** **hopper** ***has two vowel sounds.*** Say and clap the syllables in grasshopper. **Grasshopper** ***is divided into syllables between*** **grass** ***and*** **hopper,** ***between the letters*** **s** ***and*** **h,** ***and then*** **hopper** ***is divided between the two*** **p**'*s. Draw a line between the*** **s** ***and*** **h,** ***and the two*** **p**'*s.*

6. Explain: ***Hearing the syllables in words also helps you write them.*** Cover the words and have the students write *bedroom* and *grasshopper* on their dry-erase board. Check or have the students check their responses.

SCAFFOLD

1. Have students say the word *baseball* as they clap the syllables. Then write *baseball* on the board or chart paper.

2. Ask students to tell you what they notice about this word, and to locate and identify the vowel sounds and letter patterns.

3. Remind the students: ***Every syllable, or word part, has just one vowel sound. Now clap the word*** **baseball** ***once more to decide where to divide this word into syllables. Between what letters would the word*** **baseball** ***be divided?*** After the students respond, draw a line between the letters *e* and *b*.

4. Repeat using the word *rainbow*.

5. Cover the words and have the students write *baseball* and *rainbow* on their dry-erase board. Check or have the students check their responses. [Note: Encouraging students to examine the letter patterns in polysyllabic words after they have identified them in reading and/or spelled them will increase their proficiency in using spelling patterns and syllabication to identify other polysyllabic words.]

Identify other syllable patterns with which students need to become familiar, such as words with suffixes, double consonants, open first syllables, closed first syllables. Follow the same steps as above with examples of these words at another time.

REINFORCE

- Give students index cards with polysyllabic words, such as compound words and words with inflectional endings added, such as *hilltop, football, cannot, cupcake, newspaper, basketball, grasshopper, jumping, shouted, playing, boxes, hopping, swimming, started*. Have them sort them into sets with common features. Ask them to explain how they decided which words should go together.

- Give students index cards with one-, two-, and three-syllable words written on them, such as *stand, standing, play, player, night, nighttime, stop, stopping, grass, grasshopper, paper, newspaper, ball, baseball, basketball, home, homework*. Have them sort them into sets with common features. Ask them to explain how they decided which words should go together. Ask students to find other ways to sort the same group of words or use selected words in sentences.

- After word sorts, have the students record how they sorted the words and how they selected an exemplar for each category of words for future reference in their word study journals.

Structural Analysis

Purpose: To teach students to analyze how words are constructed; identify compound words, contractions, base/root words, prefixes, and suffixes; and recognize and use known word-meaning elements, such as *un, friend*, and *ly* in *unfriendly* or *n't* in *couldn't*, to help understand the meaning of the whole word

Rationale: Since it is impossible to teach the meaning of every word students will encounter in their daily reading, it is important that they learn how to determine the meaning of the majority of these words independently. If developing readers are to become independent readers, they must learn how to use context clues and structural analysis (compound words, contractions, base/root words, prefixes, and suffixes) to initially construct as well as confirm the meaning of unfamiliar words. It is also important that they learn to how use graphic aids included in informational texts to learn the meaning of and/or extend their understanding of content-related words. The use of these strategies will extend and enhance their vocabularies as well.

Tasks 28, 35, 38:
Using structural analysis to determine word meaning: suffixes I, II, & III

OBJECTIVE
The student will be able to read aloud and use each word with a suffix in a sentence to demonstrate his/her understanding of the word.

MATERIALS
- letter cards or magnetic letters
- large index cards
- marker

TEACH/RETEACH

1. Use letter cards or magnetic letters to build the word *jump*. **This word is jump. *I am going to add some endings to the word* jump *to show you how endings sometimes change what a word means and how the word is used in a sentence.***

2. Add the letter *s* to the word *jump* and say: **Jumps. The cat jumps *up on the table. When we say* jumps, *it means it is happening now.*** Write *jump* on chart paper and then write *jumps* under *jump*.

3. Remove the *s* and add the letters *e, d*. **Jumped. *Jack* jumped *over the candlestick. When we say* jumped, *it means it happened awhile ago.*** Write *jumped* on chart paper.

4. Remove the *ed* and add the letters *i, n, g* and say: **Jumping. *I am* jumping.** Jump up and down several times. **When *I say* I am jumping, *it means that it is happening right now, but if I say* I was jumping *that means, it happened awhile ago.*** Write *jumping* on chart paper.

5. Remove the *ing* and add the letters *e, r* and say: **Jumper. *The* jumper *was ready to jump out of the plane. In this sentence* jumper *means a person who jumps. Sometimes* jumper *may also mean a piece of clothing. The teacher had on a red* jumper.** Write *jumper* on chart paper.

6. Remove the *er* and add the letters *y* and say: **Jumpy. *The man was very* jumpy. Jumpy *in this sentence means the person can't sit or stand still.*** Write *jumpy* on chart paper.

7. Read the words on the list and review how the word changed when you added different endings/suffixes.

8. Cover the list of words and dictate the words for the students to spell. Check or have the students check their responses.

SCAFFOLD

1. Have the students repeat the steps above using other words. Give the students the following letter cards: *p, l, a, y, s, i, n, g, e, d, r, f, u, l*.

2. Tell them to make the word *play*. Then write *play* on the chart paper.

3. Say: **What letters would you add to make the word playing?** Give the students time to respond and then say: **Change play *to* playing.**

4. Explain: **When we add letters to a word it sometimes changes what the word means and how the word is used in a sentence.**

5. Ask one of the students to use the word *playing* in a sentence and reinforce his/her response. Then write the word *playing* on the chart paper.

6. Follow the same steps for the following words: *plays, player, played, playful*.

7. Read both sets of words (*jump* and *play*) and review how the words change when endings/suffixes are added.

8. Cover the list of words and dictate five or six of the words for the students to spell. Check or have the students check their responses.

Identify other suffixes with which students need to become familiar, such as *ly, ful, ness, en, er, est.* Continue with the same steps as above with examples of these words at another time.
[Note: See "Teaching Common Prefixes and Suffixes" on pages 156–161 in *Phonics They Use: Words for Reading and Writing,* Third Edition.]

REINFORCE

- Have students sort words with two to three different suffixes into categories, such as *helpless, homeless, hopeless, careless, endless, careful, helpful, truthful, wonderful, painful, beautiful, chosen, golden, forgotten, hidden.* Ask the students to explain how they decided which words should go together and to use selected words in sentences. After word sorts, have the students record how they sorted the words and how they selected an exemplar for each category of words in their word study journals for future reference.

- Co-construct a chart such as the following. Encourage students to add words for each category as they find them in their reading. Have students read the sentence that included the word or use the word in a sentence to reinforce their understanding of the word.

Suffix/Ending	Meaning	Examples	
s/es	"more than one"	books	babies
er, est	"comparison"	bigger	biggest
al	"related to"	magical	comical
less	"without"	helpless	hopeless
ness	"full of"	darkness	happiness
ful	"full of"	respectful	careful

Task 37: Using structural analysis to determine word meaning: prefixes

OBJECTIVE

The student will be able to read aloud each word with a prefix and tell what it means.

MATERIALS

- letter cards or magnetic letters
- large index cards
- marker

TEACH/RETEACH

1. *Today we are going to learn about prefixes. Many words begin with prefixes. If you know what prefixes are and what they mean, you can use them as clues to read new words and to figure out the meaning of the words. A prefix is a group of letters that are added to the beginning of words. I'll show you what I mean.*

2. Write the word *lock* on chart paper and say: *This word is* lock. *I will* lock *the classroom door when I go home.*

3. Write the word *unlock* beneath the word *lock*. Say and clap the syllables in unlock. Then say: *The letters* u, n *spell* un. Un *is a prefix and means "not." I will* unlock *the classroom door when I come in the morning. It means that the door will not be locked. Adding the prefix* un *changed the meaning of lock.*

4. Ask: *What other things can lock or unlock?*

SCAFFOLD

1. Write the word *tie* on chart paper and say: *This word is* tie. Ask one of the students to tell what the word means or use it in a sentence. Reinforce the meaning of *tie*.

2. Write the word *untie* beneath the word *tie*.

3. Ask: *How are these two words alike?*
   How are they different?
   Let's say and clap the syllables in this word together.
   What does the prefix un *mean?*

4. Then ask the students to use the word *untie* in a sentence.

5. Cover the list of words (*lock, unlock, tie, untie*) and dictate the words for the students to spell. Check or have the students check their responses.

6. Ask student to think of or find other words with the prefix *un* to add to the list (*unpack, undo, unsafe, unable, unzip*).

Repeat the steps with a new set of words featuring another prefix, such as *preschool/preview, reread/retell, subway/submarine, dislike/disagree, impossible/impolite*, at another time.

REINFORCE

- Have students form three prefix teams, such as *un-*, *dis-*, *re-*. Call out base words (*please, certain, order, build, happy, obey, read, open, able, cover, teach, wash*). Team members raise their hands if their prefix can be added. Write the word on the board or chart paper to verify.

- Co-construct a chart such as the following. Encourage students to add words for each category as they find them in their reading. Have students read the sentence that included the word or use the word in a sentence to reinforce their understanding of the word.

Suffix/Ending	Meaning	Examples	
un	"not"	unlock	untie
dis	"not" or "to do the opposite"	dislike	disagree
re	"back" or "again"	retell	reread
pre	"before"	preschool	preview
sub	"under"	subway	submarine

[Note: See "Prefix Sort" on pages 247–248 in *Words Their Way: Word Study for Phonics, Vocabulary, and Spelling Instruction*.]

Glossary

affix a bound (non-word) morpheme that changes the meaning or function of a base word to which it is attached, as the prefix *re-* and the suffix *-ing* in *rewriting*

alliteration the repetition of the initial sound(s) in a group of words; alliterative words may form phrases or sentences, i.e., *Lilly likes lollipops.*

alphabetic principle the assumption that letters represent sounds; understanding how print connects to different sounds

analogy the use of known words and/or word features to identify/problem-solve unfamiliar words in reading and in writing; based on an understanding that words with the same spelling pattern sound the same and words that have sounds in common frequently have the same spelling pattern

base word a word to which affixes may be added to create related words, as *view* in *viewing* or *preview*

blend to combine the sounds represented by letters to pronounce a word; sound out

closed syllable a syllable that ends with a consonant sound, such as *rab* in *rab/bit* and *jac* in *jac/ket*

compound word a combination of two or more words that functions as a single unit of meaning, such as *bookcase* and *raincoat* (single words) or *mud-covered* (hyphenated words)

contraction the shortening of a written or spoken expression by the omission of one or more letters or sounds, as *can't* for *cannot*

CVC a spelling pattern consisting of a sequence of letters in a consonant-vowel-consonant order and representing a short vowel sound as in the word *pat*

CVVC a spelling pattern consisting of a sequence of letters in a consonant-vowel-vowel-consonant order and representing a long vowel or diphthong sound as in the words *rain* and *join*

digraph two letters that represent one speech sound, as *ch* for /ch/ in *chin*, *ea* for /ē/ in *each*, or *igh* for /ī/ in *high*

diphthong a vowel sound produced when the tongue glides from one vowel sound toward another vowel in the same syllable, as in *joy* and *choice*

decode to use knowledge of grapheme/phoneme relationships to identify and pronounce written words while constructing meaning; convert the printed word into its spoken form

developmentally appropriate instruction instruction that is designed to teach students what they need to learn next, provide the right amount of support to ensure success, and at the same time reinforce what students know and can do independently

encode to change oral sounds/words/thoughts into printed letters/words/sentences; to use knowledge of phoneme/grapheme relationships and spelling patterns to identify and conventionally represent sounds in words while composing

grapheme a written or printed representation of a phoneme, as *p* for /p/, *ea* for /ē/, and *ch* for /ch/ in *peach*; a grapheme may be a single letter or a group of letters

grapheme-phoneme correspondence the relationship between a grapheme (letter or letters) and the phoneme (sound), i.e., *c* representing /k/ in *cat* and /s/ in *cent*

high-frequency word a word that appears many more times than most other words in spoken or written language

inflectional ending a suffix that expresses plurality or possession when added to a noun (*Tim's*), tense when added to a verb (*jumped*), and comparison when added to an adjective (*bigger*)

initial blend The joining of two or more consonant sounds, represented by letters, that begin a word without losing the identity of the sounds, as /bl/ in *blue*, /str/ in *stream*

key words words used as a category header during word sorts or an example in a word study journal

long vowel the vowel sounds that are also the names of the alphabet letters as /ā/ in *play*, /ē/ in *tree*, /ī/ in *vine*, /ō/ in *gold*, /ū/ in *cute*; long vowel sounds are frequently represented by two or more letters

metalanguage language (terms/vocabulary) used to describe, talk about, and analyze language, such as *word, letter, beginning sounds, prefix, syllable, phoneme*, etc.

miscue a term used to describe a deviation from the printed text during oral reading

morpheme the smallest unit of meaning, including prefixes, base/root words, and suffixes

onset the consonants preceding the vowel of a syllable, as *str* in *street*, *p* in *pea*, and *n* in *nut* and in *peanut*

onset substitution a word-identification technique in which a known consonant sound is combined with a known phonogram to facilitate pronunciation of unknown words, as replacing /m/ of *man* with /r/, /p/, or /c/ to identify *ran, pan, can*

open syllable a syllable that ends with a vowel sound, such as /bā/ in *ba/bies* and /rē/ in *rea/son*

phoneme a minimal sound unit of speech that, when contrasted with another phoneme, affects the meaning of words, as /b/ in *book* contrasts with /t/ in *took*, or /k/ in *cook*

phonics the study of letters/graphemes and sounds/phonemes relationships and how to use phonics knowledge to encode and decode words

phonogram a sequence of letters beginning with a vowel and letters that follow in single-syllable words, such as *ame* in *game* and *eet* in *street*

phonological awareness the ability to (1) hear and explicitly attend to sounds in, not the meaning of, spoken words and (2) manipulate the sounds in spoken words

polysyllabic words words with more than one syllable, such as *ta/ble, a/part/ment*, and *in/ter/est/ing*

preconsonant nasal the letters *m* and *n*, nasal sounds, when they appear before another consonant, such as in *went* and *jump*

r-controlled vowels when a vowel is followed by an *r*, the *r* influences the sound of the vowel

reliability consistency in assessment administration and results; inter-rater reliability (two teachers administering the same assessment would obtain similar results with the same student) and intra-rater reliability (a teacher administering the assessment would obtain similar results if the assessment is re-administered within a short period of time)

rhyme identical or very similar recurring final sounds in words, such as *race, face, space,* and *day, grey, sleigh*

rime a vowel and any following consonants of a syllable, as /ook/ in *shook*, /īp/ in *stripe*, and /ā/ in *play*

rime substitution a word-identification technique in which a vowel and any following consonants of a syllable are combined with a known initial consonant(s) to facilitate pronunciation of unknown words, as replacing /at/ of *hat* with /is/, /ot/, or /im/ to identify *his, hot, him*

root word often used as a synonym for base word; a Greek or Latin meaning unit to which affixes are added, such as *phon* ("sound") in *telephone* and *phonetic*

scaffold provide the right amount of support needed by learners during the process of learning; generally moves from teacher modeling and teaching to student practicing with teacher support to student gaining more control and requiring less and less teacher support to student performing independently

segmentation dividing a word into segments, i.e., syllables (*bas/ket/ball*), onset and rime (*st/air*), or phonemes (/s/ /a/ /t/)

short vowel the sound qualities of /a/, /e/, /i/, /o/, and /u/ heard in the beginning of *apple, Ed, igloo, octopus, umbrella* or the middle sound in *bat, bet, bit, boss,* and *bus*

spelling pattern a sequence of letters that present a particular sound, such as in *ch* and *ai* in *chain*, and *igh* in *night*

structural analysis the identification of word-meaning elements, as *re* and *read* in *reread*, to help understand the meaning of a word as a whole; commonly involves the identification of roots, affixes, compounds, hyphenated forms, inflected endings, and contractions

suffix an affix attached to the end of a base or root word that changes meaning (*less* in *sleeveless*) or grammatical function (*ness* in *happiness*) of the word

syllabication the process of analyzing the patterns of consonants and vowels in a word to determine where to divide a word into syllables

syllable a minimal unit of sequential speech sounds containing a single vowel sound

word analysis a general label applied to word identification; often includes (1) the analysis of words into their constituent parts, (2) sight vocabulary, (3) phonics, (4) structural analysis, and (5) the use context clues

VCe a spelling pattern consisting a sequence of letters in a vowel-consonant-*e* (long vowel marker) order and representing a long vowel sound as in the word name

word discrimination the process of noting differences and similarities in words

word hunt an activity in which students go back to texts previously read looking for other words that contain the identified spelling pattern (*ea* as in *eat*) or word feature (*re* as in *reread*)

word identification the process of determining the pronunciation and some degree of meaning of an unknown word

word recognition the quick and easy identification of the pronunciation and appropriate meaning of a word previously met in print or writing

word sort a learning activity in which students group words into categories with similar features/spelling patterns

word study journal a journal in which students record various word activities, such as recording key words as examples of spelling patterns, listing words found during word hunts, explaining how words were sorted and what was learned in word sorts, compiling lists of words with common prefixes and/or suffixes, etc.

Recommended Resourses

Developmental assessments are an integral part of the teaching-learning process when teachers analyze what students can do and know and identify what they need to learn next. What takes place after the assessment determines the amount of growth between assessments. The following books provide guidelines, rationales, and examples of how to instruct and support developing readers and writers in the elementary school.

Allington, Richard L. *What Really Matters for Struggling Readers: Designing Research-Based Programs.* New York: Longman, 2001.

Armstrong, Thomas. *The Multiple Intelligences of Reading and Writing: Making the Words Come Alive.* Alexandria, VA: ASCD, 2003.

Bear, Donald R., Marcia Invernizzi, Shane Templeton, and Francine Johnston. *Words Their Way: Word Study for Phonics, Vocabulary, and Spelling Instruction*, Second Edition. Upper Saddle River, NJ: Prentice Hall, 2000.

Chapman, Marilyn L. "Phonemic Awareness: Clarifying What We Know." In *Literacy Teaching and Learning: An International Journal of Early Reading and Writing*, 7(1&2) Edited by Emily M. Rogers and P. David Pearson, pp. 91–109. Columbus, OH: Reading Recovery Council of North America, 2003.

Clark, Kathleen F. "What Can I Say Besides 'Sound It Out'? Coaching Word Recognition in Beginning Reading." In *The Reading Teacher* 57, 5: 440–449, 2004.

Cunningham, Patricia M., Richard L. Allington. *Classrooms That Work: They Can All Read and Write*, Third Edition. New York: Longman, 1999.

Cunningham, Patricia M. *Phonics They Use: Words for Reading and Writing*, Third Edition. New York: Longman, 2000.

Dahl, Karin L., et al. *Rethinking Phonics: Making the Best Teaching Decisions.* Portsmouth, NH: Heinemann, 2001.

Dorn, Linda J., and Carla Soffos. *Shaping Literate Minds: Developing Self-Regulated Learners.* Portland, ME: Stenhouse, 2001.

Dufresne, Michèle. *Word Solvers: Making Sense of Letters and Sounds.* Portsmouth, NH: Heinemann, 2002.

Fisher, Bobbi, and Emily Fisher Medvic. *Perspectives on Shared Reading: Planning and Practice.* Portsmouth, NH: Heinemann, 2000.

Fountas, Irene C., and Gay Su Pinnell. *Voices on Word Matters: Learning About Phonics and Spelling in the Literacy Classroom.* Portsmouth, NH: Heinemann, 1999.

Fountas, Irene C., and Gay Su Pinnell. *Guiding Readers and Writers Grades 3–6: Teaching Comprehension, Genre, and Content Literacy.* Portsmouth, NH: Heinemann, 2001.

Fountas, Irene C., and Gay Su Pinnell. *Sing a Song of Poetry: A Teaching Resource for Phonics, Word Study, and Fluency.* Portsmouth, NH: Heinemann, 2004.

Fresch, Mary Jo, and Aileen Ford Wheaton. *The Spelling List and Word Study Resource Book: Organized Spelling Lists, Greek and Latin Roots, Word Histories, and Other Resources for Dynamic Spelling and Vocabulary Instruction.* New York: Scholastic Teaching Resources, 2004.

Fresch, Mary Jo, and Aileen Ford Wheaton. *Teaching and Assessing Spelling: A Practical Approach That Strikes the Balance Between Whole-Group and Individualized Instruction.* New York: Scholastic Professional Books, 2002.

Fry, Edward Bernard, Ph.D., Jacqueline E. Kress, Ed.D., Dona Lee Fountoukidis, Ed.D. *The Reading Teacher's Book of Lists,* Fourth Edition. San Francisco, CA: Jossey-Bass, 2000.

Fry, Edward Bernard, Ph.D. *Phonics Patterns: Onset and Rhyme Word Lists,* Fourth Edition. Laguna Beach, CA: Laguna Beach Educational Books, 1998.

Ganske, Kathy. *Word Journeys: Assessment-Guided Phonics, Spelling, and Vocabulary Instruction.* New York: The Guilford Press, 2000.

Ganske, Kathy, Joanne K. Monroe, and Dorothy S. Strickland. "Questions Teachers Ask About Struggling Readers and Writers." In *The Reading Teacher* 57, 2: 118–128, 2003.

Harris, Theodore L., and Richard E. Hodges. *The Literacy Dictionary: The Vocabulary of Reading and Writing.* Newark, DE: International Reading Association, 1995.

Honig, Bill, Linda Diamond, and Linda Gutlohn. *Teaching Reading Sourcebook: For Kindergarten Through Eighth Grade.* Novato, CA: Arena Press, 2000.

Kam-Wong, JoAnn, and Vivian Vasquesz, Co-editors. "Spelling Today." National Council of Teachers of English: School Talk 9, 2, 2004.

Lyons, Carol A. *Teaching Struggling Readers: How to Use Brain-Based Research to Maximize Learning.* Portsmouth, NH: Heinemann, 2003.

Marten, Cindy. *Word Crafting: Teaching Spelling, Grades K–6.* Portsmouth, NH: Heinemann, 2003.

Martinez, Miriam, Nancy L. Roser, and Susan Strecker. "I Never Thought I Could Be a Star: Readers Theatre Ticket to Fluency." *The Reading Teacher* 52, 4: 326-334, 1999.

McCarrier, Andrea, Gay Su Pinnell, and Irene C. Fountas. *Interactive Writing: How Language & Literacy Come Together, K–2.* Portsmouth, NH: Heinemann, 2000.

Moustafa, Margaret. *Beyond Traditional Phonics: Research Discoveries and Reading Instruction.* Portsmouth, NH: Heinemann, 1997.

Opitz, Michael F., and Timothy V. Rasinski. *Good-Bye Round Robin: 25 Effective Oral Reading Strategies.* Portsmouth, NH: Heinemann, 1998.

Parkes, Brenda. *Read It Again!: Revisiting Shared Reading.* Portland, ME: Stenhouse, 2000.

Prelutsky, Jack. *Read-Aloud Poems for the Very Young.* New York: Alfred A. Knopf, 1986.

Rasinski, Timothy V., and Nancy D. Padak. *From Phonics to Fluency: Effective Teaching of Decoding and Reading Fluency in the Elementary School.* New York: Longman, 2001.

Rasinski, Timothy V., and Belinda S. Zimmerman. *Phonics Poetry: Teaching Word Families.* Boston, MA: Allyn and Bacon, 2001.

Routman, Regie. *Reading Essentials: The Specifics You Need to Teach Reading Well.* Portsmouth, NH: Heinemann, 2003.

Routman, Regie. *Conversations: Strategies for Teaching, Learning, and Evaluating.* Portsmouth, NH: Heinemann, 2000.

Strickland, Dorothy, Kathy Ganske, and Joanne Monroe. *Supporting Struggling Readers and Writers: Strategies for Classroom Intervention 3–6.* Portland, ME: Stenhouse, 2002.

Taberski, Sharon. *On Solid Ground: Strategies for Teaching Reading K–3.* Portsmouth, NH: Heinemann, 2000.